Linguistic Relativity in SLA

SECOND LANGUAGE ACQUISITION
Series Editor: Professor David Singleton, *Trinity College, Dublin, Ireland*

This series brings together titles dealing with a variety of aspects of language acquisition and processing in situations where a language or languages other than the native language is involved. Second language is thus interpreted in its broadest possible sense. The volumes included in the series all offer in their different ways, on the one hand, exposition and discussion of empirical findings and, on the other, some degree of theoretical reflection. In this latter connection, no particular theoretical stance is privileged in the series; nor is any relevant perspective – sociolinguistic, psycholinguistic, neurolinguistic, etc. – deemed out of place. The intended readership of the series includes final-year undergraduates working on second language acquisition projects, postgraduate students involved in second language acquisition research, and researchers and teachers in general whose interests include a second language acquisition component.

Full details of all the books in this series and of all our other publications can be found on http://www.multilingual-matters.com, or by writing to Multilingual Matters, St Nicholas House, 31–34 High Street, Bristol, BS1 2AW, UK.

SECOND LANGUAGE ACQUISITION
Series Editor: David Singleton

Linguistic Relativity in SLA
Thinking for Speaking

Edited by
ZhaoHong Han and Teresa Cadierno

MULTILINGUAL MATTERS
Bristol • Buffalo • Toronto

Library of Congress Cataloging in Publication Data
A catalog record for this book is available from the Library of Congress.
Linguistic Relativity in SLA: Thinking for Speaking/Edited by ZhaoHong Han and Teresa Cadierno.
Second Language Acquisition: 50
Includes bibliographical references and index.
1. Second language acquisition. 2. Language and languages--Usage.
3. Psycholinguistics. 4. Language and culture.
I. Han, Zhaohong, II. Cadierno, Teresa.
P118.2.L557 2010
418.0071–dc22 2010018313

British Library Cataloguing in Publication Data
A catalogue entry for this book is available from the British Library.

ISBN-13: 978-1-84769-277-1 (hbk)

Multilingual Matters
UK: St Nicholas House, 31–34 High Street, Bristol, BS1 2AW, UK.
USA: UTP, 2250 Military Road, Tonawanda, NY 14150, USA.
Canada: UTP, 5201 Dufferin Street, North York, Ontario M3H 5T8, Canada.

The policy of Multilingual Matters/Channel View Publications is to use papers that are natural, renewable and recyclable products, made from wood grown in sustainable forests. In the manufacturing process of our books, and to further support our policy, preference is given to printers that have FSC and PEFC Chain of Custody certification. The FSC and/or PEFC logos will appear on those books where full certification has been granted to the printer concerned.

Typeset by Techset Composition Ltd., Salisbury, UK.
Printed and bound in Great Britain by the MPG Books Group.

Contents

Contributors

Teresa Cadierno is Associate Professor at the Institute of Language of Communication, University of Southern Denmark. Her research interests include instructed second language acquisition, with a special focus on the acquisition of grammar by L2 learners, L2 input processing and the role of formal instruction in L2 acquisition; and applied cognitive linguistics, especially the acquisition and teaching of L2 constructions for the expression of motion events, and the investigation of re-thinking for speaking processes in a foreign language.

Kenny R. Coventry is Professor of Cognitive Science, and the Director of the Cognition and Communication Research Centre, Northumbria University. He is also currently a fellow at the Hanse Institute for Advanced Studies, Germany. His research focuses on the relationship between language and perception from a multidisciplinary perspective. With Simon Garrod, he is the author of *Saying, Seeing and Acting: The Psychological Semantics of Spatial Prepositions* (2004).

Monika Ekiert is currently an EdD candidate at Teachers College, Columbia University, where she also teaches graduate courses in the MA TESOL and Applied Linguistics programs. Her research interests include the acquisition of L2 meaning by adult L2 learners, the acquisition of definiteness, form–meaning connections in second language learning, crosslinguistic influence in second language acquisition and conceptual transfer.

Pedro Guijarro-Fuentes is a reader in Spanish. His research interests are in the interdisciplinary field of Spanish applied linguistics, sociolinguistics, psycholinguistics and bilingualism. His current research projects include among others a study of the copula verbs *ser/estar* and a study of the acquisition of spatial prepositions by L2 learners of both English and Spanish, projects funded by the British Academy and the Art and Humanities Research Council. He has authored and co-authored numerous articles and book chapters, and his research has appeared in different international, refereed journals such as *Language Learning, Bilingualism: Language* *and Cognition, Cognition, Studies in Second language Acquisition* and *International Journal of Bilingualism* among others.

ZhaoHong Han is Associate Professor in Linguistics and Education at Teachers College, Columbia University. Her research interests lie broadly in second language learnability and second language teachability. She is the author of *Fossilization in Adult Second Language Acquisition* (2004) and the editor/co-editor of a number of volumes on the topics of the second language process, second language reading and fossilization. In addition, her work on input enhancement and input processing has appeared in scholarly journals. She is the recipient of the 2003 International TESOL Heinle and Heinle Distinguished Research Award.

Victoria Hasko is Assistant Professor in the Department of Language and Literacy Education, University of Georgia. Her areas of research include second and heritage language acquisition, language attrition and cognitive development in bilinguals. Her recent projects have addressed topics such as acquisition of motion expressions, identity repertoire, variability of emotion talk and expressive suffixation in the speech of second language and heritage language learners. She is a co-editor of *New Approaches to Slavic Verbs of Motion* (John Benjamins Publishing, 2010) and the editor of a special issue of the *Slavic and Eastern European Journal* on the teaching and learning of verbs of motion (2009).

Terence Odlin teaches courses in linguistics and English as a second language at Ohio State University. He is the author of *Language Transfer* and several articles and book chapters on the same topic. He has also served as the editor or co-editor of volumes on language contact, pedagogical grammar and fossilization. His current research projects focus on comprehension, linguistic complexity and language transfer in second language acquisition.

Gale A. Stam is Professor of Psychology at National-Louis University. Her research interests include language and culture, language and cognition, speech and gesture, and first and second language acquisition, particularly the development of first language (L1) thinking for speaking and linguistic and gestural changes in thinking for speaking with second language (L2) acquisition. She has published articles on changes in thinking for speaking, the importance of looking at gesture in L2 acquisition and lexical retrieval in an L2. Her co-edited book *Gesture: Second Language Acquisition and Classroom* (2008) is the first book on the topic of gesture and second language acquisition.

David Stringer is an Assistant Professor of Second Language Studies at Indiana University. He received his PhD in linguistics from Durham University, UK, and previously taught linguistics and English language in Spain, Italy and Japan. His experimental research is concerned with the first and second language acquisition of lexical semantics and syntax. His current work includes projects on the linguistic realization of motion events, and how mismatches between the first and second language representations of spatial predicates raise intriguing learnability issues for second language acquisition.

Berenice Valdés is currently a lecturer in the Faculty of Psychology at the Universidad Complutense de Madrid. Her PhD thesis looked at the relationship between attention and consciousness in word meaning processing. From 2006 to 2008, she collaborated with Professor Kenny Coventry and Dr Pedro Guijarro-Fuentes as a post-doctoral researcher in an AHRC-funded project about second language acquisition of spatial language in English and Spanish.

Preface

As we were putting finishing touches on this volume, the news broke that Flight 1549 crashed in the Hudson River, New York. Our attention was instantly diverted by an outpouring of online and offline news reports and commentaries to the breath-taking drama that had unfolded, in particular, the pilot's miraculous landing of the aircraft on the river, saving 154 lives. As we glanced over the reports, our eyes halted on the following lines and the similar wording:

> Many on board and watching from the shores were shocked that the aircraft did not sink immediately. Instead, *it floated, twisting and drifting south in strong currents,* as three New York Waterway commuter ferries moved in. Moments later, *terrified passengers began swarming out the emergency exits and into brutally cold air and onto the submerged wings of the bobbing jetliner,* which began taking in water. (*New York Times,* January 16; emphasis added)

Piqued by our interest in linguistic relativity, we turned to *El País,* a Spanish newspaper, and found several descriptions, and much as expected, none with the level of detail with respect to manner of motion or with such elaborate and compact path description as the above (see italics). The Spanish descriptions tend to contain a greater number of path verbs than manner verbs and abound in static descriptions of the scene rather than descriptions of the trajectories per se. The two paragraphs below illustrate these tendencies. The first paragraph includes several path verbs (*dirigirse* 'head', *volver* 'return', *amerizar* 'land on water') and one cause-of-motion verb (*evacuar* 'evacuate'), with manner information provided only by means of the periphrastic construction *quedó flotando* 'remained floating'. The second paragraph illustrates the tendency to provide static descriptions:

> La nave, un Airbus A320 que se *dirigía* a Carolina del Norte *volvía* al aeropuerto de La Guardia (Nueva York-USA) tras golpearse con unos pájaros, según las primeras versiones, *amerizó* de forma controlada y *quedó flotando* sobre las aguas. – Los pasajeros *han sido evacuados* por las salidas de emergencia. – Todos han sobrevivido, según la autoridad aeroportuaria (*El País,* January 15, emphasis added)

('The plane, an Airbus A320 that was *headed* to North Carolina *returned* to LaGuardia Airport (New York-USA) after crashing against some birds, according to early versions, *landed on water* in a controlled way and *remained floating* on the water. – Passengers were evacuated via emergency exits. – All have survived, according to airport authority')

Las imágenes emitidas en directo por canales de EEUU han mostrado a varias personas con chalecos salvavidas *sobre las alas del avión*, esperando a ser rescatadas por barcos que han rodeado enseguida el aparato (*El País*, January 15, emphasis added)

('The images broadcast live on US channels showed several people with life jackets *on the wings of the plane*, waiting to be rescued by boats that have surrounded the plane')

Apparently, the linguistic effects are pervasive: As we see from the above examples and also as has been amply documented elsewhere (e.g. Slobin, 1996a),[1] different languages predispose their speakers to view and talk about events differently. An obvious question, then, for us and indeed, for the entire second language acquisition (SLA) field, has been this double-barreled question: To what extent does a prior language (L1) affect the acquisition and use of a second language, and more profoundly, to what extent does the conceptual system that comes with the L1 affect the development of another compatible with the L2?

Precisely, this book investigates linguistic relativity in SLA. The essential idea of linguistic relativity, that is the idea that language affects the way people think, has been around for centuries, dating from the work of Roger Bacon in the 13th century and of the German 18th-century philosophers Machaelis, Herder and Leibniz, but it gained prominence in the work of the German Romantic philosophers of the 19th century, especially in the writings of the German educator, linguist and philosopher von Humboldt (1767–1835). In the 20th century, the main line of research into this hypothesis moved to America with the development of Boasian anthropology and the work of Sapir (1884–1939) and Whorf (1897–1941). (For detailed information about the historical background of the hypothesis, the interested reader can consult Gentner & Goldin-Meadow, 2003; Gumperz & Levinson, 1996; Lucy, 1992a.) The modern-day version of the idea is the so-called Sapir–Whorf hypothesis. This hypothesis has a strong and a weak version. The strong version stipulates that language *determines* cognition; that is, it assumes that speakers' thoughts can never be free from the constraints imposed by the language they speak. The weak version stipulates that language *influences* cognition; that is, it claims that the specific structure of a language influences its speakers' non-verbal habitual thought, routine ways of attending to, categorizing, and remembering objects and events (Lucy, 1992a).

The notion of linguistic relativism has fascinated scholars from a variety of disciplines, including, but not limited to, philosophers, psychologists, linguists and anthropologists. Over the centuries, the strong version of the hypothesis has lost ground to the weak version. As Pinker states, 'there is no scientific evidence that languages *dramatically* shape their speakers' ways of thinking' (Pinker, 1994: 58). The weak version has, in the last decade and a half, incited a great deal of empirical research by linguists, cognitive psychologists, psycholinguists and anthropologists (e.g. Boroditsky, 2001; Gentner & Goldin-Meadow, 2003; Gumperz & Levinson, 1996; Levinson, 2003a; Lucy, 1992b; Lucy & Gaskins, 2001; Pederson *et al.*, 1998). According to Gentner and Goldin-Meadow (2003), recent interest in the hypothesis can be traced to three major themes: (1) the work carried out by prominent cognitive linguists such as Talmy, Langacker and Bowerman, who have demonstrated the important differences in how languages partition the world; (2) the development of a series of theoretical arguments, which include the revival of Vygotsky's (1962) claim of the important role of language in children's cognitive development and Lucy's (1992b, 1994) influential empirical research on the cognitive effects of classifier grammars; and (3) the move from a focus on color to the study of new domains such as space, motion, time, number, gender, theory of mind and the nature and function of objects versus substances.

Research along these lines has provided compelling evidence of the effects of language on thought. As Hunt and Agnoli have noted:

> Models of cognition developed after Whorf's day indicate ways in which thought can be influenced by cultural variations in the lexical, syntactic, and pragmatic aspects of language. Although much work remains to be done, there appears to be a great deal of truth to the linguistic relativity hypothesis. In many ways, the language people speak is a guide to the language in which they think. (Hunt & Agnoli, 1991: 377)

Similarly, Slobin (2000) asserts that there are 'non-dramatic' influences that deserve scientific attention.

The field of SLA has seen some work on linguistic relativity, conceptual and empirical, on and off over the last 30 years and the work has concerned target languages such as German, Russian, Spanish and English by learners from a variety of L1 backgrounds (e.g. Kaplan, 1966; Kellerman, 1995; Lado, 1956; von Stutterheim & Klein, 1987; Weinreich, 1953). The last few years, however, have witnessed a notable increase of interest in linguistic relativity; more studies have invoked, or framed themselves along the lines of, the Sapir–Whorf hypothesis, and have specially based their work on Slobin's thinking-for-speaking hypothesis (for reviews, see Cadierno, 2008; Odlin 2003, 2005, 2008a).[2]

The purpose of this volume is to capture and substantiate an emerging interest among SLA researchers in Slobin's thinking-for-speaking hypothesis (1987, 1996a), a weak form of linguistic relativism, which suggests that the extant language system may operate online to influence articulation of experience. The hypothesis has received extensive support in first language, crosslinguistic research (for brief reviews, see Cadierno, this volume; Hasko, this volume; Stam, this volume), but its relevance for second language research has not been explored until recently (Kellerman, 1995; see also Cadierno, 2004; Cadierno & Lund, 2004; Cadierno & Ruiz, 2006; Han, 1998, 2004). This volume assembles seven studies, all employing the thinking-for-speaking hypothesis as (part of) their conceptual framework, although the acquisition issues dealt with herein vary from study to study.

Chapter 1 (Cadierno) addresses the impact of L1 inter- and intra-typological proximity on the way L2 learners of Danish talk about motion events, in particular, boundary-crossing events. Chapter 2 (Hasko) is driven by a similar concern. More specifically, it examines the question of whether it is possible for advanced L2 learners of Russian to fully acquire the target language thinking for speaking, as it relates to the obligatory marking of unidirectionality and non-unidirectionality of motion in motion talk. Chapter 3 (Stam) assesses the extent to which long-term experience with the target language leads to restructuring of the L1-based thinking-for-speaking pattern in L2 English verbal description and gesturing vis-à-vis motion events. Chapter 4 (Coventry, Valdés & Guijarro-Fuentes) investigates whether language (Spanish versus English) affects implicit recognition of spatial relations. Chapter 5 (Stringer) raises and examines the issues surrounding glossing in crosslinguistic syntactic analyses, as a result of lexical relativity, and their implications for SLA. Reporting findings from a small-scale study, Chapter 6 (Ekiert) tackles the problem of consistent omission of articles in certain discourse environments among native speakers of Polish learning English as the L2. Chapter 7 (Han) provides an in-depth investigation, by virtue of a longitudinal case study, a prevalent problem in adult SLA, namely, inadequate command of grammatical morphemes and its oft-manifested persistency and variability. Chapter 8 (Odlin) concludes the volume by reflecting on the studies in relation to conceptual transfer, contemplating definitional issues and providing an outlook for the linguistic relativity research in SLA.

Disparate as they are for their samples and methodology, the studies overwhelmingly claim to have found artifacts of L1-based thinking for speaking in L2 production (including gesturing). From these studies it appears that Slobin's thinking-for-speaking hypothesis not only has validity for SLA, but it also holds the promise of offering a parsimonious account for a number of SLA conundrums, such as the recalcitrant nature of select influences of native language, inter- and intra-learner variable acquisitional outcomes, fossilization and even seemingly random alternation of target-like and non-target-like behaviors (see e.g. Han, this volume). For the latter, extant accounts have been many, yet piecemeal and incongruent.

A paramount gain from the present collection of studies is that it has driven home the tasks confronting future research: in order to establish the thinking-for-speaking hypothesis as a contending theoretical approach to resolving outstanding acquisitional problems, it is imperative to form a consensus among researchers on the operationalization of the construct of 'thinking for speaking', to ascertain the types of data that are the most pertinent and, by the same token, the kinds of measures that are the most sensitive to tapping thinking for speaking (see Coventry *et al.*, this volume, for an insightful discussion), and last but not least, to tease out thinking for speaking from potentially confounding factors such as learner proficiency, context and +/− language-mediated cognition.

The studies reported in this volume raise numerous interesting questions for future research, of which five are particularly worth noting:

(1) To what extent is restructuring of L1-based thinking for speaking possible in SLA?
(2) What learning conditions, including pedagogy, are likely to spur changes?
(3) Given the right conditions, what changes are inevitable and what are not?
(4) What contributions do individual difference variables (e.g. aptitude, memory, motivation and personality) make to the extent of restructuring possible?
(5) How does L1-based thinking for speaking influence L2 input perception and comprehension?

Due to its pioneering nature, this book is best suited for use as a textbook for theme-based graduate seminars in SLA, as a reference for bilingualism and SLA researchers, especially those whose work is concerned with crosslinguistic influence, and as a general reader for those interested in language acquisition, the relationship between cognition and behavior, and the second language production process.

This volume would not have been possible without the dedication and hard work of its contributors, to whom we owe our respect and gratitude. We also want to take this opportunity to thank Vera Regan for her insightful and constructive comments on an earlier version of the manuscript. And finally, we wish to acknowledge Carly Tam for her assistance with the index.

ZhaoHong Han
Teresa Cadierno

Notes

1. As noted by Slobin (1996a), Sapir took sometimes the strong view associated with Whorf, whereas at other times he embraced a weaker version of the hypothesis, which is more similar to Slobin's own view of the role of language in the expression of thought.
2. A related type of research within SLA has been framed within the framework of conceptual transfer (e.g. Jarvis, 1998; Jarvis & Pavlenko, 2008; Odlin, 2005, 2008a; Pavlenko & Jarvis, 2001). According to Jarvis and Pavlenko (2008), the basic distinction between research on linguistic relativity and conceptual transfer is that whereas the former starts with language and ends with cognition, the latter begins with language and ends, via cognition, with language, and thus examines the influence of language-mediated conceptual categories of one language on the learner's *verbal performance* in another language. A slightly different notion of conceptual transfer is offered by Odlin (e.g. Odlin, 2008a) who sees the assessment of learners' *non-verbal performance* as a prerequisite for work under this framework. For a detailed review of the historical background of work on conceptual transfer, the interested reader can consult Jarvis (2007).

Chapter 1

Motion in Danish as a Second Language: Does the Learner's L1 Make a Difference?

TERESA CADIERNO

Introduction

The linguistic relativity hypothesis, that is, the possibility that language can influence thought, has constituted an important part of Western intellectual and philosophical discussions over the centuries (see Gumperz & Levinson, 1996; Lucy, 1992a, for some historical background on the hypothesis).[1] The hypothesis, however, is best associated with the work of Benjamin Whorf (1956), whose ideas can be traced back to Sapir and Boas, as well as to the German linguist and philosopher von Humboldt. Even though the hypothesis fell into disfavor in the 1960s with the predominant view in linguistics of language as separate from cognition, and the emphasis in cognitive psychology on the universality of human conceptual structures, the last decade and a half has witnessed a renewed interest in this important issue, as evidenced by the methodologically rigorous empirical work developed by Lucy (1992a, 1992b) and the influential volumes edited by Gumperz and Levinson (1996) and Gentner and Goldin-Meadow (2003).

One important outcome of this renewed interest in the linguistic relativity hypothesis has been Slobin's (1996a) thinking-for-speaking hypothesis, which focuses on the influence of language on the kind of thinking that goes on, online, while we are using the language. According to this hypothesis, the language that we speak directs our attention, while speaking, to particular ways of filtering our experiences of the world. In other words, our experiences of the world are filtered into verbalized events not only through the choice of the individual speaker's perspective, but critically through the particular set of options provided by the language that we speak as well. Thinking for speaking thus entails 'picking those characteristics of objects and events that (a) fit some conceptualization of the event, and (b) are readily encodable in the language' (Slobin, 1996a: 76).

Slobin's thinking-for-speaking hypothesis has received empirical support in research showing that native speakers (NSs) of typologically different languages (Talmy, 1985, 1991, 2000b) tend to pay different kinds of attention to particular details of motion events when talking about them (e.g. Berman & Slobin, 1994; Slobin, 1996a, 1996b, 1997, 1998, 2000, 2003, 2004, 2006). This empirical research as well as Slobin's thinking-for-speaking hypothesis have important implications for second language acquisition. Under such a perspective, learning another language entails learning another way of thinking for speaking (Cadierno & Lund, 2004; Han, 1998, 2004, 2008; Stam, 1998), a hypothesis that has been investigated in a number of studies on how adult L2 learners with typologically different L1s and L2s come to talk about motion in an L2 (see Cadierno, 2008; Stam, this volume, for a detailed review). The present chapter contributes to this line of inquiry by reporting an investigation that takes into account both inter- and intra-typological differences between the learners' L1 and L2 with respect to (a) the description of one particular type of motion event, namely motion events involving boundary-crossing situations, and (b) the productive and receptive vocabulary of L2 motion verbs, in general, and of manner-of-motion verbs, in particular, of the L2 learners examined.

Thinking for Speaking and the L1 Expression of Motion Events

Empirical research into the expression of motion in L1 acquisition and use has been inspired by Talmy's (1985, 1991, 2000b) typological work, which describes the characteristic lexicalization patterns involved in the expression of motion events in different languages of the world. In satellite-framed languages (S-languages), such as Chinese and all branches of the Indo-European languages except Romance languages, the core schema of a motion event, that is the Path, is characteristically coded in a satellite, whereas Motion and Manner are expressed in the verb root. In verb-framed languages (V-languages), on the other hand, Motion and Path are typically expressed in the verb, whereas Manner and Cause tend to be coded in a separate constituent such as an adverbial or a gerund. This pattern is characteristic of Romance, Semitic and Polynesian languages. The following English and Spanish examples taken from Talmy (1985) illustrate the contrast between the two types of languages: *The bottle floated into the cave* versus *La botella entró a la cueva flotando* ('The bottle entered the cave floating').

However, in order to fully account for the lexicalization patterns of the two types of language, we need to take into account the so-called boundary-crossing constraint (Aske, 1989; Slobin & Hoiting, 1994), that is whether or not a Path involves the crossing of a spatial boundary (motion into/out of/ over a bounded region). Thus, whereas in S-languages the conflation of

Motion and Manner into the main verb is possible in both boundary and non-boundary-crossing situations (e.g. *Mary ran into the house* [+boundary-crossing]; *Mary ran up to the house* [–boundary-crossing]), in V-languages this conflation is only possible in non-boundary-crossing contexts (e.g. *María corrió hasta la casa* 'Mary ran up to the house' [without entering]). In boundary-crossing situations, Manner must be expressed in a separate constituent (e.g. *María entró a la casa corriendo* 'Mary entered the house running'). This is due to the fact that in these languages '... crossing a spatial boundary is conceived of as a change of state, and (that) state changes require an independent predicate ...' (Slobin, 1997: 441). In V-languages, a change of state is marked by means of path verbs such as the Spanish verbs *entrar* 'enter', *salir* 'exit', *subir* 'go up' and *bajar* 'go down'. The only exception to this pattern is verbs that express high-energy motor patterns such as the equivalents of English *throw oneself* and *plunge*, which are more likely conceived of as punctual and instantaneous acts than as activities extended in time (Slobin, 2004). Given the particular force dynamics encoded in this type of verbs, sudden boundary-crossing situations such as 'plunging into a swimming pool' can then be conceptualized as changes of states, a conceptualization that would license the possibility of using manner verbs in V-languages. The following Spanish example illustrates this possibility: *El niño se sumergió en la piscina* 'The child plunged into the swimming-pool'. It is important to mention, however, that in a language like Spanish the possibility of using manner-of-motion verbs in sudden boundary-crossing events is also dependent on factors such as the type of ground that is described (e.g. whether it is three dimensional or not) and the speaker's background knowledge of the motion event at hand (Iraide Ibarretxe-Antuñano, personal communication).

Crosslinguistic research into the expression of motion events in different languages (e.g. Berman & Slobin, 1994; Slobin, 1996a, 1996b, 1997, 1998, 2000, 2003, 2004, 2006) has shown systematic differences in how NSs from S- and V-languages talk about motion. Speakers of S-languages tend to provide more elaborated and tightly packaged descriptions of paths within a clause than speakers of V-languages, who, in turn, tend to provide descriptions of the static scene in which the movement takes place. Important differences have also been found with respect to manner of motion. Speakers of S-languages tend to provide more elaborated manner descriptions than speakers of V-languages, an elaboration that is reflected both in terms of the frequency with which manner information is supplied and in terms of the variety of manner distinctions made. Speakers of V-languages typically use neutral motion verbs to designate a creature's normal way of moving, thus providing manner information only when this is communicatively important in a given context (Slobin, 2004). Furthermore, when describing motion events that involve boundary-crossing, speakers of V-languages often fail to provide manner information in a separate constituent unless, again, manner is somehow at issue. This is, according to Slobin (2004, 2006), due to language processing constraints, as the resulting construction would be syntactically heavy and would add processing load in terms of comprehension and production. Ease of processing is therefore an important factor to take into account when accounting for the use of simpler constructions over more complex ones by speakers of V-languages.

Özçalişkan (under review) attempted to overcome this tendency of V-speakers to leave out manner information by requiring speakers of Turkish – a V-language – as well as speakers of English – an S-language – to perform an experimental task that involved the description of a series of boundary-crossing motion events where both path and manner were presented as salient elements. The results of the study showed clear cross-linguistic differences with respect to the type of verbs, and the types of event segmentation employed by the two groups of NSs. Overall, NSs of English used manner verbs in their descriptions, whereas NSs of Turkish displayed a more varied pattern of verb use, which included a higher proportion of path verbs and path verbs with subordinate manner adjuncts. Manner verbs were also used by Turkish NSs, but, in agreement with Slobin's (2004) claims, their use was restricted to descriptions of pictures that depicted punctual or instantaneous boundary-crossing events (e.g. *diving into a pool of water, leaping over a hurdle*). With respect to event segmentation, English speakers predominantly described the boundary-crossing motion events in single clausal segments (e.g. *he crawls into the house*), whereas Turkish speakers tended to use multiple clausal segments, especially when describing stimuli that depicted temporally extended types of boundary-crossing events such as *running into a house* or *crawling over a carpet*. In this type of events, both manner and path information were included in the Turkish descriptions, but this was done in a sequential fashion: first by encoding manner as an activity towards a boundary, then marking the boundary-crossing with a path verb and, finally, describing manner again as an activity away from the boundary. The following English example illustrates this pattern of use: *He crawls towards the carpet, and he crosses it, then he crawls away*. According to Özçalişkan (under review), this result suggests that when manner is particularly salient, speakers of V-languages may employ elaborated types of expression that allow them to mention this component within the constraints of the semantic structure of their language.

In addition to inter-typological differences between speakers of S- and V-languages, important intra-typological distinctions within a given type of language have also been identified in crosslinguistic research. For example, studies by Özçalişkan and Slobin (1998), Ibarretxe-Antuñano (2004) and Engberg-Pedersen and Trondhjem (2004) have shown that speakers of three V-languages, Turkish, Basque and West-Greenlandic, provide more elaborated path descriptions than those found in other more 'prototypical' V-languages such as Spanish. Likewise, differences have been found between speakers of different S-languages with respect to the expression of manner. When describing the emergence of the owl in the 'owl exit scene' in the frog story, speakers of Russian tended to use manner verbs to a greater extent than speakers of Mandarin and Tai, who, in turn, used these verbs more frequently than speakers of three Germanic languages, namely English, German and Dutch (Slobin, 2004, 2006). These intra-typological differences seem to be largely due to the different morpho-syntactic structure and the lexical availability of the languages in question, such as the expression of path by means of verb particle in German languages versus prefixes in Slavic languages.[2] In fact, the noticing of these differences has led several authors (e.g. Slobin, 2004; Zlatev & Yangklang, 2004) to argue for the existence of a third type of typological pattern that would include, among others, serial-verb languages such as Tai and Mandarin Chinese, that is languages previously categorized by Talmy (1985, 2000b) as S-languages. This type of languages, referred to as equipollently framed languages by Slobin (2004, 2006), would be characterized by the expression of both manner and path via elements that are equal both in formal linguistic terms and in their force of significance.

On the basis of these intra-typological differences, Slobin (2004, 2006) has suggested that, at least with respect to manner of motion, languages should be categorized on a cline of manner salience rather than in a strict bipartite typology. Manner salience, which is defined by Slobin (2006: 64) as '... the level of attention paid to manner in describing events', can be assessed through various means, including ease of lexical access (i.e. the easiness with which speakers of different languages can list manner-of-motion verbs in a specific time span), the frequency and diversity with which manner information is provided by speakers of different languages in both natural conversational use and elicited speech, and the imagery and understanding of manner verbs by these speakers. In high-manner-salient languages, there is an accessible slot for manner in the language (e.g. in the main verb in S-languages and in the manner verb in serial-verb languages), whereas in low-manner-salient languages, such as V-languages, manner is subordinated to path and is thus typically expressed in a separate constituent. Speakers of high-manner-salient languages are from childhood exposed to more frequent and more varied manner information in the input, tend to regularly and easily provide frequent and varied manner information when describing motion events, and end up consequently with a highly differentiated conceptualization of manner. Speakers of low-manner-salient languages, on the other hand, tend to provide manner information when manner needs to be contextually foregrounded for some reason. As indicated by Slobin (2004), NSs of these languages do pay attention to manner, as this is too important a dimension of experience to ignore, but they are not led by their grammars to focus and elaborate on it to the same extent as speakers of S-languages.

In sum, languages differ with respect to the linguistic means with which they encode given domains of experience, and if a language provides a more accessible and more readily codable means of expression for a particular domain, as is the case of manner of motion in high-manner-salient languages, its speakers will attend to and elaborate on that domain to a larger degree than speakers of languages where that domain is less accessible and less readily codable. Each language thus trains its NSs to pay different kinds of attention to particular domains of experience when talking about them. Or formulated in terms of Slobin's thinking-for-speaking hypothesis, the language that we speak influences our thinking-for-speaking patterns, that is the kind of thinking that goes on while we are using the language. According to Berman and Slobin (1994), when acquiring a native language, a child learns particular ways of thinking for speaking, a claim that, as discussed below, has important consequences for second language acquisition.

Thinking for Speaking and the L2 Expression of Motion Events

If, as stated by Berman and Slobin (1994), acquiring a native language involves learning particular ways of thinking for speaking, which means, for the purposes of the present study, learning to attend to particular aspects of a motion event and learning to relate them verbally in ways that are in consonance with them, it follows that learning a foreign language must then involve learning alternative ways of thinking for speaking, that is (a) learning which particular details of a motion event must be attended to in input and expressed in the L2 (e.g. attention to trajectories versus static descriptions, and relatively more or less attention to manner of motion), and (b) learning the characteristic lexicalization patterns of the L2, both with respect to +/− boundary-crossing situations (Cadierno & Lund, 2004). In other words, the L2 learner must learn the particular verbalized orientation to experience that is expressed in the grammatical resources of the foreign language s/he is attempting to learn, and which may differ from his/her L1 orientation. As indicated by Slobin himself (1996a), the thinking-for-speaking patterns acquired during first language acquisition may well turn out to be rather resistant to restructuring in adult second language acquisition.

Two crucial and closely related questions to ask are, then, whether and to what extent adult L2 learners are able to learn the appropriate L2 thinking-for-speaking patterns, and whether and to what extent this learning is influenced by the specific verbalized orientation of their L1s. In the last few years, several studies have attempted to address these questions by comparing the expression of motion events in a given foreign language by learners with typologically different L1s and L2s and the NSs of the L2 in question (e.g. Cadierno, 2004; Cadierno & Ruiz, 2006; Kellerman & Van Hoof, 2003; Navarro & Nicoladis, 2005; Tsekos Phillips, 2007). The results of these studies have shown that the learners investigated, who were pre-dominantly intermediate and advanced L2 learners[3] with L1 S-languages, such as English and Danish, and L2 V-languages, such as Spanish, were able to restructure their thinking-for-speaking patterns when talking about motion in an L2 that was typologically different from their L1. There were, however, some traces of the learners' L1 thinking-for-speaking pat-terns. For example, in a study by Cadierno (2004), intermediate level Danish learners of Spanish tended to provide more complex and elabo-rated path descriptions than Spanish NSs, a tendency that was evidenced in a 'satellization' of the Spanish motion constructions, that is the use of inaccurate constructions incorporating anomalous path particles not found in the Spanish NS data (e.g. *El niño fue arriba de una roca* 'The boy went on top of a rock'), and in the more frequent inclusion of ground adjuncts in motion descriptions. Another example of the influence of the L1 thinking-for-speaking patterns can be found in the studies conducted by Harley (1989) and Harley and King (1989), who found that English learners of French used certain manner-of-motion verbs (e.g. *courir* 'run', *sauter* 'jump' and *marcher* 'march') more frequently than French NSs, who, in turn, tended to use verbs conflating motion and path (e.g. *monter* 'go up', *descendre* 'descend' and *sortir* 'go out'). Furthermore, studies examin-ing the simultaneous use of language and gesture (e.g. Kellerman & Van Hoof; 2003; Negueruela *et al.*, 2004; Stam, 2001, this volume) have shown that L2 learners sometimes rely on the L1 gesturing patterns even at advanced levels of proficiency, thus evidencing L1-based thinking-for-speaking patterns in otherwise fluent and target-like L2 speech (Kellerman & Van Hoof, 2003).

A further issue to consider in the light of the thinking-for-speaking hypothesis is whether the attainment of appropriate L2 thinking-for-speaking patterns is dependent on (or related to) the relative degree of similarity or difference between the learners' L1 and L2 thinking-for-speaking patterns. In respect of the conceptual domain of motion, the issue would then be whether adult learners with typologically similar L1s and L2s are able to exhibit more target-like lexicalization patterns and more appropriate L2 ways of thinking for speaking than comparable learners with typologically different L1s and L2s. According to Kellerman's (1995) transfer-to-nowhere principle, this would be the case, as large linguistic differences between the learners' L1 and L2 can lead to large learning difficulties, especially when these differences relate to '... the way languages predispose their speakers to conceptualize experience' (Kellerman, 1995: 137). In cases like this, the L2 learners may fail to notice that the foreign language they are learning favors a conceptualization and verbalization of a given event that is different from the one preferred in their native language.

In a study by Cadierno and Ruiz (2006), however, this hypothesis received limited empirical support. With respect to the expression of manner of motion, Danish learners of Spanish (i.e. where the L1 and the L2 are typologically different) did not, as expected, exhibit a higher degree of elaboration of this semantic domain when compared to Italian learners of Spanish (i.e. where the L1 and the L2 are typologically similar). No significant differences were found between the two groups with respect to the amount of manner-of-motion verbs used and the use of alternative means of expressing manner of motion (e.g. subordinated manner clauses and adverbial expressions) when describing the frog story.

One possible explanation for these findings may be the proficiency level of the two groups of learners, who were at the advanced stages of language acquisition. It might be the case that the influence of the L1 thinking-for-speaking patterns is stronger at the initial and intermediate stages of language acquisition and that such an influence disappears as the process of acquisition advances. Another possible and complementary explanation may be found in the intra-typological differences mentioned above. Italian seems to be closer to the S-languages than other Romance languages in relation to both the expression of path and manner of motion. In fact, NSs of Italian have been found to use a wider variety and more frequent manner-of-motion verbs than speakers of other V-languages such as French and Spanish (Slobin, 2004). What is needed then are studies that take both inter-typological and intra-typological differences into account when examining the issue of whether the process of learning a new way of thinking for speaking is affected by the degree of similarity or distance with respect to the L1 and L2 thinking-for-speaking patterns, an issue that is addressed in the present investigation.

The Study

The present study constitutes a partial replication of Özçalişkan (under review) and thus focuses on the expression of boundary-crossing motion events by three different groups of adult L2 learners of Danish as a second language: speakers of a V-language – Spanish, and speakers of two different S-languages, a Germanic language – German – and a Slavic language – Russian. A comparison group of Danish NSs was also included in the investigation. In addition, the study explored possible differences between the participant groups with respect to their productive and receptive knowledge of motion verbs, in general, and of manner-of-motion verbs, in particular. Given that the learners' L1s differed with respect to manner salience, it was of interest to examine whether such difference had an effect on the learners' ease of lexical access and on the degree of recognition of manner-of-motion verbs in the L2. Specifically, the study addressed the following research questions:

(1) Are there inter- and intra-typological differences between the three learner groups of Danish (L1 Spanish, L1 German and L1 Russian) with respect to:
   (a) The preferred patterns of expressions, that is types of constructions, used when describing boundary-crossing motion events?
   (b) The proportion of manner-of-motion verb types used when describing boundary-crossing motion events?
   (c) The learners' productive and receptive vocabulary of motion verbs, in general, and of manner-of-motion verbs, in particular?

(2) How does the performance of the three learner groups compare to that of Danish NSs?

Description of the languages involved in the study

Applying the typology suggested by Talmy (1985, 1991, 2000b), German, Danish and Russian, on the one hand, and Spanish, on the other, represent two different typological patterns. German and Danish – both Germanic languages – and Russian – a Slavic language – are all characterized as S-languages, where Motion and Manner are generally coded in the main verb, and Path is typically expressed by means of a satellite. The following examples, which are 'equivalent' in meaning to the English sentence *He crawled into the house*, exemplify this pattern: German: *Er krabbelte ins Haus*; Danish: *Han krawlede ind i huse*; and Russian: Он вполз в дом. There are, however, crucial intra-typological differences between the three S-languages. A full characterization of the motion construction types of the three languages would be beyond the scope of this chapter, so only the relevant characteristics are briefly noted here.

As shown in the examples above involving boundary-crossing events, one difference is that path of motion is coded by means of unbound path particles in the two Germanic languages (i.e. German *ins* and Danish *ind*) and by means of bound path prefixes in Russian (i.e. *в;*). This difference has consequences for the rhetorical style concerning the expression of manner (see e.g. the discussion in note 2). However, as indicated by Hasko (2009), path of motion in Russian can also be encoded by unprefixed verbs + unbound path satellites when coding non-boundary-crossing motion events. In addition, Russian possesses a grammaticized category in relation to certain motion verbs, which is absent in the two Germanic languages, namely the distinction between unidirectional and multidirectional motion (for a detailed explanation of this distinction and other characteristics of Russian expression of motion, see Hasko, 2009).

The two Germanic languages also exhibit morphological differences with respect to the distinction between translocative and locative motion. German uses a case system to differentiate between motion to a goal (accusative case) and motion at a fixed location (dative case). The following two examples taken from De Knop and Dirven (2008) illustrate this contrast: *Er geht auf die Straße* 'He walks into the street' (translocative) versus *Er geht auf der Straße* 'He is walking in the street' (locative). In Danish, on the other hand, the opposition between translocative and non-translocative/ locative motion is coded by means of an elaborate system of verb particles (e.g. *ud-ude* 'out (translocative)-outside' and *ind-inde* 'in (translocative)-inside'). The following examples illustrate this contrast: *Manden kravler ind i huset* 'He crawls into the house' (translocative) and *Manden kravler inde i huset* 'He crawls inside the house' (non-translocative/locative).

Spanish is, on the other hand, a Romance language characterized as a V-language, where Path tends to be encoded in the verb (e.g. *entrar* 'enter', *salir* 'leave', *bajar* 'go down' and *subir* 'go up'), whereas Manner and Cause of motion tend to be encoded separately, often via an adverbial or prepositional phrase (e.g. *Entró a la casa corriendo* 'He entered the house running'). However, since typologies are not rigidly fixed, Spanish also has verbs that conflate Motion and Manner (e.g. *caminar* 'walk', *correr* 'run' and *volar* 'fly'), which are used in non-boundary situations (e.g. *Corrió hasta la casa* 'He run up to the house [without entering]').

Participants

There were 48 participants in the study: 12 NSs of Spanish, 12 NSs of German, 12 NSs of Russian and 12 NSs of Danish. At the time of data collection, the Danish NSs were all first-year students at a Danish university, whereas the NSs of the different L1s (i.e. Spanish, German and Russian) were all instructed learners of Danish as a second language in Denmark. The courses that the learners were taking were part of a nationally based teaching program offered to foreigners who live in Denmark, and who have completed medium or long cycle educational training programs (e.g. vocational qualification, upper secondary education or higher education) in their home countries.[4] Within this program, the learners under investigation were all placed in classes belonging to the so-called '4th module', which corresponds to the Common European Framework of Reference (CEFR) Independent User B1 level.[5] Their level of language proficiency in Danish can be therefore characterized as low intermediate. According to the information provided in a background questionnaire administered to them at the beginning of the study, the learners' length of stay in Denmark at the time of data collection ranged from 1.5 to 2.5 years. Most of the learners reported either being married or living with a Danish person. With respect to their use of Danish outside the classrooms, the majority of the learners reported using the language frequently (i.e. most of the days in the week and several times during the day) and a few learners reported using the language very frequently (i.e. every day) or once in a while (i.e. once or twice a week).

Data collection procedures

Data for this investigation were collected in the participants' regular classes. All the participants were asked to perform three tasks consecutively. The first task was a picture description task,[6] which was designed to elicit the learners' preferred means of expression when describing motion scenes depicting boundary-crossing situations. There were 12 pictures depicting three types of boundary-crossing motion events: (a) motion into a bounded space (e.g. *running into a house*); (b) motion out of a bounded space (e.g. *sneaking out of a jar*); and (c) motion over a line or plane (e.g. *crawling over a carpet*). Each picture depicted a man moving in a particular direction and in a particular manner into/out of/over a given bounded region. The list of boundary-crossing events in the order in which they were presented to the participants is presented in Table 1.1, and the 12 pictures used as stimuli are presented in Appendix A. Participants were instructed to look through a series of 12 pictures that depicted a man moving in a particular direction and in a particular manner with respect

Table 1.1 List of boundary-crossing events in order of presentation

Order of presentation	Type of boundary-crossing	Event description
1	INTO a bounded space	Run into a house
2	OUT of a bounded space	Fly out of a jar
3	OVER a plane	Crawl over a carpet
4	INTO a bounded space	Dive into a pool
5	OUT of a bounded space	Dash out of a house
6	OVER a plane	Flip over a bar
7	INTO a bounded space	Tumble into a net
8	OUT of a bounded space	Creep out of a house
9	OVER a plane	Leap over a hurdle
10	INTO a bounded space	Crawl into a house
11	OUT of a bounded space	Sneak out of a sack
12	OVER a plane	Jump over a cliff

to a particular object (e.g. a house, a jar and a carpet), and then write in their own words a short description of what they saw in each picture. A list of Danish words for the objects depicted in the pictures (e.g. *huset* 'the house' and *tæppet* 'the carpet') was provided to the learners in order to ensure that a possible lack of knowledge of these words would not prevent them from completing the task successfully. Learners were asked to use those words in their descriptions. After reading the instructions and making sure they understood them, the participants proceeded with the task. A maximum of 25 minutes was allotted for this task.

The second and third tasks concerned vocabulary knowledge, and their purpose was to determine the range of lexical options that the participants possessed with respect to motion verbs, in general, and manner-of-motion verbs, in particular, both in terms of production and reception/recognition. The production task was administered before the recognition one. It required the participants to write all the motion verbs they could think of in five minutes, whereas the vocabulary recognition task required the participants to circle the verbs that they knew from a list of verbs that was provided to them. Participants were specifically instructed to circle only those verbs whose meaning they were completely sure of. The list, which contained a total of 83 verbs, was taken from Pedersen's (2000) corpus-based taxonomy of Danish motion verbs, and can be found in Appendix B. The taxonomy divides motion verbs into two broad categories. One category subsumes 18 motion verbs that express direction, which are subdivided into verbs that express path (e.g. *kydse* 'cross' and *passere* 'pass'), source verbs (e.g. *afgå* 'depart' and *skride* 'take off'), goal verbs (e.g. *ankomme* 'arrive' and *falde* 'fall') and chase verbs (e.g. *følgje* 'follow' and *jagte* 'chase'). The other category contains 65 verbs that express manner, which are subdivided into verbs where the motion involves a vehicle (e.g. *cykle* 'cycle' and *sejle* 'sail'); verbs where the motion involves moving specific body parts such as the feet, such as walking verbs[7] (e.g. *gå* 'walk', *liste* 'tiptoe' and *spadsere* 'promenade'), running verbs (e.g. *sprinte* 'sprint' and *galoppere* 'gallop') and jumping verbs (e.g. *hoppe* 'hop' and *springe* 'jump'); motion verbs utilizing other parts of the body, such as the wings (e.g. *flyve* 'fly'), the knees (e.g. *kravle* 'crawl') or the stomach (e.g. *mave sig* 'crawl forward on one's stomach'); verbs involving motion of the body that is necessarily related to any specific body part (e.g. *danse* 'dance' and *styrte* 'rush'); and verbs involving motion of large groups of entities moving around rather quickly (e.g. *myldre* 'swarm').

Data analysis

Three types of analyses were conducted on the data. The first analysis examined the preferred means of expression, that is type of constructions, used by the participants when performing the picture description task. On the basis of the descriptions, the following classification scheme was developed and then used as a basis for categorizing the participants' preferred means of describing the boundary-crossing events in question:

(a) A construction containing a manner verb + a path satellite (MV + PS construction), such as *manden løber ud af huset* 'the man runs out of the house' (picture 5) or *manden flyver ud af dåsen* 'the man flies out of the jar' (picture 2). This type of construction follows the characteristic lexicalization pattern of S-languages and thus constitutes the target-like Danish type of expression.

(b) A construction containing a non-manner verb + a path satellite (–MV + PS construction), such as *manden kommer ud af huset* 'the man comes out of the house' (picture 5) or *manden falder ned ind i nettet* 'the man falls down into the net' (picture 7).[8] This type of construction follows the characteristic lexicalization pattern of V-languages for the expression of boundary-crossing motion events in that manner is not expressed in the main verb. However, it is idiosyncratic in that path is expressed in a satellite and not in the verb, as is characteristic of V-languages. In fact, in Danish, with a few exceptions, it is not possible to express path in the verb as this language lacks latinate verbs such as the English *enter* or *exit*.

(c) A construction consisting of a non-manner verb + a manner adjunct + a path satellite (–MV + MA + PS), such as *manden kommer hemmeligt ud af sækken* 'the man comes secretly out of the jar' (picture 11) or *manden kommer langsomt hen over tæppet* 'the man comes slowly over the carpet' (picture 3). This type of construction differs from the previous one in that manner information is provided by means of a separate constituent, typically an adverbial. This construction again resembles the type of expression found in V-languages where manner, if expressed at all, must be coded outside the main verb when describing boundary-crossing motion events.

(d) Finally, a type of expression that did not mark boundary-crossing (–BC). This category included two types of expressions: expressions that did not convey boundary crossing at all, and expressions that marked boundary crossing in an implicit fashion. With respect to the former, two sub-types of descriptions were identified: one, which included expressions such as *manden laver gymnastik* 'the man does gymnastics' (picture 6) or *han spiller circus* 'he plays circus' (picture 7), where the participants' descriptions somehow fit what is depicted in the pictures but do not actually describe the translocative motion depicted in them; and a second sub-type, which included descriptions such as *manden kravler på tæppet* 'the man crawls on top of the carpet' (picture 3) or *manden løber inde i huset* 'the man runs inside the house' (picture 1) where the lack of boundary-crossing expressions is due to the use of inappropriate path particles (e.g. *på* 'on top of' instead of *hen over* 'over'; *inde* 'inside' versus *ind* 'into'). The expressions that marked boundary crossing in an implicit fashion consisted of descriptions where the motion event in question was divided into two sub-events by means of two clauses, the first one describing the motion towards the boundary, and the second the motion away from the boundary: *manden kravler til tæppet og så bevæge sig fra tæppet* 'the man crawls to the carpet and then moves (away) from the carpet' (picture 3) or *manden forlader en kløft og ankommer på en anden* 'the man leaves a cleft and arrives on the other' (picture 12). This type of description somewhat resembles the multiple clausal descriptions provided by the Turkish NSs in Özçalişkan (under review). However, they differ in two crucial aspects. The first is that whereas in Özçalişkan's study these expressions were basically used when describing pictures that depicted temporally extended types of boundary crossing, in our study they were also used to describe pictures depicting events of a more punctual nature (e.g. picture 12). The second is that whereas in the Turkish native data these expressions included segments describing the movement towards and away from the boundary (usually by means of manner-of-motion verbs) and a segment describing the actual crossing of the boundary (by means of a path verb), as in *He crawls towards the carpet, and he crosses it, then he crawls away*, the expressions found in our data never included the latter type of segment.

After coding the data into the above categories, the data analysis then proceeded to examine the proportion of Danish manner-of-motion verb types used by the four participant groups when performing the picture description task. In this analysis, therefore, the manner-of-motion verb types were computed in relation to the total amount of motion verb types used by each participant. Finally, the data analysis focused on the participants' knowledge of Danish motion verbs, in general, and of manner-of-motion verbs, in particular, at the levels of production and recognition. For both the vocabulary production and recognition tasks, the total number of motion verbs produced and recognized by the participants was computed and the manner-of-motion verbs were identified.

Results

Types of constructions used in the picture description task

The distribution of types of constructions used by the four participant groups is graphically represented in Figure 1.1. This figure shows that the German and the Russian groups used the characteristic S-language construction, that is the construction consisting of a manner verb + a path satellite, to a larger extent than the Spanish group, who, in turn, used the construction involving a non-manner verb + a path satellite more frequently. In addition, the three learner groups made use of the non-boundary-crossing type of expression, even though the German learners used this type of expression to a lesser extent than the two other learner groups. As shown in Figure 1.2, the expressions that did not convey boundary crossing at all were used more frequently by all learner groups than those where boundary crossing was conveyed in an implicit fashion. Finally, Figure 1.1 shows that the construction involving the use of a non-manner verb + a manner adjunct + a path satellite was very rarely used, even by the Spanish learner group.

If we focus on Figure 1.1, it is also worth noting that the Spanish learner group exhibited a more varied pattern of distribution than the other two learner groups. Whereas the German and the Russian learners, like the Danish NSs, clearly showed a predominant use of the construction involving a manner verb + a path particle, the Spanish learners made use of three major types of constructions, namely the constructions respectively involving the

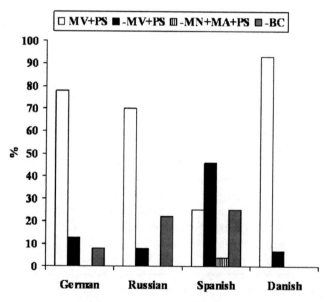

Figure 1.1 Picture description task: Mean percentages of types of constructions used. *Note*: MV + PS = construction involving a manner verb + a path satellite; −MV + PS = construction involving a non-manner verb + a path satellite; −MV + MA + PS = construction involving the use of a non-manner verb + a manner adjunct + a path particle; −BC = non-boundary-crossing type of expression.

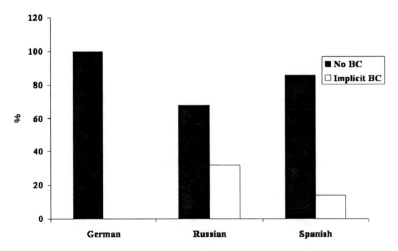

Figure 1.2 Picture description task: Mean percentages of non-boundary-crossing type of expression.

use of a non-manner and a manner verb + a path satellite, and the non-boundary-crossing type of expression.

In order to check for significance in the use of the different types of constructions by the four participant groups, a multinomial logistic regression model was applied to these data. The results of this analysis showed significant differences between the types of construction used by the groups ($p = 0.00$) as well as significant differences between all the pairwise comparisons performed, comparisons that were adjusted for multiple testing by application of a Bonferroni correction (Danish versus German: $p = 0.00$; Danish versus Russian: $p = 0.00$; Danish versus Spanish: $p = 0.00$; German versus Spanish: $p = 0.00$; Russian versus Spanish: $p = 0.00$; German versus Russian: $p = 0.01$). In order to check whether these significant contrasts were due to the differential use of specific types of constructions by the participant groups, a Fisher's exact pairwise test was conducted on the data. These comparisons, which again were adjusted for multiple testing by the application of a Bonferroni correction, showed that with respect to the MV + PS (manner verb + path satellite) and –MV + PS (non-manner + path satellite) constructions, the two L1 S-language groups, that is the German and the Russian learners, were significantly different from the V-language group, that is the Spanish learners (for both constructions: German versus Spanish: $p = 0.00$; Russian versus Spanish: $p = 0.00$), but not significantly different from each other (MV + PS: German versus Russian: $p = 0.11$; –MV + PS: German versus Russian: $p = 0.25$). When the Danish NSs versus the three learner groups were compared, the results showed that with respect to the MV + PS (manner verb + path satellite) construction, the Danish NS group was significantly different from all the three learner groups (Danish versus German: $p = 0.00$; Danish versus Russian: $p = 0.00$; Danish versus Spanish: $p = 0.00$). In contrast, with respect to the –MV + PS construction, the performance of the Danish NS group was only significantly different from the Spanish learner group. (Danish versus Spanish: $p = 0.00$; Danish versus German: $p = 0.7$; Danish versus Russian: $p = 0.5$).

With respect to the construction that included manner information in a separate adjunct (i.e. the –MV + MA + PS construction), no significant differences were found between all the contrasts performed (German versus Spanish: $p = 0.18$; Russian versus Spanish: $p = 0.18$; German versus Russian: $p = 1.0$; Danish versus German: $p = 1.0$; Danish versus Russian: $p = 1.0$; Danish versus Spanish: $p = 0.18$).

Finally, the pairwise comparisons made with respect to the non-boundary-crossing type of expression revealed a significant difference between the German and the Spanish learner groups ($p = 0.00$) and between the German and the Russian learner groups ($p = 0.00$), but not between the Russian and the Spanish learner groups ($p = 0.58$). The comparisons involving the Danish NS group versus the three learner groups revealed significant differences with respect to all the contrasts made (Danish versus German: $p = 0.00$; Danish versus Russian: $p = 0.00$; Danish versus Spanish: $p = 0.00$).

Proportion of manner-of-motion verb types used in the picture description task

Table 1.2 shows the proportion of manner-of-motion verb types used in relation to the total number of motion verb types employed by the four participant groups in the picture description task. A one-way analysis of variance (ANOVA) performed on the data revealed a significant main effect for type of participant group ($F = 69.78$, MSE = 5307.52678, $p < 0.01$). A post-hoc Scheffe's pairwise test revealed that the two L1 S-language groups were again significantly different from the Spanish L1 group (German versus Spanish: $p = 0.00$; Russian versus Spanish: $p = 0.00$), but

Table 1.2 Picture description task: Proportion of manner-of-motion verb types

	Mean	*SD*
German	81.25	6.50
Russian	83.23	10.92
Spanish	43.06	10.77
Danish	89.22	5.17

not significantly different from each other (German versus Russian: $p = 0.96$). In addition, the Danish NS' performance was not significantly different from the two L1 S-language groups (Danish versus German: $p = 0.19$; Danish versus Russian: $p = 0.43$) but was significantly different from the Spanish language group (Danish versus Spanish: $p = 0.00$).

Knowledge of motion verbs and manner-of-motion verbs in production and recognition vocabulary tasks

Vocabulary production task

Table 1.3 shows the results for the proportion of manner-of-motion verbs produced by the four participant groups in the vocabulary production task. A one-way ANOVA conducted on the data showed a significant main effect for type of participant group ($F = 60.60$, MSE = 5676.29357, $p < 0.01$). Furthermore, a post-hoc Scheffe's test revealed that the two L1 S-language groups were significantly different from the Spanish L1 group (German versus Spanish: $p = 0.00$; Russian versus Spanish: $p = 0.00$) but not significantly different from each other (German versus Russian: $p = 0.90$). Additionally, the Danish NS group was significantly different from the Spanish learner group (Danish versus Spanish: $p = 0.00$) but not significantly different from the two other learner groups (Danish versus German: $p = 0.78$; Danish versus Russian: $p = 0.36$).

Table 1.4 shows the results for the total number of motion verbs produced by the participant groups in the vocabulary production task. These results are quite similar to the ones just described. A one-way ANOVA

Table 1.3 Vocabulary production task: Proportion of manner-of-motion verbs

	Mean	*SD*
German	92.84	7.44
Russian	89.82	7.99
Spanish	50.11	15.72
Danish	96.96	2.91

Table 1.4 Vocabulary production task: Total amount of motion verbs used

	Mean	*SD*
German	11.58	2.43
Russian	10.58	1.38
Spanish	6.75	1.36
Danish	21.33	3.23

revealed a significant main effect for type of participant group ($F = 92.16$, MSE = 462.354167, $p < 0.01$), and a post-hoc Scheffe's test again revealed that the two L1 S-language groups were significantly different from the Spanish L1 group (German versus Spanish: $p = 0.00$; Russian versus Spanish: $p = 0.00$) but not significantly different from each other (German versus Russian: $p = 0.76$). The Danish NS group, however, was significantly different from all three learner groups (Danish versus Spanish: $p = 0.00$; Danish versus German: $p = 0.00$; Danish versus Russian: $p = 0.00$).

Vocabulary recognition task

Tables 1.5 and 1.6, respectively, show the proportion of manner and non-manner-of-motion verbs recognized by the participant groups in relation to the total number of manner and non-manner motion verbs included in the list the participants were presented with. Two separate one-way ANOVAs conducted on these two sets of data revealed a significant difference between the groups with respect to the proportion of manner-of-motion verbs recognized ($F = 315.69$, MSE = 14295.9243, $p = 0.00$) and the proportion of non-manner verb recognized ($F = 42.02$, MSE = 6037.38003, $p = 0.00$). A Scheffe's post-hoc test conducted on the proportion of manner-of-motion verbs data showed that both the German and the Russian learner groups recognized a larger proportion of the manner verbs presented in the vocabulary list than the Spanish learner group (German versus Spanish: $p = 0.00$; Russian versus Spanish: $p = 0.01$).

Table 1.5 Vocabulary recognition task: Proportion of manner-of-motion verbs recognized

	Mean	*SD*
German	40.51	8.81
Russian	31.92	5.33
Spanish	21.54	8.58
Danish	98.59	1.22

Table 1.6 Vocabulary recognition task: Proportion of non-manner-of-motion verbs recognized

	Mean	*SD*
German	48.61	15.19
Russian	57.41	12.38
Spanish	59.72	13.63
Danish	99.07	2.16

Table 1.7 Vocabulary recognition task: Total amount of motion verbs recognized

	Mean	*SD*
German	35.08	5.76
Russian	31.08	3.03
Spanish	24.75	6.44
Danish	81.92	0.90

In addition, the German group recognized a larger proportion of this type of verbs than the Russian learner group (German versus Russian: $p = 0.03$). Furthermore, when the learner groups were compared with that of the Danish NSs, the results showed that the Danish NS group recognized a larger proportion of manner-of-motion verbs than the three learner groups (Danish versus Spanish: $p = 0.00$; Danish versus German: $p = 0.00$; Danish versus Russian: $p = 0.00$).

With respect to the recognition of the non-manner motion verbs, the only contrasts that turned out to be significant were the Danish NS group versus the three learner groups (Danish versus German: $p = 0.00$; Danish versus Russian: $p = 0.00$; Danish versus Spanish: $p = 0.00$). Even though the Spanish learners tended to recognize a larger proportion of non-manner-of-motion verbs than the other two learner groups, the contrasts did not reach significance (German versus Spanish: $p = 0.18$; Russian versus Spanish: $p = 0.97$). In addition, no significant differences were found between the German and the Russian learner groups (German versus Russian: $p = 0.37$).

Finally, Table 1.7 shows the results for the total number of motion verbs recognized from the list given to the participants. A one-way ANOVA revealed a significant difference between the groups with respect to the total number of motion verbs recognized ($F = 387.93$, MSE $= 8208.30556$, $p = 0.00$). A post-hoc Scheffe's test showed that the two L1 S-language groups were significantly different from the Spanish learner group (German versus Spanish: $p = 0.00$; Russian versus Spanish: $p = 0.02$), but not significantly different from each other (German versus Russian: $p = 0.23$). The Danish NS group, as was the case with the vocabulary production task, was significantly different from all the three learner groups (Danish versus Spanish: $p = 0.00$; Danish versus German: $p = 0.00$; Danish versus Russian: $p = 0.00$).

Discussion and Conclusion

The main aim of this study was to examine possible inter- and intra-typological differences in how L2 learners from three different linguistic backgrounds – German, Russian and Spanish – described boundary-crossing motion events in Danish as a second language. In addition, the study examined possible differences between the three learner groups with respect to the degree of productive and receptive knowledge of motion verbs, in general, and of manner-of-motion verbs, in particular. The performance of these learner groups was in all cases compared to that of a group of Danish NSs.

The results of the study showed clear inter-typological differences between the learners whose L1 is an S-language, that is the German and the Russian learners, on the one hand, and the learners whose L1 is a V-language, that is the Spanish learners, on the other, with respect to (a) the type of construction used in the picture description task; (b) the proportion of manner-of-motion verbs used in both the picture description task and the vocabulary production task; and (c) the total amount of motion verbs produced and recognized in the vocabulary production and recognition tasks. In contrast, no such significant differences were observed between the two intra-typological S-language groups, that is the German and the Russian learner groups.

With respect to the type of construction used when describing the boundary-crossing motion events in the picture description task, the German and the Russian learner groups used the characteristic Danish construction consisting of a manner verb + a path particle (e.g. *manden løber ind i huset* 'the man runs into the house') to a larger extent than the Spanish learner group, who, in turn, exhibited a predominant use of the construction involving a non-manner verb + a path particle construction (e.g. *manden kommer ind i huset* 'the man comes into the house'). This result points to the influence of the learners' L1 typological patterns, because the type of construction used by the two learner groups in L2 Danish closely resembles the characteristic expression employed in their respective native languages. Specifically, for the German and the Russian speakers, the characteristic Danish construction involving the use of a manner verb + a path satellite follows the general lexicalization pattern of their native languages where motion and manner are typically conflated in the main verb, with path expressed in a satellite. However, the closer resemblance between the types of path satellites found in Danish and German – unbound particles – as compared to Russian – bound prefixes – for the expression of boundary-crossing events (Hasko, 2009) did not lead to any intra-typological differences between the two L1 S-language groups. For the Spanish learners, on the other hand, the construction involving the use of a non-manner verb + a path satellite more closely resembles the characteristic Spanish expression for boundary-crossing events, where manner information cannot be coded in the main verb. This expression is, nevertheless, idiosyncratic in that it contains a satellite expressing path. It seems then that the Spanish learner group under investigation has managed to learn a constructional pattern that could be described as S (Figure) + V (Motion) + Satellite (Path) + PP (Ground), a pattern that resembles the appropriate target language pattern in its general form or makeup, but which often lacks the co-expression of manner in the verb.

One finding that seems to support the above conclusion is that the Spanish learner group tended to use the Danish manner-of-motion verb *gå* 'walk' in a non-manner sense to describe target pictures that clearly depicted other manners of moving (e.g. running, dashing, crawling, and creeping). The following examples illustrate this usage: *manden gå ind i huset* 'the man goes into the house' (picture 1); *manden går ud af dåse* 'the man goes out of the jar' (picture 2); *manden går over tæppet* 'the man goes over the carpet' (picture 3); and *manden går ud af huset* 'the man goes out of the house' (picture 5). Because in none of these pictures the figure, that is the man, is performing the locomotion act of walking but rather he is running into, flying out of, crawling over and dashing out of a bounded space, the verb *gå* in these contexts seems to have a general meaning of pure translational motion along a path, equivalent to the meaning of the English verb *go*.

These usages on the part of the learners can be partly explained by the fact that in Danish the verb *gå* can, in given contexts, be used to refer to general translational motion across a path, as in *jeg går ud og handler* 'I go out and shop' where the figure does not necessarily need to go shopping on foot. It is important to note, however, that neither the Danish NS group nor the German and the Russian learner groups used this verb to refer to the pictures that explicitly depicted other manners of motion such as running, flying or crawling. Another potential explanation for the treatment of the Danish verb *gå* as a non-manner verb by the Spanish L1 learners is L3 English influence. The crosslinguistic influence of one foreign language on another has been widely documented in the literature (e.g. Cenoz *et al.*, 2001). Given the phonetic and graphemic similarity between the Danish verb *gå* and the English verb *go*, the learners might have identified their meanings. This explanation is certainly possible, as all the learners in the study reported having studied English for several years during their primary and/or secondary education. What is interesting, however, is that whereas all the learners were likely to have knowledge of the meaning of the English verb *gå*, only the learners with Spanish linguistic background used the Danish verb *gå* in the general sense of pure translational motion. This fact thus seems to point to a third explanation, namely the fact that these usages by the Spanish L2 learners seem to reflect a lack of online attention – while describing the pictures – to the actual manner of movement depicted in them. The learners' attention at the moment of verbally describing the pictures seems to be on the path of motion, that is on the fact that the man is entering, exiting or crossing a given bounded region in space.

This relative lack of online verbal attention to manner of motion by the Spanish learner group is also reflected in their infrequent mention of manner information in a separate constituent, that is in their scarce use of the construction that was described as consisting of a non-manner verb + a manner adjunct + a path satellite (e.g. the –MV + MA + PS construction). A possible explanation for this result may be ease of processing. As indicated by Slobin (2004), and discussed in the first part of this chapter, NSs of V-languages often fail to code manner information in a separate constituent, presumably because the resulting construction is both syntactically and psycholinguistically heavy. Manner information tends to be provided by these speakers only when it is communicatively important in a given context. However, in our investigation, even though the stimuli used in the picture description task depicted both path and manner of motion as salient elements (Özçalişkan, under review), the manner component was frequently ignored by the Spanish learner group when performing this task.

Inter-typological differences between the German and the Russian learners, on the one hand, and the Spanish learners, on the other, were also observed with respect to the proportion of manner-of-motion verb types used in both the picture description and the vocabulary production tasks. Again, learners with German and Russian linguistic backgrounds produced a significantly larger proportion of this type of verbs than learners with a Spanish linguistic background. Thus, whereas the descriptions made by the Spanish learners tended to include only basic level manner-of-motion verbs such as *løbe* 'run', *flyve* 'fly', *svømme* 'swim', *hoppe* 'jump' and *kravle* 'crawl', the descriptions provided by the German and the Russian learners also included the use of more specific and fine-grained manner-of-motion verbs, such as *springe* 'leap', *krybe* 'creep', *liste* 'walk softly, steal' and *klatre* 'clamber'.

The difference in performance between the German and the Russian learners, on the one hand, and the Spanish learners, on the other, can be attributed to the different degree of manner salience in their respective native languages (Slobin, 2004). As speakers of high-manner-salient languages, the German and the Russian learners are used to paying relatively more attention to manner information, and make finer manner distinctions when describing motion events in their L1s than speakers of low-manner-salient languages, that is speakers of Spanish. The basic argument is that the more highly differentiated conceptualization of manner that the German and the Russian speakers have by virtue of their L1 would facilitate the noticing and ulterior acquisition of the different manner distinctions expressed in the Danish manner-of-motion verbs. For Spanish learners, on the other hand, the relative lack of attention to highly differentiated manners of motion in their native language would lead to difficulties in learning the manner distinctions encoded in Danish manner-of-motion verbs. When acquiring this type of verbs, the Spanish learners need to develop highly differentiated conceptual representations of manner of motion, that is representations that include a greater deal of fine-grained manner distinctions than their L1-based ones.

Yet another important inter-typological difference between the German and the Russian learners, on the one hand, and the Spanish learners, on the other, relates to the number of manner and non-manner-of-motion verbs recognized in the vocabulary recognition task. The German and the Russian learners recognized a larger proportion of manner-of-motion verbs than the Spanish learners, whereas the opposite tendency was observed with respect to the non-manner verbs: the Spanish learners recognized a larger proportion of this type of verbs than the German and the Russian learners. Even though this last pattern did not reach statistical significance, the two tendencies suggest that the learners' L1 may enhance the likelihood of recognizing similar semantic patterns in the L2.[9] Finally, inter-typological differences between the two learner groups with L1 S-languages and the learner group with an L1 V-language were found with respect to the total amount of motion verbs produced and recognized in the two vocabulary tasks. The former groups of learners produced and recognized a larger amount of motion verbs in the vocabulary production and recognition tasks. This result is closely related to, and can be partially explained by, the finding discussed above, namely that the German and the Russian learner groups produced and recognized a larger proportion of manner verbs than the Spanish learner group in the two vocabulary tasks and the fact that the Danish lexicon contains a much larger proportion of manner verbs as opposed to non-manner verbs (Pedersen, 2000).

Intra-typological differences between the German and the Russian learner groups, that is the two groups of learners with L1 S-languages, were found with respect to both the number of non-boundary-crossing type of expressions used in the picture description task and the proportion of manner-of-motion verbs recognized in the vocabulary recognition task. With respect to the former, the Russian learners used a significantly larger number of the non-boundary-crossing type of expressions than the German learners, even though their use was still surpassed by the learners with a Spanish linguistic background. The use of this type of expressions, which mainly consisted of descriptions such as *manden laver gymnastik* 'The man does gymnastics' (picture 6) and *manden løber og det er nogle forhindringe på vej* 'The man runs and there are some obstacles in the way' (picture 9), seems to reflect a type of communication strategy on the part of the L2 learners: When the learners do not know or are unsure about the appropriate target-like construction, they provide descriptions that somehow fit what is depicted in the pictures, but do not actually describe the translocational motion depicted in them. On the other hand, descriptions such as *manden løber inde i huset* 'The man runs inside the house' (picture 1) or *manden kravler udenfor huset* 'The man crawls outside the house' (picture 5) could be attributed to the learners' inability to make the Danish distinction between translocative and locative path particles, a distinction that frequently differentiates boundary from non-boundary-crossing motion events in Danish, as illustrated in *Manden løber ind i huset* (translocative) 'The man runs into the house' versus *Manden løber inde i huset* (locative) 'The man runs outside the house'.[10]

With respect to the proportion of manner-of-motion verbs recognized in the vocabulary recognition task, the German learner group was able to recognize a larger proportion of this type of verbs than the Russian learner group, a result that could be attributed to greater similarity between the Danish and the German lexicon of motion verbs in comparison with the Russian lexicon. Hence, even though the German learners did not use a significantly higher proportion of manner-of-motion verbs than the Russian learners in the vocabulary production task, they were nevertheless able to recognize a larger number of this type of verbs in the vocabulary recognition task.

Finally, when the three learner groups are compared with the Danish NS group, the results show that even though the German and the Russian speakers attempted more use of the characteristic Danish manner verb + path construction relative to the Spanish speakers, they did so significantly less than the Danish NS group. The Danish NSs were also better than the three learner groups at producing and recognizing motion verbs in the vocabulary production and recognition tasks, and at recognizing manner-of-motion and non-manner-of-motion verbs in the vocabulary recognition task. In contrast, in terms of use of manner-of-motion verb types in the picture description and vocabulary production tasks, the Danish NSs' performance was only significantly different from the Spanish learner group. These results suggest that even though the performance of the German and the Russian learner groups was generally closer to that of the Danish NSs than to that of the Spanish learner group, these learners had not fully acquired the appropriate L2 thinking-for-speaking patterns, a result that was expected, given their level of language proficiency. Future research could examine L2 learners of more advanced levels of proficiency and from L1 S- versus V-languages to see the extent to which they approximate NS performance.

In sum, the results of this study point to two main inter-related findings. The first is that, in learning to talk about motion events in a foreign language, the inter-typological differences between the learners' L1 and L2 seem to play a more important role than the intra-typological differences within a given type of language. The second is that these results provide evidence for the influence of the learners' L1 thinking-for-speaking patterns in their L2 expressions of motion.[11] Speaking about motion in an L2 thus seems to be influenced by the specific verbalized orientation to experience that is characteristic of the learners' L1. Even though the present study did not include comparable L1 data, the differences observed between the learner groups in relation to the three tasks employed seem to suggest the following: In cases where there is a greater degree of similarity between the thinking-for-speaking patterns in the L1 and the L2, that is learners with typologically similar L1s and L2s – like the German and the Russian learners of Danish investigated in the present study, the acquisition of the L2 patterns is facilitated. In contrast, when the learners' L1 and L2 present larger differences in their preferred ways of verbalizing experiences, that is learners with typologically different L1s and L2s – like the Spanish learners of Danish examined in the present study, the process of learning the specific L2 patterns presents larger acquisitional difficulties. This pattern provides empirical evidence for Kellerman's (1995) transfer-to-nowhere principle, according to which transfer from the learners' L1 into the L2 may be more apparent when the learners fail to realize that there can be crucial differences in the way experience is verbalized in different languages. Consequently, when verbalizing events in a foreign language, the learners '. . . may not look for the perspectives peculiar to that language; instead, they may seek the *linguistic tools* which will permit them to maintain their L1 perspectives' (Kellerman, 1995: 141).

To conclude, the results of this study show that the learners' L1 does make a difference when learning to talk about motion in a foreign language that is typologically different from one's own. When learning an S-language such as Danish, learners with typologically similar L1s and L2s, that is learners with German and Russian linguistic backgrounds – make use of more target-like motion constructions, use a wider variety of manner-of-motion verbs, and are able to both produce and recognize a larger amount of motion verbs than learners with typologically different L1s and L2s, that is learners with a Spanish linguistic background. This study thus provides a clearer role for the learners' L1 thinking-for-speaking patterns than earlier studies that had focused on the L2 expression of motion by learners with L1 S-languages and L2 V-languages (e.g. Cadierno, 2004; Cadierno & Ruiz, 2006; Navarro & Nicoladis, 2005). The divergence in results between learners with L2 V-languages, on the one hand, and learners with L2 S-languages, on the other, may be explained by the different degree of saliency with which the semantic components of a motion event are expressed in S- versus V-framed languages. As indicated by Talmy (2000b), more semantic information is presented in a backgrounded fashion in S-languages compared to V-languages. According to this author, other things being equal, a semantic element is backgrounded if it is expressed in the main verb root or in any other closed-class element such as a satellite. Manner of motion is then generally less salient in

S-languages as compared to V-languages given its characteristic lexicalization in the verb root. L1 V-language speakers acquiring an L2 S-language thus face a double challenge, namely (a) learning to pay relatively greater attention to manner information than what they are used to in their native language, including learning to categorically discriminate among many new manners of motion; and (b) the need to do so on the basis of a type of L2 input where manner information is not particularly salient. The results of this study seem to provide evidence for this double challenge.

Future research in this area may benefit from studies that focus more closely on comprehension processes and examine how L2 learners from various linguistic backgrounds interpret L2 motion constructions. Whereas the present study included a recognition task that attempted to elicit the learner's receptive knowledge of motion verbs, this task only asked the learners to mark the L2 motion verbs they knew, without, therefore, checking whether the learners actually knew the meaning of the verbs in question or to what degree they knew their meaning.[12] The use of other methodologies, such as picture matching tasks, category judgment goodness tasks (e.g. Miller, 1995; Rosch & Mervis, 1975) and intermodal preferential looking tasks (e.g. Golinkoff *et al.*, 1987; Hirsh-Pasek & Golinkoff, 1996) may help us address these questions.[13]

Notes

1. I would like to thank Betina Abrahamsen, Brøndum-Nielsen, Esben Lydiksen, Betina Rohr and Lars Skov for their invaluable help in the data collection process. Also, many thanks to Werner Vach for his help in the statistical analyses of the data, and to ZhaoHong Han and Terence Odlin for their insightful comments on the chapter.
2. According to Slobin (2004, 2006), narrators of both Germanic languages (i.e. Dutch, German and English) and of Russian chose to take the viewer's perspective when describing the 'owl exit scene', that is they chose to focus on the owl's emergence from the tree rather than on the manner in which the emergence took place. In the Germanic languages, one must opt for a manner verb such as *fly* or *pop* or a deictic verb such as *come* plus the particle *out* that expresses path (e.g. *fly/pop/jump out* versus *come out*) when describing this scene, and it was the latter option that was preferred by the speakers of the Germanic languages. If these speakers would have added manner information to this viewer's perspective, they would have had to use a heavier construction such as 'come flying out'. Speakers of Russian also opted for a simple construction with a single verb, but the morpho-syntactic structure of this language allows for an easier and more readily available expression of manner of motion. Russian, in contrast to the Germanic languages, lacks an independent verb such as 'come', and the expression of motion towards the speaker must be expressed by the deictic prefix *pri*; in fact, in this language, path is always expressed by means of prefixes, which cannot be stacked. So when describing the owl exit scene in Russian, one must opt for *pri-letet* 'come-fly' or *vy-letet* 'out-fly', and the majority of the Russian speakers chose, like their Germanic counterparts, the latter option. What is crucial here is

that both options contain a manner verb, which accounts for the more frequent use of manner verbs by Russian speakers as compared to speakers of Germanic languages.

3. A noteworthy exception is the study by Tsekos Phillips (2007) who looked at beginning and low-intermediate English-speaking learners of Spanish.

4. Adult foreigners living in Denmark are entitled to Danish language tuition for up to three years. Three different types of programs are available depending on the level of formal schooling of the students in question. The program attended by the learners in the present study emphasizes the need for learners to acquire diverse oral and written language skills, knowledge of Danish culture, history and society, and to learn to discuss given themes from different perspectives. In addition to this, two other programs exist: one is for participants who do not read or write in their own language or who do not master a European script, and the other is for participants with basic schooling from their home country.

5. The three teaching programs described in note 4 are divided into six modules, each with specific aims. In order to move up a module, learners must pass a test that shows that they have acquired the required skills of the previous one. The modules are characterized in agreement with the CEFR, a guideline developed by the Council of Europe to describe the achievements of foreign language learners across Europe. According to this guideline, learners are placed into three broad divisions with two sub-levels in each: (a) a basic user, which comprises the A1 (breakthrough) and A2 (Waystage) levels; (b) an independent user, which comprises the B1 (Threshold) and B2 (Vantage) levels; and a proficient user, which comprises the C1 (Effective Operational Proficiency) and the C2 (Mastery) levels. At the B1 (Threshold) level, that is the proficiency level of the students who participated in the present study, a learner 'can understand the main points of clear standard input on familiar matters regularly encountered in work, school, leisure, etc.; can deal with most situations likely to arise whilst travelling in an area where the language is spoken; can produce simple connected text on topics which are familiar or of personal interest; can describe experiences and events, dreams, hopes & ambitions and briefly give reasons and explanations for opinions and plans' (http://www. linguanet-europa.org/pdfs/global-scale-grid-en.pdf).

6. I would like to thank Şeyda Özçalişkan for kindly letting me use her stimulus pictures in this investigation.

7. The sub-category of walking verbs is particularly dense in Danish. According to Pedersen's (2000) taxonomy, it involves sound verbs, that is walking with little or much noise (e.g. *liste* 'tiptoe', *snige sig* 'sneak' and *trampe* 'stomp'), verbs that involve walking in specific surroundings, usually walking in step within a specific group of people, or wearing specific shoes or clothes (e.g. *defilere* 'march' and *spankulare* 'strut about'), and verbs involving walking slowly with uncertainty, aimlessly or clumsily (e.g. *drysse* 'saunter', *slentre* 'stroll' and *jokke* 'plod').

8. The verb *fall* has been categorized differently by different authors. For researchers such as Slobin (1996b) and Özçalişkan (under review), *fall* is mainly considered a path verb as its primary meaning is downward direction of motion. In contrast, Zlatev and Yangklang (2004) consider this verb to conflate both path and manner information. Given that the present investigation constitutes a partial replication of Özçalişkan (under review) and that this researcher categorized the English verb *fall* as a path verb, the Danish verb *falde* 'fall' received the same type of classification.

9. For another study that clearly supports the influence of the learners' L1 on the noticing of L2 lexis, the interested reader might consult Paribakht (2005). Thanks to Terence Odlin for providing me with this reference.

10. As indicated earlier in the chapter, Danish possesses an elaborate satellite system consisting of verb particles that indicate an opposition between translocative and locative function, such as *ud-ude* 'out (translocative)-outside', *ind-inde* 'in (translocative)-outside', *op-oppe* 'up (translocative)-upstairs', *ned-nede* 'down (translocative)-downstairs' and *hjem-hjemme* 'home (translocative)-at home'. The suggested inability on the part of the learners to make the distinctions between the translocative and locative uses of these particles can be, at least partially, explained by the subtle phonetic differences that exist between them, which include the presence or absence of glottal stop and stress, as well as differences in vowel length (Cadierno & Lund, 2004).

11. The results of all three tasks included in the present investigation provide evidence for the thinking-for-speaking hypothesis, as they all examine the possible effects of the learners' L1 lexicalization patterns and ways of thinking for speaking on L2 language use. As indicated by Slobin (2003), the label of 'thinking for speaking' embraces all forms of linguistic production and reception as well as a range of mental processes such as remembering and imaging.

12. The issue of what it means to know a word has been the subject of much theoretical and empirical work on vocabulary acquisition. Numerous researchers (e.g. Ellis, 1995; Haastrup & Henriksen, 2000; Harley, 1995; Henriksen, 1999; Meara, 1996; Nation, 1990, 2001; Read, 1993, 2000) have stressed the complexity and multidimensionality of word knowledge, suggesting that various kinds of knowledge are associated with a word, ranging from knowledge related to its pronunciation, spelling and morphological features to knowledge of its syntactic and semantic relationships with other words in the language such as paradigmatic (antonomy, synonomy, hyponymy) and syntagmatic relations (collocational restrictions). Henriksen (1999) describes vocabulary acquisition as development along three dimensions: (a) from partial to precise comprehension, that is the fact that the learner's knowledge of a lexical items moves from mere word recognition through different degrees of partial knowledge towards a more precise comprehension; development along this dimension is primarily associated with the mapping process, which is related to the processes of labeling and packaging (Aitchison, 1994); (b) the depth of knowledge, which is related to the process of network building (Aitchison, 1994), that is discovering the sense relations or intensional links between words; and (c) from receptive to productive control, which refers to a control continuum describing levels of access or use ability (Bialystok & Sharwood Smith, 1985).

13. In fact, methodologies such as these are being used in a NordForsk Infrastructure (Joint Nordic Use of Research Infrastructure)-funded project on 'Spatial categorization and language across populations'. The project, whose main aim is to optimize research in the field of spatial cognition and language carried out in research units across the Nordic and Baltic countries (Norway, Denmark, Finland, Sweden and Estonia) and to link this research to similar units in other European countries such as Great Britain, examines spatial language and cognition from a crosslinguistic perspective in different populations, including L1 and L2 speakers, and normal versus deficient individuals, such as autistic speakers. For more information on the project, visit http://www.nordforsk. org/text.cfm?id=508&path=67,68

14. The English translations were not provided to the participants. They are only included here for the benefit of the non-Danish reader.

Appendix A: Stimulus pictures used in the picture description task

1.   Run into a house

2.   Fly out of a jar

3.   Crawl over a carpet

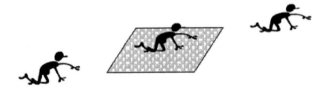

4.   Dive into a pool

5. Dash out of a house

6. Flip over a bar

7. Tumble into a net

8. Creep out of a house

9. Leap over a hurdle

10. Crawl into a house

11. Sneak out of a sack

12. Jump over a cliff

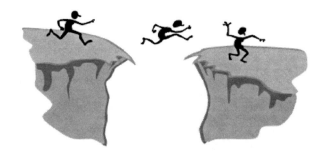

Appendix B: List of Danish motion verbs in vocabulary recognition task[14]

krydse 'cross'	*cykle* 'cycle'	*kravle* 'crawl'
passere 'pass'	*køre* 'drive'	*mave sig* 'crawl on stomach'
forlade 'leave'	*ride* 'ride'	*svømme* 'swim'
skride 'take off'	*ro* 'row'	*rutsche* 'slide'
ankomme 'arrive'	*skøjte* 'skate'	*danse* 'dance'
Dale 'descend'	*sejle* 'sail'	*steppe* 'tap dance'
dratte 'flop down'	*surfe* 'urf'	*valse* 'waltz'
falde 'fall'	*stå på ski* 'ski'	*fare* 'rush'
komme 'come'	*gå* 'walk'	*haste* 'hurry around'
returnere 'return'	*liste* 'tiptoe'	*ile* 'hasten'
stige 'ascend'	*snige sig* 'sneak'	*piske* 'dash'
styrte 'fall'	*trampe* 'stomp'	*ræse* 'rush'
tage 'go'	*defilere* 'march'	*flakke* 'wander about'
følge 'follow'	*marchere* 'march'	*føjte* 'gad about'
forfølge 'pursue'	*spadsere* 'promenade'	*strejfe* 'roam about'
jagte 'chase'	*spankulere* 'strut about'	*svanse* 'flounce'
jage 'chase'	*vade* 'wade'	*tulre* 'blunder about'
vandre 'wander'	*galoppere* 'gallop'	*vimse* 'bustle about'
drysse 'saunter'	*rende* 'run'	*vrikke* 'wiggle'
jokke 'plod'	*sprinte* 'sprint'	*myldre* 'teem/swarm'
sjokke 'shamble'	*spurte* 'spurt'	*sværme* 'swarm'
sjoske 'shamble'	*trave* 'trot'	*vrimle* 'teem/crawl'
slentre 'stroll'	*hinke* 'hop on one leg'	*drive* 'stream'
traske 'plod'	*hoppe* 'hop'	*strømme* 'pour'
trisse 'trundle'	*springe* 'spring'	*sive* 'ooze'
tøffe 'chug'	*flyve* 'fly'	*vælde* 'gush'
bevæge sig 'move'	*futte* 'scurry'	*løbe* 'run'
afgå 'depart'	*drøne* 'race'	

Chapter 2

The Role of Thinking for Speaking in Adult L2 Speech: The Case of (Non)unidirectionality Encoding by American Learners of Russian

VICTORIA HASKO

Introduction

The expression of motion events has gained increasing prominence in the areas of crosslinguistic, cross-typological and acquisitional research and is currently being investigated by theoretical, cognitive and applied linguists working with diverse languages. Perception of the physical characteristics of motion events is an integral component of our daily functioning, and linguistic encoding of motion meanings is an important and necessary semantic domain in all world languages. Recent studies have attested that surface structures used in different languages to encode motion exhibit distinctive lexicalization patterns (Talmy, 2000a, 2000b, 2006). Because the semantic domain of motion is universally expressed, on the one hand, but relies on diverging lexicalization patterns and grammatical constructions, on the other, motion talk presents an interesting case for analysis. Surface structures expressing motion meanings have been used to study the inter-relationship between preferred linguistic patterns and meanings that emerge in the process of speaking in children acquiring their first language (L1), as well as adult monolingual speakers and second language (L2) learners (Gagarina, 2009; Cadierno, this volume). The study reported in this chapter investigated the influence of the diverging linguistic patterns for encoding motion on adult L2 learners' online thinking-for-speaking (TFS) processes, as they filtered their perceptions of visually portrayed motion scenes into verbalized events during a communicative task of storytelling.

Linguistic relativity and the encoding of motion domain

Irrespective of the language that we speak, all humans are equipped with the same biological characteristics, which allow us to process motion events and spatial characteristics of our surroundings. Hence, linguistic studies investigating spatial semantics and event structure often begin with the argument that the basic components of human perception and cognition (including those related to the conceptualization of motion and spatial relations) are shared by all humans and are independent of language and culture (Fodor, 1975; Landau & Jackendoff, 1993; Li & Gleitman, 2002; Pinker, 1994). Thus, the argument that follows is that it is only 'commonsensical' to regard the relevant linguistic categories and structures as 'more-or-less straightforward mappings from a preexisting conceptual space, programmed into our biological nature' (Li & Gleitman, 2002: 266).

However, recently, numerous studies have posited that languages vary greatly in the means they employ to express spatial meanings and that there is no universal formula for describing motion events syntactically or semantically (Berman & Slobin, 1994; Bowerman & Levinson, 2001; Cadierno, this volume; Filipović, 2007; Gentner & Goldin-Meadow, 2003; Gumperz & Levinson, 1996; Hasko & Perelmutter, 2010; Hickmann & Robert, 2006; Lucy, 1992a, 1992b; Slobin, 2006). The surface structures and systematic patterns used by speakers of various languages to express motion meanings have been analyzed most extensively through the typological lens developed by Talmy (1985, 2000a, 2000b). Talmy identified several conceptual core schemas, or components, involved in the expression of motion events, including *Figure, Manner, Path, Ground,* etc.[1]; he further proposed a crosslinguistic typology based on the variability that exists among individual languages in the encoding of these core components. Of these, *Manner* and *Path* form the basis of the inter-typological dichotomy within which each language could be placed.[2] Talmy refers to the languages in which the main verb is used to encode path as 'verb-framed languages' (V-languages; e.g. Romance, Semitic and Polynesian languages), and the languages in which the main verb encodes manner and a satellite is used to convey path information as 'satellite-framed languages' (S-languages; e.g. Germanic and Slavic languages).

Several conclusions have emerged from the cross-typological research on motion talk. First, there exists linguistic variability across languages in the encoding of motion events and the description of spatial relations, which refutes the universal view. Second, there is a link between the cross-linguistic variability and the characteristics of spatial reference and motion events that speakers of the languages habitually attend to or ignore. This evidence revitalizes the linguistic relativity debate by virtue of its support for the 'weaker' Neo-Whorfian view suggesting that online processes of language production are influenced by linguistic patterns characteristic of individual languages (Slobin, 1996a, 2003, 2004, 2006).

Based on his extensive crosslinguistic research on motion talk, Slobin has developed a so-called TFS framework for the study of the relationship between language and the mind. In this approach, language is treated and analyzed as a human activity (hence, *thinking* and *speaking* as opposed to *thought* and *language*). In this view, linguistic differences and rules play a role in language production, as they force speakers to fit thoughts into available linguistic frames during the process of speaking:

> We encounter the contents of the mind in a special way when they are being accessed for use. That is, the activity of thinking takes on a particular quality when it is employed in the activity of speaking. In the evanescent time frame of constructing utterances in discourse one fits one's thoughts into available linguistic frames. (Slobin, 1996a: 76)

Slobin and other researchers (e.g. Berman & Slobin, 1994; Filipović, 2007; McNeill, 2005; Naigles *et al.*, 1998; Negueruela *et al.*, 2004; Özçalişkan & Slobin, 2000; Slobin, 1996a, 2003, 2004, 2006; Zlatev & Yangklang, 2004) have conducted experiments with speakers of multiple languages using linguistic and non-linguistic tasks. The data suggest that variability in lexicalization patterns for encoding motion has consequences for TFS, that is online production of motion descriptions by speakers of these languages. These studies also point to effects of language on categorization, attention, mental imagery, memory, learning and evaluation, although the influence of the language-specific lexicalization patterns on non-linguistic performance has been contested (Gennari *et al.*, 2002; Papafragou *et al.*, 2001). The studies offer evidence for robust TFS effects during online communicative performance as a result of the crosslinguistic lexicalization dichotomy. For instance, the studies have shown that speakers of S-languages (a) attend to and encode manner more frequently and variedly, (b) offer more detailed descriptions of motion path within a single clause and (c) provide more dynamic, rather than static, descriptions of motion paths in comparison to speakers of V-languages.

While Slobin emphasizes thought processes during *linguistic* production, he has explored *non-linguistic* consequences of TFS effects, for example mental imagery in speakers of S- and V-languages. Slobin (2006) conducted an experiment in which monolingual speakers of English[S] and Spanish[V] were given parallel passages to read (from Spanish novels and their English translations) and were later asked to report mental imagery for the novel-based events. Reports given by English speakers contained manner-rich descriptions of the protagonists' movements, while Spanish participants generally reported little or no imagery of the motion manner, even though they could recall physical surroundings of the scene. Balanced Spanish–English bilinguals were also recruited and subjected to the same task in both languages. Slobin (2006) found that their preferences changed based on the language in which they read/recalled passages: after reading in English, the bilinguals' reports consistently contained more mental imagery for manner of motion, whereas their reports following reading in Spanish had fewer descriptions of manner and more accounts of physical surroundings. These data provide support for TFS effects – depending on the language in which the participants were performing the task, the lexicon and grammar of the language shaped bilinguals' speech (and cognition in general, i.e. memory and attention).

Other recent studies have uncovered similar effects of habitual attention to manner versus path in memory, recall and non-verbal tasks. Oh (2003, reported in Slobin, 2006) showed his English[S]-speaking and Korean[V] participants a series of video clips, which included diverse motion events rich in manner nuances. When subjects were given surprise questions about the details of the video clips, their responses revealed that English monolinguals were significantly more precise in recalling the details of the manner of motion, including sensorimotor nuances specific to the motion manner. Experiments by Kersten and his colleagues (Kersten *et al.*, 2003, reported in Slobin, 2006) suggest that habitual attention to manner can surface in non-linguistic learning tasks as well. In a categorization task, English[S]- and Spanish[V]-speaking participants were shown cartoons in which alien creatures moved along paths in a fashion difficult to name in either language. When the participants had to categorize the creatures into four groups on the basis of their path and manner of motion, Kersten *et al.*, found that while both participant groups were similar in how long it took them to distinguish the creatures based on the path of motion, English monolinguals were significantly faster at categorizing the creatures on the basis of manner. The balanced bilinguals who participated in the study performed similarly to either the monolingual Spanish or the monolingual English group, depending on the language in which they were trained for the experiment.

Mixed results are offered by a series of experiments conducted by Gennari *et al.* (2002) who investigated whether the different lexicalization patterns of motion events in English[S] and Spanish[V] could predict how speakers of these languages would perform in non-linguistic tasks involving recognition, similarity judgments and descriptions of a series of video clips. Gennari *et al.* found no effect of language in the recognition memory tasks; however, based on the results of the similarity tasks, they conceded that 'language-specific regularities available in the experimental context may mediate speakers' performance in making non-linguistic judgments' (Gennari *et al.*, 2002: 77).

Although most studies draw on mature linguistic systems, that is monolingual speakers and balanced bilinguals, the TFS argument can be further strengthened by citing evidence from research investigating *the dynamics of developmental L2 systems in adult learners.* In fact, Slobin (1996a) has suggested that the habitual patterns of TFS developed through L1 exposure have direct consequences for L2 acquisition because L1 'training carried out in childhood is exceptionally resistant to restructuring in adult second language acquisition' (Slobin, 1996a: 89). Following this line of thinking, it is logical to assume that if learners' L1 and L2 belong to different typological groups, inter-typological differences should manifest themselves in L2 spontaneous production, and conversely, that if L1 and L2 share similarities, a facilitation effect should be observed. Motion talk has been used in several studies as a testing platform for this conjecture.

Harley (1989) described an acquisitional investigation in which the pattern of path segmentation proved to cause acquisitional difficulties for learners of a typologically different language. In this study, native speakers of English[S] learning French[V] in an immersion environment exhibited a tendency to rely heavily on prepositional phrases to provide directional information in L2 writing. This tendency is not consistent with the French pattern, as path is already incorporated into the motion verb in French. This characteristic of the L2 learners' inter-language is attributed to the habitual surface structures used to encode motion in English, which elaborates path through stackable satellite phrases.

Yu (1996) conducted a study testing both the hypotheses that (a) acquisition of motion talk can be facilitated if L1 and L2 belong to the same typological group and (b) acquisition can be inhibited due to inter-typological differences. Yu recruited advanced L1 Japanese[V] and L1 Chinese[S] learners of English[S] to explore these questions. While Japanese and English belong to two different groups according to Talmy's typology, Chinese and English are more similar in that both have extended manner-of-motion lexicons for habitual encoding of manner.[3] Both learner groups performed three tasks (storytelling, picture description and translation). The results confirmed once again that intra-typological similarities or inter-typological divergences can facilitate or impede, respectively, adult L2 acquisition of motion talk: comparison of the two language groups (L1 Chinese and L1 Japanese) revealed that the first group did significantly better than the second group on all three tasks. Yu (1996) reported the novel finding that even when L1 and L2 are as different as English and Chinese beyond the patterns for encoding motion meanings, intra-typological similarities in the expression of motion meanings can facilitate L2 learning of these structures. When it comes to encoding manner, Chinese is closer to English than it is to Japanese and other East Asian languages, which explains the facilitation in the acquisition of the motion domain by Chinese learners of English.

So far, however, studies investigating the effects of L1 TFS on L2 motion talk are relatively scarce, and several studies report mixed evidence. Navarro and Nicoladis (2005) focused on L2 acquisition of Spanish[V] by

English[S]-speaking adults who had more than two years of university-level instruction and experience in Spanish-speaking countries. The L2 participants were compared to L1 speakers of Spanish on a narrative task (with video segments used as stimuli). Navarro and Nicoladis reported that the L2 participants started to approximate the native speaker group in favoring path verbs over manner verb, which can be viewed as evidence against TFS mediation in adult L2 acquisition of motion constructions. However, this conclusion is not convincing, given that the number of manner versus path verbs in Spanish is rather limited and thus automatically restricts participants' freedom to encode manner even if they attended to it. The analysis of post-verbal particles would, in fact, be a more reliable measure. As already described in the foregoing analysis of Harley's (1989) study, English-speaking learners of V-languages tend to plug in path satellites after motion verbs, a typical construction in English that is often unnecessary in V-languages in which path is encoded through verbs. Indeed, the count of post-verbal particles in Navarro and Nicoladis' study showed divergences from the L1 Spanish pattern in the L2 speakers' greater use of post-verbal phrases, which suggests resistance to a complete shift to L2.

Cadierno (2004) examined the use of motion talk by intermediate and advanced learners of Spanish[V] whose L1, Danish[S], is a typologically different language. Her results did not show a consistent picture with respect to the role of TFS in the encoding of motion events in the L2. On the one hand, Cadierno found that Danish learners exhibited a higher degree of complexity and elaboration of path descriptions in Spanish than the L1 Spanish group, which suggests L1-based TFS interference. On the other, the study did not confirm that Danish learners would pay more attention to the dynamics of movement than to static setting descriptions or that they would conflate manner and path. In a follow-up study, Cadierno and Ruiz (2006) included an additional means of contrast – the incorporation of a second learner group, Italian[V] learners of Spanish[V]. Similar to the study of Yu (1996), this study investigated whether inter-typological differences (and, consequently, diverging L1 TFS patterns) would surface in the speech of Danish learners of Spanish and account for the differences in the L2 performance of the Danish learners and the Italian learners of Spanish. The token and type analysis showed (a) no significant differences between the two groups of learners and (b) that the Danish learner group did not make use of alternative means of expressing manner information, such as subordinate clauses or descriptions of internal states. These results led the researchers to argue for a limited role of L1 TFS patterns in adult second language acquisition (SLA). However, the researchers did find that the Danish learner group, unlike the Italian learner group, used a significantly higher number of path segments than the other two groups and tended to produce ungrammatical constructions, likely influenced by typological differences related to the encoding of path.

A study by Negueruela *et al.* (2004) makes an interesting contribution to the research on TFS effects in adult L2 acquisition. Negueruela *et al.*, investigated the inter-relationship between gesture and L2 motion talk proficiency in English-speaking adult learners of Spanish and found that their participants learned to follow the rhetorical style characteristic of their target language verbally: the learners did not encode manner in descriptions of manner-rich motion scenes. Yet, the analysis of partici-pants' gestures established that 'giving up' the encoding of manner carries cognitive costs: participants hesitated in their lexical choices, paused, relied on idiosyncratic circumlocution, and still marked manner through gestures in a fashion characteristic of L1-English TFS patterns. Thus, the study, once again, shows that variation in lexicalization patterns has observable consequences for L2 learners depending on the similarities/ differences between the L1 and the L2.

The body of research reviewed so far offers irreconcilable conclusions: it supports and yet simultaneously refutes the effects of TFS influence on adult L2 acquisition of motion talk. The study reported in this chapter con-tributes to the ongoing debate on L2 TFS effects in adult SLA in several ways. First, it delineates and draws upon a unique case of intra-typological variation in the encoding of motion (specifically, the obligatory marking of unidirectionality versus non-unidirectionality of motion, as defined in the next section) that exists in Russian[S] but not in other non-Slavic S- or V-languages. Second, it investigates whether this characteristic of Russian motion talk has a bearing on the L2 TFS processes of English-speaking adult learners of Russian. Thus, the present study not only investigates a previ-ously unexplored aspect of motion talk (i.e. the encoding of unidirectional-ity and non-unidirectionality of motion), but also attempts to evaluate TFS effects that stem from a fine *intra*-typological difference that exists between two S-languages, Russian and English, rather than focusing on more pro-nounced inter-typological distinctions as previous studies have done.

Encoding of motion in Russian and English: Recent findings

Both Russian and English are identified within Talmy's typology as S-languages. There are undeniable similarities on how manner and path are expressed in the two languages. With regard to manner, both boast an extended inventory of manner verbs that are habitually used. English is often used as a classic example of a manner-rich language, as the verbal repertoire for the encoding of manner is particularly robust in English even in comparison to other S-languages, such as German, Dutch or Swedish (Slobin, 2006). Typological research focusing on Russian is not as plentiful as studies investigating English, but the Russian manner-of-motion lexicon has been shown to be of equal, if not greater, richness than that of English (Hasko, 2007; Slobin, 2006). Yet, as more comparative studies emerge, it is becoming clear that the size of the lexicon (or the number of manner verbs) alone may not be the best point for comparison. In spite of their similar richness, verbal repertoires for the expression of motion manner in these two languages appear to be quite dissimilar. Sub-domains such as motion on foot, aquamotion, rotation, saccadic motion, placement and locomotion have been shown to differ between Russian and English and, in fact, between Slavic and non-Slavic S-languages (e.g. Hasko & Perelmutter, 2010; Kopecka, 2010; Majsak & Rakhilina, 2007).

There are additional subtle differences with regard to the specificity and frequency of manner encoding between the two languages. For instance, Russian lacks generic verbs of motion such as the English *come*, *go* and *get* that can refer to walking, climbing, flying, swimming, driving, etc. A sentence such as *I went to Europe last summer* can only be rendered in Russian through the verb *ezdit'* 'go by vehicle or drive'. Whereas in the case of English, generic manner-free verbs are frequently used with various satellites in reference to manner-rich scenes (as in *get up the ladder, get over the fence, get out of the garage, get up in the air*) to highlight path versus manner, Russian does not typically allow for a manner-free option.

As for the encoding of path, the typological literature highlights the common pattern that characterizes both Russian and English as S-languages, namely the expression of path through particles-satellites, with the only difference being that Russian relies on bound path prefixes and English relies on unbound path satellites. In the Slavic research literature, the role of prefixes in encoding spatial meanings and their interaction with the semantics of verbs of motion is widely acknowledged (e.g. Cienki, 1989; Janda, 1988; Titelbaum, 1990). However, recent studies suggest that the expression of path in Russian is more multifarious, semantically and structurally, than in other S-languages, including English (cf. Hasko & Perelmutter, 2010).

Russian and English differ in the encoding of path in several important aspects. One of the major differences is that both bound prefixes *and* unbound prepositions play an important role in path descriptions in Russian (e.g. Murav'eva, 2006; Skvortsova, 2004), while English overwhelmingly relies on unbound satellites. Thus, in the case of English, the predominant lexicalization pattern for encoding manner is 'an unprefixed verb + path satellite(s)', for example:

(1)   *The girl is **running**^{MANNER} **to**^{PATH}. the park.*

The lexicalization pattern characteristic of English is also possible in Russian, for example:

(2)   *Devochka **bezhit**^{MANNER} v^{PATH} park.*
      [girl   runs   to   park]
      'The girl is running to the park'.

Yet the pattern illustrated in Example (2) is neither the only pattern for encoding motion in Russian nor even the most common. Drawing on the work of Filipović (2007) on Serbo-Croatian, Driagina (2007) has shown that the range of meanings expressed by Russian satellites encompasses the encoding of how spatiotemporal boundaries of motion events interact with the path of motion, which is achieved through the use of prefixation. A prefix-satellite is obligatory in boundary-crossing and boundary-reaching events. Consider, for example, Examples (3) and (4):

(3) *Sobaka   vbezhala*^{MANNER/PATH}   *v*^{PATH}   *dom.*
     [dog   in-ran   into   house]
     'The dog ran in the house'.

(4) *Sobaka   podbezhala* ^{MANNER/PATH}   *k*^{PATH}   *devochke.*
     [dog   up to-ran   toward   girl]
     'The dog ran up to the girl'.

Note that both prefixed satellites and unbound satellites function as conceptual units in boundary-crossing and boundary-reaching descriptions to explicate motion path and its interaction with ground. Unprefixed verbs of motion [as in Example (2)] are reserved for non-boundary-crossing and non-boundary-reaching motion events only, events that imply no interaction between the path of motion and the spatial boundaries of motion events.

Additionally, Russian and English differ markedly in how they encode temporal characteristics of motion events. The slot for prefixes in Russian verbs of motion can be used to encode aspect, and in fact, many procedural motion verbs are derived through the process of perfectivizing prefixation (Forsyth, 1970). When the satellite slot is taken by an aspectual prefix, the path of motion has to be encoded by unbound satellites. This specifies yet another possible lexicalization pattern in Russian: a prefixed verb with an aspectual prefix plus an unbound path satellite. An example is given in Example (5).

(5) *Sobaka **pobezhala***^{AKTIONSARTEN/MANNER} *za*^{PATH} *devochkoi.*
     [dog   beginning of action-ran   after   girl]
     'The dog took off running after the girl'.

Lastly, and most importantly for this investigation, a select group of manner verbs in Russian formally expresses unidirectionality and non-unidirectionality of motion in space. The rigid boundaries for inclusion into this group of (non)unidirectional verbs are based on a seemingly isolated 'pairedness' phenomenon. The primary semantic feature of this verbal class is that when unprefixed, these verbs come in imperfective pairs that essentially state the same type of motion manner (roughly corresponding to English *run, crawl, climb, wander, drive,* etc.), but still provide different information about the motion event (Foote, 1967; Isachenko, 1960). Specifically, one group of verbs expresses motion *in one direction*, while the verbs serving as their paired counterparts lack this meaning of unidirectionality (Ward, 1965). While a variety of terms have been proposed to capture this opposition, the terms that best capture this dichotomy, in my view, are 'unidirectional' and 'non-unidirectional' [hereafter, (non)unidirectional]. Table 2.1 presents the lists of these two groups of verbs of motion.

The opposition expressed by the verbs in Table 2.1 has been argued to be not only of directional but also of sub-aspectual nature (Kagan, 2010; Zalizniak & Shmelev, 2000), as all of the (non)unidirectional verbs are imperfective. According to Vinogradov (1960), unidirectional verbs refer to motion events that 'flow' or 'unfold' not only (a) in one direction, but also (b) continuously and (c) at a particular moment. These characteristics are exemplified in Example (6), retrieved from the Russian National Corpus (www.ruscorpora.ru).

(6)   *Nu vot, **idu**   ia po ulitse Gor'kogo.*
      [so   go-UNI, IMP I   on Street Gorky]
      'So, I am walking down Gorky Street'.

Table 2.1 (Non)unidirectional verbs of motion

Unidirectional	*Non-unidirectional*	*Translations*
idti	*khodit'*	'to go; move along on foot'
bezhat'	*begat'*	'to run'
bresti	*brodit'*	'to wander'
vezti	*vozit'*	'to carry by vehicle/to convey'
vesti	*vodit'*	'to lead'
gnat'	*goniat'*	'to chase; drive (a herd, etc.)'
ekhat'	*ezdit'*	'to move by vehicle; to drive'
katit'	*katat'*	'to roll'
lezt'	*lazit'*	'to climb'
letet'	*letat'*	'to fly'
nesti	*nosit'*	'to carry (usually in hands)'
plyt'	*plavat'*	'to swim'
polzti	*polzat'*	'to crawl'
tashchit'	*taskat'*	'to drag'

In contrast, non-unidirectional verbs refer to motion that is (a) not in a single direction, (b) not in one take and (c) not at the same time at once. Non-unidirectional verbs can be viewed as providing a 'complex' view of a motion event (Foote, 1967) by presenting it as a series of unidirectional events forming a non-unidirectional trajectory [as in Example (7)] or as a roundtrip (as in Example (8)].

(7) **Khozhu**   *ia znakomymi zakoulkami*   *po   liubimomu   tsentru.*
     [go-NON, IMP I   familiar   backstreets   in   favorite   center]
     'I am walking up and down familiar backstreets in my favorite city center'.

Because non-unidirectional verbs of motion cannot refer to motion in one direction, when they are used with a clearly marked goal of motion they signify completed roundtrips [as in Example (8)] or habitual events referring to multi-leg trips [as in Example (9)].

(8) *Priznavaisia, nebos', **khodili***   *v cheshskii klub, pivo pit'?*
     [confess,   probably,   went-NON, IMP to Czech   pub   beer drink]
     'Tell me the truth, you probably went to the Czech pub to drink beer?'

(9) *On chasto **khodil***   *v   teatr,   prochel mnogo   knig.*
     [he often   went-NON, IMP   to   theater   read   many   books]
     'He often went to the theater, read many books'.

It is not accidental that the group of (non)unidirectional verbs of motion includes only unprefixed verbs of motion. The reason is that, due to their semantics, that is focus on directionality and imperfectivity rather than the reaching or crossing of spatial and temporal boundaries, they refer to imperfective non-boundary-crossing and non-boundary events. Arguably, when a prefix is added to a motion verb, the spatial or aspectual information that the prefix communicates subdues the directionality nuance and highlights the reaching/crossing of spatial boundaries (when a prefix-satellite is added) or temporal boundaries (when a perfectivizing prefix is added). Thus, the use of (non)unidirectional verbs commands Russian speakers' attention not only to the unidirectionality or non-unidirectionality of motion path, but also to the temporal characteristics of a motion event and the overall appropriate lexicalization pattern in which the verb is employed, as well as the manner of motion.

It is without dispute that (non)unidirectionality of motion can potentially be encoded in all languages implicitly (e.g. contextually) and explicitly through various types of circumlocution. However, (non)unidirectionality is habitually and obligatorily expressed in Russian when certain common types of motion events are described (i.e. the ones listed in Table 2.1). For example, if one wanted to describe a running figure in Russian, the speaker would obligatorily need to attend to the directionality of the figure's path and verbally frame the event as either unidirectional or non-unidirectional by choosing between *bezhat'*-UNI and *begat'*-NON 'run'. On the basis of the TFS hypothesis formulated by Slobin, one would argue that this idiosyncratic characteristic of Russian verbs of motion trains its speakers to obligatorily attend to, differentiate between and explicitly encode unidirectional and non-unidirectional events. Since English does not require consistent encoding of this distinction, the TFS hypothesis would predict that English-speaking learners of Russian would experience marked difficulties in shifting to the L2-specific TFS pattern due to their lack of experience attending to and encoding (non)unidirectionality of motion, despite the fact that Russian and English share general typological characteristics of S-languages. On the other hand, the universal, non-relativistic view would suggest that L2 learners, especially those at advanced levels of proficiency, should not have marked difficulties in expressing (non)unidirectionality in a fashion consistent with the L2 grammar, since (non)unidirectional verbs refer to common types of motion events (such as motion on foot, driving, flying, swimming, etc.), which can be perceived through the pre-existing conceptual space programmed into our biological nature (cf. Li & Gleitman, 2002).

The present study sought to test the two competing views outlined above by comparing the verbal behaviors of monolingual Russian speakers to highly proficient L2 learners of Russian in quantitative and qualitative terms. Quantitatively, the frequency with which the two speaker groups attended to and encoded (non)unidirectionality of motion was measured, and qualitatively, the contexts of use and lexicalization patterns within which (non)unidirectional descriptions occurred during a spontaneous oral production task were compared. Specifically, the following questions were asked:

(1) Do highly proficient, adult L2 learners of Russian employ (non)-unidirectional verbs with the same frequency as monolingual Russian speakers?

(2) Do highly proficient, adult L2 learners of Russian employ (non)unidirectional verbs in the same contexts, that is in reference to the same motion events, as monolingual Russian speakers?

(3) Do highly proficient, adult L2 learners of Russian employ (non)unidirectional verbs within the same lexicalization pattern for encoding motion that characterizes the speech of monolingual Russian speakers?

The Study

Participants

Sixty participants took part in the study: 30 American learners of Russian attending a liberal arts college in the northeastern United States and 30 native speakers of Russian residing in Eastern Russia. The mean age of the monolingual Russian participants, all of whom were undergraduate students, was 19 years. The L2 learners of Russian ($M = 26.5$ years) were enrolled in advanced-level Russian courses in a highly intensive summer immersion program to which they had applied from various universities from across the United States, most of them being undergraduate and graduate majors in various fields of Slavic Studies. The learners had been placed into advanced courses after taking a series of rigorous institutional entrance tests, which included a simulated Oral Proficiency Test and computerized grammar, speaking, listening and writing tests. On average, the learners had studied Russian for 5.3 years. They reported using Russian professionally and/or socially on a regular basis, and all deemed Russian important for their future professional plans.

Procedure

The goal of the study was to investigate the inter-relationship between online thinking and speaking. Accordingly, a *spontaneous oral production task* was chosen for data elicitation. The wordless picture book *Frog, Where Are You?* (Mayer, 1969) served as a stimulus for eliciting motion-rich descriptions. Prior to the onset of storytelling, participants were given five minutes to look through the book, at which time they were allowed to consult a list of select nouns that included animals and objects significant for the flow of the story. The actual storytelling took 20 minutes, on average, and was audio recorded.

Data analysis

To analyze the use of (non)unidirectional motion verbs, the study adopted *contrastive learner corpus analysis (CLCA)*, a methodological approach in which electronic corpora comparable in size, domain, genre and other characteristics are formed from L1 and L2 speakers, with all participants being similar in age, socio-economic and educational background, etc. Two corpora were, therefore, created from the monolingual speakers group and the L2 learners group, respectively, and they were compared in quantitative and qualitative terms, the purpose being to uncover their similarities and differences (cf. Granger, 2002; Pavlenko & Driagina, 2007).

Upon completion of the storytelling task, all audio recordings were transcribed and stored electronically. To ensure quick and easy retrieval of motion verbs, all (non)unidirectional verbs, corresponding path satellites (bound and unbound) and aspectual prefixes marking temporal boundaries of motion events were tagged as such in both corpora.

Results

Frequency counts of L1 and L2 corpora

The word count showed that the L2 learners were on a par with the monolingual Russian speakers in their ability to produce extended narratives. Thus, in terms of narrative length, there were no significant differences between the Russian monolinguals and the learners of Russian $[t(29) = 1.39, p > 0.05]$, with the latter producing stories only slightly shorter (mean = 356 words) than those told by the native speakers (mean = 399 words). However, with regard to the encoding of motion, the native speakers' and the learners' narratives showed important differences.

Analysis of the two corpora in terms of motion richness, that is the number of motion verbs per narrative, revealed a significant difference between the monolinguals' and learners' narratives ($t = 2.57$, df = 29, $p < 0.05$), with the Russian monolinguals producing stories richer in motion descriptions. Thus, on average, verbs of motion account for 11.3% of all words in the monolinguals' narratives (SD = 2.6), and for 9.7% in the learners' stories (SD = 2.5). The significance of the language group effect was also confirmed by an analysis of variance (ANOVA) ($F = 5.4$, df = 1, $p < 0.05$). This translates to about 43 verbs of motion per narrative in the monolingual corpus and 34 verbs of motion in the L2 learner corpus. These findings are summarized in Table 2.2.

The most interesting result, however, comes from the (non)unidirectional verbs, the target of the present study. These verbs constitute only a small group in both the monolingual and learner narratives, which is not surprising considering that these verbs only refer to durative, non-boundary-crossing or -reaching events. The percentage of (non)unidirectional verbs in the monolingual narratives averages 4.3% (SD = 4.2) relative to the total number of motion verbs per narrative. In the L2 learners' stories, however, this number is significantly higher (mean = 12.3%, SD = 8.5) (see Table 2.2; Mann–Whitney *U*-test, $p < 0.001$). This finding is

Table 2.2 Length and motions characteristic of L1 and L2 corpora

	Narrative length (words)	*Verbs of motion (tokens) per narrative*	*Motion richness of corpus, %*	*(Non) unidirectional richness per corpus, %*	*Ratio of UNI to NON verbs of motion*
L1 Russian	Mean = 399	Mean = 43	Mean = 11.3	Mean = 4.3	5:1
	SD = 135.5	SD = 13	SD = 2.6	SD = 4.2	
L2 Russian	Mean = 356	Mean = 34	Mean = 9.7	Mean = 12.3	1:1
	SD = 108.2	SD = 13	SD = 2.5	SD = 8.5	

unexpected: One would expect to discover underuse of the notoriously difficult (non)unidirectional verbs, and yet the data show that while the overall motion richness is lower in the L2 corpus, the (non)unidirectional verbs are overrepresented in the learners' narratives. This will be further explained through SLA.

Aside from the significant overuse of (non)unidirectional verbs by the learners, Table 2.2 shows that the L2 corpus is also characterized by a marked difference, vis-à-vis the native speaker corpus, in the frequency of unidirectional and non-unidirectional motion verbs. The monolingual speakers heavily favored unidirectional verbs to describe the motion story (the ratio of unidirectional to non-unidirectional verbs is 5:1), but the L2 learners used the verbs with a 1:1 ratio. The diverging verbal portrayals (predominantly unidirectional descriptions in the L1 corpus versus evenly mixed unidirectional/non-unidirectional descriptions in the learner corpus) are reflective of diverging TFS patterns. It therefore seems that the highly proficient L2 adult learners of Russian had not completely shifted to the target language TFS.

Encoding of individual directional episodes

The storybook, which served as a stimulus for motion talk in the present study, is a collection of static pictures. Intended for children, the pictures are straightforward and allow the 'reader' to make easy inferences about the basic structure of the plot portrayed in the story. Therefore, it was possible in the present study to focus on each individual motion event and compare the monolinguals and learners with respect to how they encoded (non)unidirectionality in each episode. Table 2.3 provides descriptors of each motion episode narrated by the participants as either unidirectional or non-unidirectional (listed in the plot-based order) and the numbers assigned to the episodes.

Inferences can be made about the learners' ability to differentiate between the conceptual schemas underlying the expression of (non)unidirectionality through intra- and inter-group consistency analyses of the level of agreement within/between the participant groups in framing each motion episode as either unidirectional or nonunidirectional. Logically, a high level of agreement within the learner corpus would be indicative of a stable mature TFS pattern that learners share in attending to and verbalizing (non)unidirectionality of motion. A high level of agreement between the learner corpus and the monolingual corpus would suggest that the two participant groups share a TFS pattern for encoding (non)unidirectionality, or that a shift to the target language TFS has occurred. Figures 2.1 and 2.2 graphically represent how (non)unidirectional verbs were used by the monolingual group and the learner group, respectively, in the encoding of the individual episodes under analysis.

Table 2.3 Motion events portrayed as directional by L1 and L2 speakers

Number of the episode	Source corpus	(Non)unidirectional episode
1	L2	The frog escaping from the jar
2	L2	The boy crawling on the ground
3	L1	The boy and the dog wandering in the woods
4	L1/L2	The boy and the dog moving along
5	L1	The dog under the tree
6	L1/L2	The bees near the swarm
7	L1/L2	The chase (the bees after the dog)
8	L1/L2	The chase (the dog from the bees)
9	L2	The owl's emergence from the tree
10	L2	The boy climbing the tree
11	L1/L2	The owl following the boy
12	L1/L2	The boy climbing the rock
13	L1/L2	The deer carrying the boy
14	L1/L2	The dog following the deer
15	L1/L2	The boy and the dog in the swamp
16	L1/L2	The boy carrying the frog home

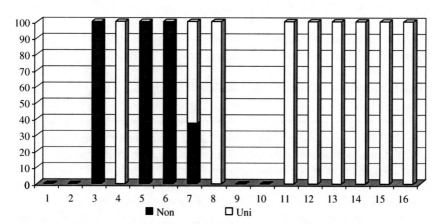

Figure 2.1 Directionality of the contexts in monolinguals' narratives

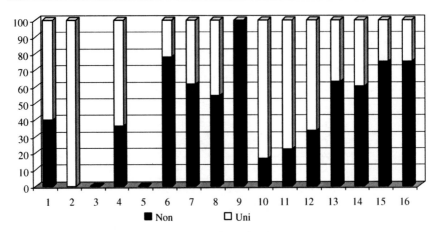

Figure 2.2 Directionality of the contexts in the learners' narratives

Figure 2.1 shows that the native Russian speakers' stories are characterized by a high degree of consistency. The monolingual participants consistently shared a common interpretation and framing of individual events as having either a unidirectional or a non-unidirectional trajectory. This confirms that the frog story is a reliable and unambiguous instrument for eliciting unidirectional versus non-unidirectional descriptions. Figure 2.2, on the other hand, demonstrates that such within-group consistency is lacking in the L2 corpus; the same episodes were encoded as both unidirectional and non-unidirectional in the L2 corpus by different L2 learners. This lack of within-group consistency suggests that the learners did not share a stable and mature TFS pattern for encoding non-unidirectionality and that they failed to recognize and encode (non)unidirectionality in the systematic manner characteristic of the Russian TFS pattern. For a deeper understanding of the choices made by the L1 and L2 speakers, the perceptual characteristics of all motion events marked as (non)unidirectional, their linguistic encoding and the lexicalization patterns within which the verbs were used by the native speakers and the L2 learners were analyzed.

L1 speakers' narratives: Sentence-level analysis

Unidirectional verbs

As the frequency analysis showed, the monolingual Russian speakers narrated the episodes in question as unidirectional five times more frequently than as non-unidirectional. This is not surprising: after all, the underlying idea of the plot is inherently unidirectional – the boy and the dog are on a quest to find the lost pet frog. Most of the episodes in the story are pictorially presented as trips from one point to the other with the starting point and the endpoint of these trajectories explicitly provided, excluding the possibility of a non-unidirectional interpretation.

Unidirectional verbs abound in the monolingual frog stories, particularly in the descriptions that represent the boy's journey *as the sum of short, goal-oriented trips in one direction*: first, a trip from the house to the forest, then from the forest to the swamp, etc. The following two examples illustrate Episodes 10 and 15, 'the boy climbing the rock' and 'the boy and the dog swimming towards the shore', respectively (see Table 2.3):

(10) *On* **lezet**   *na kamen'.*
     [he climbs-UNI, IMP on rock]
     'He   climbs the rock'.

(11) *Sobaka   zdes'* **plyviot**   *i mal'chik ei pokazyvaet vrode kak, Ne shumi!*
     [Dog   here swims-UNI, IMP]
     'Here the dog is swimming (to the boy) and the boy is gesturing to it like, "Quiet!" '

The most salient type of unidirectional motion event in the native speaker corpus is that of a 'chase'/'flight'. Chasing and fleeing are narrated in Episode 7 'the bees chasing the dog', Episode 8 'the dog running away from the bees', Episode 11 'the owl following the boy', Episode 13 'the deer carrying the boy' and Episode 14 'the dog following the deer'. These episodes account for 70% of all unidirectional descriptions in the native speakers' stories. Based on our world knowledge, chasing and fleeing are most easily conceptualized as having a unidirectional trajectory from one point to the other. The consistency with which the chases were framed as unidirectional in the native speaker corpus, in fact, proves that they were overwhelmingly perceived and presented by the native speakers as one-leg trips with trajectories unfolding in one direction towards some endpoint, as shown in Example (12).

(12) *Kogda oni* **bezhali,**   *natknulis'*   *na*   *bol'shoi kamen'.*
     [when they ran-UNI, IMP]
     'When they were running (away from the bees), they stumbled upon a big rock'.

Forty-six percent of the native speakers explicitly encoded either the goal or the source of motion in their unidirectional descriptions through goal-oriented directional satellites, which include prepositions *za* 'after', *na* + ACC 'on', *v* + ACC 'in', and adverbs such as *domoi* 'home' and *dal'she* 'further'. In 54% of all the descriptions given by the native speaker group, however, the path was not encoded through any other means than the directional verb itself. In other words, the semantics of the verbs alone seemed to suffice for forefronting the unidirectionality of the motion trajectory [as in Examples (11) and (12)].

Non-unidirectional verbs

Non-unidirectional verbs were used by the native speakers to describe only a limited number of motion scenes. It can easily be inferred from the non-unidirectional descriptions (and, naturally, from the pictures in the storybook upon which the descriptions are based) that the motion events in these episodes do not have simple one-leg trajectories in one direction. Therefore, it is the lack of unidirectionality that is at the semantic nucleus of the non-unidirectional descriptions in the native speaker corpus.

In encoding Episode 3, 'the boy and the dog wandering in the woods', the use of non-unidirectional verbs highlights the multiplicity of the mini-segments into which the search in the woods can be broken:

(13) *Krichali, krichali oni, bespolezno.* **Khodili,**   **brodili**   *oni.*
                              [went-NON, IMP wandered-NON, IMP they]
      'They called and called, but to no avail. They walked, wandered around'.

Non-unidirectional Episodes 5 and 6 are based on the pictures that portray events with *un*directed trajectories: the dog running around under the tree trying to get the attention of the bees and the swarming bees flying in no particular direction collectively. Example (14) below illustrates the description of Episode 6:

(14) *Visel   ulei   i*   ***letali***   *ogrnomnye pchely.*
                           [flew-NON, IMP huge   bees]
      'A beehive was hanging and huge bees were flying'.

Episode 7 refers to a chase, which is the only chase in the storybook that lacks an explicit depiction of the endpoint. Thus, a non-unidirectional framing of the event, which suggests that the bees were following the fleeing dog all through the woods and/or a roundtrip, is acceptable, as in Example (15).

(15) *V eto   vremia za   sobachkoi* **gonialas'**   *staia   os.*
      [at this time   after the dog   chased-NON, IMP swarm wasps]
      'In the meanwhile, the swarm of wasps was chasing after the dog'.

Two-thirds of the non-unidirectional descriptions include locative phrases with the preposition *nad* 'over' and directional phrases with such prepositions as *vokrug* 'around' and *za* 'after', while one-third offer no elaboration of path through satellites at all. When satellites are omitted, the use of the verbs alone is sufficient for encoding (non)unidirectionality of the motion path.

In sum, the encoding of (non)unidirectionality is highly consistent throughout the native speaker corpus and reveals distinct lexicalization patterns and conceptual core schemas upon which TFS patterns for expressing unidirectionality versus non-unidirectionality are based. The next section presents the analysis of the L2 learners' descriptions of the same events during the spontaneous oral production task.

L2 speakers' narratives: Sentence-level analysis

While the level of agreement for each episode is strikingly high among the native speaker narrators, the learners' stories reveal a lack thereof: the

L2 corpus contains both unidirectional and non-unidirectional descriptions for 14 out of 16 episodes.

As has been discussed earlier, most of the episodes in the storybook naturally lend themselves to a unidirectional, goal-oriented interpretation. Episode 4, which portrays the boy and the dog advancing along the path of their journey from the house to the woods, is one of the most obvious candidates for the unidirectional framing. Yet, one-third of the learners portrayed such descriptions as non-unidirectional, as shown in Example (16).

(16) *I mal'chik   *khodil /* khodil*   *dal'she.*
   [and boy   went-NON, IMP/went-NON, IMP   further]
   'And the boy *went-NON further'.

The use of *khodit* 'go-NON' in Example (16) is inappropriate not only because it misrepresents the directionality of the motion episode, but also because it is incompatible with the lexicalization pattern and the context of the description semantically: the adverb *further* presupposes a bound vector, that is unidirectionality, and the phrase 'to look for a frog' implies a goal-oriented path verb. Similarly, incongruent directional descriptions are found in the learners' encoding of the 'chase'/'flight' in Episodes 7, 8, 11, 13 and 14. As reported earlier, the native speakers predominantly portrayed these events as simple one-leg trips from point A to point B through the use of unidirectional verbs. Yet, in the learner corpus, the chase/flight episodes comprise a salient *non*-unidirectional category in that they account for 56% of all episodes narrated as non-unidirectional.

The lack of consistency persists in all learner descriptions of motion events, including those that are unambiguously and explicitly portrayed in the storybook as one-leg trips, for example, Episode 12 in which round-trip interpretation is not possible since the boy is carried away by the deer off the rock, and Episode 15 in which the boy and the dog are swimming towards the shore after their fall into the swamp. These two episodes were framed as non-unidirectional by 31% and 72% of the learners, respectively.

(17) *Tam liagushki net.   On [mal'chik] *polzal   na kamen' i nashel olen'.*
   [he [boy]   crawled-NON, IMP on rock]

   'There is no frog there. He [the boy] *crawled-NON on the rock and found the deer'.

(18) *A   potom mal'chik i   sobaka *plavali   do   berega.*
   [and then boy   and dog   swam-NON until shore]
   'And then the boy and the dog *swam-NON to the shore'.

The inconsistencies in the encoding of directionality are true not only for the learner corpus as a whole, but also for intra-sentential descriptions within individual narratives, as shown in Example (19), where a chase/flight episode was simultaneously described as uni- and non-unidirectional:

(19) *Bednaia sobaka **bezhit**   potomu chto pchely za nim *letaiut*   vdogonku.*
     [Poor   dog   runs-UNI because   bees   after it fly-NON   in a chase]
     'The poor dog is running because the bees are *chasing-NON after it'.

The above example contains a compound sentence expressing the shared path of two motion figures (the Chaser and the Fleer). The simple sentences within it refer to the same path and trajectory (otherwise, it would not be a chase). Consequently, the use of the unidirectional verb *bezhat'* 'run-UNI' in the first clause and the use of the non-unidirectional verb *letat'* 'fly-NON' in the second clause make the sentence internally conflicting, suggesting that the L2 narrators were using the verbs unsystematically, with little access to the schemas underlying the encoding of uni- versus non-unidirectionality characteristic of Russian motion talk. Therefore, it is clear that the highly proficient, adult L2 learners of Russian had not completely shifted to the target language TSF pattern, with respect to their capacity to employ (non)unidirectional verbs in the same contexts, that is in reference to the same motion events.

The differences in the use of directional verbs between the native speaker and L2 learner corpora are even more prominent when the verbs are analyzed within the context of the overall lexicalization pattern characteristic of Russian motion talk. As analysis of the native speaker narratives showed, the unidirectional verbs of motion were used in conjunction with goal-specifying satellites (e.g. $v + ACC$ 'in' and $na + ACC$ 'on'). However, goal-oriented satellites prevailed in the non-unidirectional descriptions of the learners, as shown in Example (20).

(20) *Olen' *begaet   v   krai s   molodym chelovekom na golove.*
     [deer runs-NON to edge with young   man   on head]
     'The deer is *running-NON to the edge with the young man on its head'.

The description in Example (20) denotes an actual (i.e. not habitual) event that is goal-oriented AND non-unidirectional at the same time. As discussed in the literature review, such descriptions are nonsensical, as the only time non-unidirectional events can contain descriptions of goal and source of motion in Russian is when they refer to non-actual 'complex' events such as habitual actions or completed roundtrips in the past. Such non-actual descriptions are naturally missing from the native speaker corpus due to the nature of the stimulus: the pictorially represented frog story invites actual, 'here-and-now' interpretations of the portrayed episodes. By using satellites that express goal-oriented path in conjunction with the non-unidirectional verbs, L2 learners showed their inability to verbally differentiate between the lexicalization patterns appropriate for unidirectional versus non-unidirectional framing of motion events.

Analysis of the L2 lexicalization patterns also shows that the learners attempted to use (non)unidirectional verbs to encode the crossing and reaching of spatial boundaries, a pattern not permitted by the target language, as shown in Example (21).

(21) *Liagushka *polzala   iz   banki   i ischezla cherez okno.*
     [Frog   crawled-NON from jar]
     'The frog *crawled-NON from the jar and disappeared through the window'.

The non-unidirectional verb *polzat'*-NON 'crawl' in Example (21) highlights duration, non-boundary-crossing, and non-unidirectionality – all inappropriate for the completed event they refer to, namely, the frog getting out of the jar (Episode 1). Compare Example (27) with the description of the same episode by a native speaker:

(22) *Ona vylezla   iz banki   i napravilas' izuchat' dom.*
     [It   PATH-out + crawled-PERF from jar]
     'It crawled out of the jar and headed to explore the house'.

Incidents of omission of prefixes-satellites [as in Example (21)] may explain the observed overuse of (non)unidirectional verbs by the L2 learners as reported earlier. The semantics of (non)unidirectional verbs does not permit encoding of crossing or reaching of spatiotemporal boundaries. In accordance with the required pictorial stimuli, the native speakers marked boundary-crossing and reaching through prefixed verbs of motion, hence, the lower number of unprefixed (non)unidirectional verbs in the monolingual corpus. The learners, however, did not appear to be sensitive to these requirements of Russian lexicalization patterns, producing descriptions that were semantically, contextually and grammatically inappropriate.

In sum, with respect to their use of (non)unidirectional verbs for encoding motion, the highly proficient, adult L2 learners of Russian did not converge on the target language TFS pattern.

Discussion

The present study intended to investigate frequency, contexts of use and lexicalization patterns underlying the expression of (non)unidirectionality in L1 and L2 Russian corpora. We saw that in terms of the frequency of use, the learners heavily overused non-unidirectional verbs, and SLA additionally revealed that both unidirectional and non-unidirectional verbs were not used in a fashion consistent with the Russian TFS pattern. The learners failed to perceive and verbalize the inherent unidirectionality of the plot, and almost all episodes were marked both as unidirectional and non-unidirectional in the L2 corpus. This lack of consistency with respect to the (non)unidirectionality of the individual episodes is suggestive of the lack of systematic conceptual structuring of (non)unidirectional motion on the part of the L2 learners. In fact, it appears that the learners made random lexical choices, treating both verbs in (non)unidirectional pairs as viable alternatives when using (non)unidirectional verbs, as evident in the 50:50 ratio of non- to unidirectional verbs in the L2 narratives. Incongruent lexicalization patterns through which (non)unidirectional events were expressed by the learners further make clear that it would be highly unlikely that the learners fully adapt to the new way of thinking about motion, in general, and (non)unidirectionality, in particular. The narrative data are indicative of the opposite, namely, marked difficulties in acquisition of Russian motion talk, manifested as consistent, inappropriate (semantically, contextually and grammatically) descriptions involving the use of (non)unidirectional verbs. In short, the L2 learners' performance on the narrative task did not show a systematic shift to the new, more multifaceted and complex pattern for encoding motion events that Russian, the target language, necessitates.

Shifting to a new TFS pattern does not amount to an easy switch for L2 learners (cf. Cadierno, 2008; Navarro & Nicoladis, 2005; Negueruela & Lantolf, 2006; Stam, 2006b), especially when such patterns involve conceptual domains that are expressed markedly differently in the L1 and the L2, as is the case with the inter-typological differences that exist between S- and V-languages in the domain of motion talk. With regard to the encoding of motion in Russian and English, the differences are intra-typological and, as such, more subtle. Nevertheless, to encode (non)unidirectionality English-speaking learners of Russian have to develop a somewhat more complex and elaborate system for expressing motion. Because Russian forces its speakers to encode (non)unidirectionality obligatorily in select contexts, directionality of path must be attended to, perceived and verbalized within appropriate lexicalization patterns. Due to the intra-typological differences between their L1 and L2, the advanced L2 learners, as shown in the present study, were not able to do so, in spite of their extensive histories of studying Russian.

The transcripts of the narratives offer secondary evidence that the encoding of motion talk presented a pronounced challenge for the L2 learners of Russian. The high percentage of false starts, repetitions, prolonged pauses and self-corrections in the L2 corpus is also demonstrative of the fact that expression of motion meanings proved to be a cognitively taxing task, even for the highly advanced L2 participants. The finding that the expression of motion [and, specifically, (non)unidirectionality] is a domain particularly resistant to change and acquisition is in line with the long-held conviction of L2 teachers of Russian that the topic warrants particular pedagogical treatment and attention (Pahomov, 1977; Rifkin, 1996; Stilman, 1951). This study additionally showed that English-speaking learners need continued pedagogical interventions and practice with Russian verbs of motion even at advanced levels of proficiency.

Overall, the study of L2 learners' online performance provides support for the view that surface structures mediate our thinking in a non-trivial way. The level of difficulties experienced by the highly proficient L2 learners contradicts the universal view expressed by Li and Gleitman (2002) that 'linguistic systems are *merely* [their emphasis] the formal and expressive medium that speakers devise to describe their mental representations and manipulations of their reference world' (p. 290). While the researchers find the relationship between the linguistic and cognitive processes trivial, the case of the (non)unidirectionality encoding in Russian shows that, even for proficient L2 speakers, 'devising' new ways to describe motion meanings is not a trifling undertaking. Levinson *et al.* (2002) opine – and present ample evidence to support their reasoning – that linguistically motivated categories *pervade, change* and *facilitate* our thought. The linguistic experiment reported in this chapter shows that differences in the linguistic systems between two languages, specifically in the semantic domain of motion, can also *prevent* L2 learners from developing an L2-based TFS pattern if the new language requires attending to and verbalizing conceptual categories that their L1 does not encode. On the surface, the differences between English and Russian in how they express motion events may not appear dramatic (Russian *merely* has a more extended motion lexicon), but the two languages call for different TFS patterns from their speakers, and the L2 participants exhibited notable difficulties in making the shift. Of course, the differences in the linguistic structuring of the conceptual domain of motion in Russian and English go well beyond the frequency with which the terms for falconry were used during the Elizabethan times or the lexicon for snow terms characteristic of the speech of vacationers at Aspen and Vail, the examples that Li and Gleitman (2002) drew on in their discussion of the cognitive effects of linguistic coding.

The findings of the present study have significant implications for the field of L2 education, as they suggest that successful L2 acquisition by adult learners is dependent not only on the internalization of broad grammar rules (such as expression of aspect and time, for example) or separate lexicon items, but also on the learners' ability to systematically adapt to new ways of attending to, and TFS about, conceptual domains that may be encoded differently in their L1 and L2, as is the case of (non)unidirectionality of motion in Russian and English. The fact that the advanced L2 learners participating in the study continued to struggle with the expression of (non)unidirectionality suggests that traditional methods of teaching may not suffice for adult learners. The study offers compelling support for the argument that the structurally oriented methodology for teaching languages needs to be complemented by conceptually driven and immersive approaches and activities (cf. Negueruela & Lantolf, 2006), which would make the divergences in the encoding of conceptual domains of the

L1 and the L2 visible to the learners and would allow them to experiment with tailoring existing meaning-making processes to L2 TFS patterns through contextualized discourse-level production tasks.

With regard to the field of motion talk research, this study, with its focus on (non)unidirectionality as an important conceptual component of encoding motion path, shows that the broad categories of manner and path and their instantiations in individual languages need to be refined, empirically studied, and described in greater depth if we are to make conclusions about L2 acquisition of these categories with any degree of precision. Future in-depth analyses and contrasts of crosslinguistic conceptual schemas would not only enrich the wealth of evidence for crosslinguistic variation in the domain of motion talk, but also allow us to operate with validated and more precise analytical contrasts in SLA research, including the investigations of L2 TFS effects in the domain of motion meanings and associated pedagogical implications.

Acknowledgments

This research was supported by Robert L. Baker Summer Research Fellowship for Second Language Acquisition in an Environment of Immersion. I thank the Editors for this opportunity to contribute to this volume and for their insightful comments. I also appreciate the suggestions of the anonymous reviewers on the previous draft of this chapter. All the remaining errors are strictly my own.

Notes

1. Talmy's typology has been extensively described in the literature and, therefore, will not be summarized again here. A recent chapter (Talmy, 2006) provides a brief overview of the conceptual categories and the dichotomy he described in his earlier work.
2. The dichotomy has been recently revised to include equipollently framed languages in which manner and path receive equal weight (e.g. see Slobin, 2006).
3. Chinese is considered to be an E-framed language in a revised motion talk typology; both groups utilize manner verbs. In reference to Chinese, some still argue that Chinese is in fact an S-famed language (see, e.g. Peyraube, 2006).

Chapter 3

Can an L2 Speaker's Patterns of Thinking for Speaking Change?

GALE A. STAM

Introduction

Language and culture are intricately related. Language is both a by-product of and a transmitter of culture. It is the means by which concepts of space and time are mastered and has a direct influence on the cognitive development of individuals (Klein, 1986). What is the relationship between language, culture and thought? The answer to this question is fundamental to an understanding of not only human culture and mind, but also second language acquisition. In this chapter, I will explore this question from the perspective of thinking for speaking; Slobin's (1987, 1991, 1996a) hypothesis that languages not only provide speakers with a framework for the expression of experiences, events and thoughts but also guide how experiences, events and thoughts are expressed at the time of speaking, and my extension of the hypothesis to second language acquisition – second language learners must learn a different pattern of thinking for speaking when their native language's pattern differs from the second language's pattern (Stam, 1998). I will use spontaneous gestures, the gestures speakers make when they speak, as a means to investigate whether a second language learner's thinking for speaking changed as her proficiency in her second language, English, increased.

First, I will discuss what spontaneous gestures are. Then, I will discuss the linguistic relativity hypothesis and thinking for speaking. Next, I will discuss thinking for speaking as it applies to motion events in first language (L1) and second language (L2). Afterwards, I will discuss the study I conducted to investigate whether a second language learner's patterns of thinking for speaking changed in both her first language (L1) and second language (L2) with increased L2 proficiency.

Gestures

The gestures discussed in this chapter are movements of the arms and hands that people make to accompany their speech. These spontaneous gestures are phonologically, semantically and pragmatically synchronic with speech (McNeill, 1992). They are not culturally specific (emblems) or lexicalized gestures, such as the thumbs-up sign whose meaning is well known to all members of a cultural group or gestures that complete an utterance by filling a grammatical slot. Rather, they are external manifestations of a speaker's online thinking for speaking (McNeill & Duncan, 2000). Sometimes speech and gesture represent the same entities, and sometimes they complement each other, where the gestures indicate an aspect of the speaker's thought that is present but not expressed through speech.

Speech and gesture express two aspects of thought – the verbal and the imagistic (McNeill, 1992). They arise from the same underlying mental process and form a single-integrated system in which thought, language and gesture develop over time and influence each other (McNeill, 2005).

Empirical research (Goldin-Meadow, 2000, 2003; Marcos, 1979; McNeill, 1992, 2000; McNeill & Duncan, 2000; Stam, 1998, 2006a, 2006b, 2008) has shown that gestures provide researchers with an enhanced window onto the mind through which mental representations can be observed, and they provide information about speakers' thinking that speech alone does not.

Since the 1970s, the use of gestures in second language acquisition has been explored by a growing number of gesture and second language researchers (for reviews, see Gullberg, 2006, 2008; Gullberg & McCafferty, 2008; Stam, 2006a; Stam & McCafferty, 2008). One area where the concept that gestures offer an enhanced window onto the mind has been applied is in the investigation of the thinking-for-speaking hypothesis and second language acquisition (Stam, 2007).

Linguistic relativity hypothesis and thinking for speaking

Although the linguistic relativity hypothesis is most closely associated with Whorf, the idea that language influences thought can be traced back to von Humboldt (see Gumperz & Levinson, 1996; Lucy, 1992a, 1996; Stam, 2006a, for reviews), who viewed language and thought as an inseparable unit with each language giving its speakers a particular 'worldview' (von Humboldt, 1836/1999: 60).

Whorf (1956) proposed that language not only influenced thought, but also that the language people spoke and the habitual linguistic patterns that they used caused the speakers of different languages to think differently about the world around them. By habitual linguistic patterns, Whorf meant more than merely grammatical patterns of a language. These were general patterns of language use and included the analogies and metaphors that are shaped by the language that is spoken and by the culture of the speakers.

Since the mid-1970s, there has been a renewed interest in the linguistic relativity hypothesis (see Lucy, 1992a, 1996, for a review of studies and Gentner & Goldin-Meadow, 2003, for representative studies), and research has focused on two versions – a strong version advocated by Lucy (1992a, 1996) and a weak version proposed by Slobin (1991) called the thinking-for-speaking hypothesis.

Thinking for speaking represents the type of thinking that occurs online in the process of speaking (McNeill & Duncan, 2000; Slobin, 1991; Stam, 1998). Languages differ typologically in how semantic domains such as motion, space and temporality are indicated lexically and syntactically. Building on Talmy's (1985) work in cognitive linguistics, Slobin (1991) proposed that 'in acquiring a native language, a child learns a particular way of thinking for speaking' (Slobin, 1991: 12). Children learn grammatical constructions and lexicon that not only provide them with a framework for the expression of thoughts, events and feelings but also guide their expression as they engage in the online thinking process related to speaking.

Slobin (1991) has claimed that one of the ways that the thinking-for-speaking hypothesis can be investigated is by looking at second language learners and the difficulties they have in mastering aspects of second languages (Stam, 2006a, 2006b; see also Han, 2004, this volume). He has hypothesized that many language patterns acquired in childhood are 'resistant to restructuring in adult second language acquisition' (Slobin, 1996a: 89). Here, the typological differences between languages are important. If different patterns of thinking for speaking exist in the L1 and the L2, then learners must learn another pattern of thinking for speaking in order to be proficient speakers in their L2 (Stam, 1998). This involves 'learning which particular details of a motion event must be attended to in the input and expressed in the L2' (Cadierno & Lund, 2004: 145; see also Cadierno, this volume; Hasko, 2009). At issue is how to ascertain when learners are speaking their second language whether they are thinking for speaking in their L1, the L2, or somewhere in between.

Motion events

To test the thinking-for-speaking hypothesis, crosslinguistic research has been conducted in the domain of motion events – movements of entities through space – in a number of different languages (Danish, Dutch, English, German, Hebrew, Icelandic, Korean, Japanese, Mandarin, Russian, Spanish and Turkish). Motion events include the following components (Aske, 1989; Talmy, 1985, 1991, 2000b): *motion* – the movement, *figure* – the moving object(s), *ground* – the reference object(s) in relation to which the figure moves, *path* – the direction or trajectory of the motion and *manner* – the way in which the motion is performed (cf. Stam, 2006a, 2006b, 2008).

On the basis of where a language encodes path, Talmy (1985, 1991, 2000b) has classified languages into two types: verb-framed and satellite-framed (for discussions, see also Cadierno, this volume, and Victoria Hasko, 2009). In verb-framed languages (Romance, Semitic and Japanese), path or directionality is encoded on the verb, whereas in satellite-framed languages (Indo-European except Romance, Finno-Ugric and Chinese) it is encoded on a satellite, a particle.

Spanish and English exemplify these two typologically different languages (Talmy, 1991). Spanish is a verb-framed language, while English is a satellite-framed language. In Spanish, motion and path are indicated by the verb, and manner if present in speech is indicated outside the verb by an adjunct, an adverbial such as a gerund or a phrase. For example, in *él entra corriendo* 'he enters running', the verb *entra* 'enters' indicates path, while the gerund *corriendo* 'running' indicates manner. In English, motion and manner are indicated by the verb, and path is indicated by a satellite, a particle. For example, in *he runs in*, the verb *runs* indicates manner, while the particle *in* indicates path.

Aske (1989) has pointed out that although Spanish verbs tend not to have motion and manner and to have only motion and path, there are instances of motion and manner verbs. He attributes this to two different types of path phrases: one a locative path phrase, which denotes a one-dimensional location in which an activity takes place, and the other a telic path phrase, which denotes the path of motion + an end-of-path location/state of figure. Spanish allows motion and manner verbs with locative path phrases but not with telic ones (Stam, 2006a, 2006b, 2008).

L1 thinking for speaking in motion events

Studies examining speech in motion events (Aske, 1989; Berman & Slobin, 1994; Cadierno, 2004; Choi & Bowerman, 1991; Hohenstein *et al.*, 2006; Slobin, 1996a, 1996b, 2004, 2007; Slobin & Hoiting, 1994; Talmy, 1985, 2000b) have found that speakers of typologically different languages have different patterns of thinking for speaking about motion linguistically.

In particular, research on Spanish and English speakers' narrations of motion events show that Spanish speakers tend to describe states and expound descriptions of settings, whereas English speakers tend to describe processes and accumulate path components (Berman & Slobin, 1994; Slobin, 1991, 1996a, 1996b, 2003; Slobin & Hoiting, 1994). For Spanish speakers, crossing a spatial boundary is equivalent to a change of state and requires a new predicate. This is not the case for English speakers. A boundary crossing can be expressed in English by an additional prepositional phrase indicating path and ground, such as *the boy went through the door, up the stairs* and *into his room*.

Studies examining both the speech and gesture of the speakers of various languages (Duncan, 1996, 2001, 2002; Kita & Özyürek, 2003; McNeill, 1997, 2000; McNeill & Duncan, 2000; Özyürek & Kita, 1999; Özyürek *et al.*, 2005; Schulman, 2004) have found that speakers of typologically different languages have different patterns of thinking for speaking about motion not only linguistically, but also gesturally.

Looking at the narrations of native-Spanish and native-English speakers, McNeill and Duncan (2000) found that there was speech–gesture synchrony in their expression of motion events. Spanish speakers' path gestures tended to fall on the verb, and English speakers' path gestures tended to fall on the satellite. They also found that Spanish speakers had manner in gesture when there was none in the accompanying speech, whereas English speakers almost never had manner in gesture when there was none in the accompanying speech. In addition, McNeill (2000, 2005) pointed out that English speakers modify the importance of the manner aspect of the verb in their narrations through their gestures by either reinforcing the manner by producing an accompanying manner gesture or downplaying the manner by producing a path gesture or no gesture at all.

Native speakers' speech–gesture synchrony and use of gesture to express or downplay manner are important for second language research as they provide a way to investigate learners' thinking for speaking.

Thinking for speaking and L2 learners

As Cadierno and Lund (2004) pointed out, L2 learners need to learn which aspects of a motion event are important in the L2. In terms of the expression of motion in English, 'Spanish learners of English need to learn that in English the satellite encodes path, the satellite is obligatory, motion verbs encode manner, and path components are often accumulated within a single clause' (Stam, 2006a: 174). Where learners are in this process and what aspects of the L1 and L2 are present in their conceptualization of motion in their L2 are indicated by both their speech (see Cadierno, 2008, for a review of speech and writing studies investigating L2 thinking for speaking) and their gestures (Stam, 1998, 2006a, 2006b, 2007, 2008).

Several studies have looked at the speech and gesture of second language learners to investigate how their thinking for speaking about motion changes with second language acquisition (Brown, 2007; Brown & Gullberg, 2008; Choi & Lantolf, 2008; Kellerman & van Hoof, 2003; Negueruela *et al.*, 2004; Özyürek, 2002; Stam, 1998, 2006a, 2006b, 2008; Yoshioka, 2008; Yoshioka & Kellerman, 2006). These studies have concentrated on different aspects of the motion event, with some investigating the expression of path, others manner and still others ground.

Stam (1998, 2006a, 2006b, 2008), Kellerman and van Hoof (2003) and Negueruela *et al.* (2004) looked at Spanish and English speech and gesture to investigate whether learners' thinking-for-speaking patterns about path undergo changes when they acquire a second language. These studies replicated previous findings regarding Spanish and English native speakers' thinking-for-speaking patterns in both speech and gesture (McNeill & Duncan, 2000) – Spanish speakers express path linguistically with a verb, and their path gestures tend to occur with the verb, while English speakers express path linguistically with a satellite, and their path gestures tend to occur with the satellite. However, their results on second language learners varied as a result of differences in their study designs. Kellerman and van Hoof (2003) and Stam (1998, 2006a, 2006b, 2008) had both between-participant and within-participant designs, while Negueruela *et al.* (2004)[1] did not. In addition, Kellerman and van Hoof (2003) and Negueruela *et al.* (2004) used the frog story, *Frog, where are you?* (Mayer, 1969), as their stimulus and examined only the frequency of gestures co-occurring with verbs and satellites and did not examine different levels of proficiency among the L2 learners.

Kellerman and van Hoof (2003) looked at three groups of participants: Dutch, Spanish and English speakers, whereas Negueruela *et al.* (2004) looked at two groups of learners (Spanish learners of English and English learners of Spanish) in addition to native-Spanish and native-English speakers. On the basis of the frequency of gestures co-occurring with verbs and satellites, Kellerman and van Hoof (2003) and Negueruela *et al.* (2004) concluded that L2 learners were still thinking for speaking in their first language. In particular, Kellerman and van Hoof found that the same percentage of path gestures (65%) of the Spanish learners of English fell on the verb in both their L1 and their L2 narrations, while Negueruela *et al.* found that 23–33% of the path gestures of the Spanish learners of English fell on the verb.

Stam (2006a, 2006b, 2008) used the cartoon *Canary Row* (Freleng, 1950) as her stimulus and looked not only at the frequency of gestures co-occurring with motion event speech elements, but also at the expressions used linguistically to express path and the interaction of speech and gesture among native speakers of Spanish and English and two groups of Spanish learners of English (intermediate and advanced). She found that, linguistically, the L2 learners sometimes expressed path with a satellite in English, but they did not accumulate path components within a single clause in speech with the exception of one instance by one learner. She also found that gesturally, there was a decrease in the percentage of path gestures co-occurring with verbs and an increase in the number of path gestures co-occurring with satellites in the learners' L2 narrations compared to their L1 narrations. However, the percentages alone were misleading because they did not take into account missing speech elements such as omissions of subjects, verbs and prepositions that occurred in the speech of the intermediate learners as a result of their language proficiency, for example, 'and the cat the ball in the mouth'.

In addition, she found developmental aspects in the L2 learners' speech and gesture use in terms of what aspects of motion events were focused on compared to L1 English speakers, such as interiority of ascent or setting. She concluded that the L2 learners' thinking-for-speaking patterns were a mixture of L1 (Spanish) and L2 (English) thinking-for-speaking patterns, reflecting their interlanguage systems.

These studies were all cross-sectional and although Stam (2006a, 2006b, 2008) found developmental aspects to the L2 learners' thinking-for-speaking patterns, cross-sectional studies provide us with only a snapshot of learners' thinking, they do not give us information on how individual learners' patterns of thinking for speaking change as they become more proficient in their L2. To ascertain these changes, longitudinal studies are needed.

The Study

This longitudinal study[2] investigated how thinking-for-speaking patterns about motion changed for an advanced Spanish learner of English[3] in nine years. It sought answers to the following questions:

(1) How does the learner express path and manner linguistically and gesturally in Spanish and English in 2006?
(2) How does this compare with her expression of path and manner in both languages in 1997 and with native speakers of both languages?
(3) What are the implications for thinking for speaking in an L2?

Participant

The participant was a Mexican-Spanish-speaking learner of English at the advanced proficiency level[4] at National-Louis University at the time that she was originally videotaped in 1997. At that time, she had been studying English for two years and working at a bank in the balances department for nine months. She reported that she used English 40% of the time and Spanish 60% of the time. By the time she was subsequently videotaped in 2006, she had graduated from the university with a degree in computer information systems management and had been working at a bank as an accounting specialist for seven years. She reported that she used both English and Spanish equally: English at work and socially in dating situations and with non-Spanish-speaking friends and Spanish at home with her family and sometimes at work with Spanish-speaking customers.

Procedures

The same procedures were followed in 1997 and 2006. The participant was shown a Sylvester and Tweety Bird cartoon, *Canary Row* (Freleng,

1950), in two segments and was asked to narrate each segment in Spanish and English to two different listeners: a Spanish-speaking and an English-speaking one. The order was counterbalanced, with the initial order for the narration of the first segment randomly assigned in 1997 and the same order followed in 2006 (Spanish-English, English-Spanish). The narrations were videotaped, and the participant was not told that thinking for speaking or gestures were a focus of the study.

Coding

One episode that contained three motion events – (1) Sylvester climbs up inside the drainpipe, (2) the ball goes inside Sylvester and (3) Sylvester and the bowling ball move/roll down and out of the drainpipe, across/down the street and into a bowling alley – was coded using McNeill's (1992) coding scheme to determine how path and manner were expressed both linguistically and gesturally in Spanish and English.

First, speech was transcribed including filled, unfilled and breath pauses; self-interruptions or self-corrections; and non-speech sounds. Next, gestures including the gesture phrase (the entire movement from preparation to retraction), the stroke (the part of the gesture with meaning) and any holds (prestroke or poststroke) were coded for hand shape and movement using both regular and slow motion speed (see Table 3.1, for coding conventions).

Then, the gestures were classified by type according to McNeill's (1992) classification system of iconic, metaphoric, beat, cohesive, deictic and Butterworth gestures. Iconic gestures are gestures that represent an action or object. Metaphoric gestures are gestures that represent an abstract idea. Beats are quick movements of the hand that occur at the meta-level of discourse to introduce new characters and new themes, summarize action and accompany repairs. Cohesive gestures are gestures that tie together thematically related material but temporally separated parts of discourse. Deictic gestures are pointing gestures, which are used to indicate places in

Table 3.1 Speech and gesture coding conventions

Speech coding	*Gesture coding*
* self interruption, repetition, repair	[gesture phrase]
% non-speech sound: swallow, laugh	[[gesture] [unit]]
<> filled pause and lengthening	stroke
/ unfilled pause	<u>hold</u>
# breath pause	

Source: Stam (2006a: 108)

real or abstract space, and Butterworth gestures are gestures that occur with lexical retrieval problems. This classification is useful for talking about gestures, but it should be remembered that the classification represents dimensions, not absolute categories of gesture. Gestures may be classified as both iconic and deictic or iconic with superimposed beats depending on the level of discourse.

Subsequently, the function of the gesture in terms of motion event component (path, manner, ground) and the meaning of the gesture were noted (e.g. Sylvester climbing up the drainpipe).[5]

Data analysis

Three types of data were analyzed and compared for the 1997 and 2006 narrations: speech, gesture rate, and speech and gesture. These data were then compared with those of monolingual-Spanish speakers and native-English speakers from Stam (2006a).

Speech analysis

Counts were made of the number of clauses in each narration, and the narrations were analyzed for how path and manner were expressed linguistically. Each finite or non-finite verb unit was counted as a clause, with aspectual and modal verbs counted with the main verbs as one clause in accordance with Berman and Slobin (1994). For example, constructions with *begin, go, try* and *want* were counted as one clause: *begin to climb, go rolling* and *try to go*. Self-referential, paranarrative clauses such as 'I mean', 'I think', 'I don't know how to say it' in English and *o sea* 'I mean' in Spanish were excluded from this count.

Gesture rate

To establish the gesture rate, counts were made of the number of gestures in each narration, and the number of gestures per clause was calculated. Excluded from these counts were any unclear gestures and gestures that occurred with self-referential and paranarrative clauses.

Speech and gesture analysis

To investigate the relationship of speech and gesture across narrations, the synchrony of the gesture in relation to speech was established by watching the video recording in slow motion and frame-by-frame (30 frames/s) with the accompanying audio to establish the onsets and offsets of gesture strokes (Duncan, 2002; Kita, 1993).

Path (path, path and ground), manner (manner, path and manner) and ground gestures were identified and counted. Next, what motion event speech element the stroke of the path gesture co-occurred with (verb, satellite, ground noun phrase, more than one element and *other*) was noted and counted, and percentages for the co-occurrence were calculated and compared (see Table 3.2, for motion event speech categories). Also, whether

Table 3.2 Motion event speech categories

Speech element	Examples
Verb = V, SV, VO, conjunction (S) V	goes; he goes; throws the ball; and he goes
Satellite = adverbs, prepositions of path	through; up; to; into
Ground noun phrase	the drainpipe
More than one = V + satellite, V + satellite + ground noun phrase, satellite + ground noun phrase	comes out; comes out the drainpipe; out the drainpipe
Other = conjunctions, subjects (alone), prepositional phrases, adjectives, pauses	he, with the ball inside

Source: Stam (2006a: 111)

or not manner gestures occurred with manner in speech was noted and tabulated. Finally, how speech and gesture interacted, that is, which aspects of the motion event the speech and gesture emphasized, for example, interiority of ascent versus ground setting description, were examined.

Several decisions were made in order to be able to compare across languages. For example, in Spanish, the subject can be omitted, and the verb without a subject in Spanish is the same as one with a subject in English. Therefore, it was necessary to consider verbs, subjects and verbs, verbs and objects, and conjunctions (subjects) and verbs as verbs. Also, gestures can express complementary information to speech; consequently, all verbs that had co-occurring path gestures were counted, not just motion verbs. Additionally, both adverbs and prepositions of motion were included as satellites because these prepositions can also express direction (Talmy, 2000b) and were necessary to consider in examining speech and gesture (Stam, 2006a, 2006b, 2008). Furthermore, although Spanish does not technically have satellites, for consistency in comparison across English and Spanish, the preposition *por* was considered a satellite. Therefore *por adentro de la canal* 'through inside of the canal' was counted as satellite + ground.

Lastly, to deal with gestures sometimes falling on incomplete words and grammatical constituents, 'the following decisions were made: (1) if the gesture fell on a syllable of the word, it was counted as co-occurring with the full speech element, for example, *co* from *come* was counted as a verb; (2) if it was a case of co-articulation, for example, *s in* from *gets in*, it was counted as a satellite; (3) and if the gesture fell on a preposition and an article, for example, *to the*, it was counted as a satellite' (Stam, 2008: 239–240).

Results

For each of the areas of data analyzed, I will present the results for both Spanish and English.

Speech

The number of clauses the participant produced in her narrations in both Spanish and English did not change much between 1997 and 2006. In Spanish she produced nine clauses in 1997 and 10 clauses in 2006, while in English she produced 15 clauses in 1997 and 14 clauses in 2006 (Table 3.3).

However, the number of clauses she produced in Spanish was less than the number the monolingual-Spanish speakers produced and more than the number that the native-English speakers produced. The number of clauses for the monolingual-Spanish speakers ranged from 12 to 21 with a mean of 15.8, and the number for the native-English speakers ranged from 6 to 13 with a mean of 8.6. The difference between the mean number of clauses for the monolingual-Spanish speakers and the native-English speakers as previously reported by Stam (2006b: 154) was statistically significant, $t(1, 8) = 3.286$, $p = 0.011$. The results suggest that the number of clauses the participant produced follows the opposite language pattern: her number of clauses in Spanish is more similar to the English pattern, and her number of clauses in English is more similar to the Spanish pattern.

In terms of the participant's linguistic expression of path and manner, there were no differences in how she expressed path and manner linguistically in Spanish. In both 1997 and 2006, she expressed path with verbs such as *subir* 'ascend' and manner with constructions such as *ir(se) rodando* 'go rolling'. This was similar to how the monolingual Spanish speakers expressed path and manner with verb constructions (Table 3.4).

There was a difference in how she linguistically expressed path but not manner in English during the period between 1997 and 2006. In 1997, she expressed path 33% of the time with just the verb *go* without an accompanying satellite or prepositional phrase. This is something that native-English

Table 3.3 Number of clauses

Language	Year	Clauses
Spanish	1997	9
	2006	10
English	1997	15
	2006	14

Table 3.4 Motion verbs + satellites[a]

Spanish 1997 (N = 6)		English 1997 (N = 9)	
aventar 'throw'	17% (1)	come + out	11% (1)
bajar 'descend'	17% (1)	go Ø	33% (3)
ir subiendo 'go ascending'	17% (1)	go + down, through	22% (2)
ir(se) rodando 'go rolling'	17% (1)	go + upstairs	11% (1)
poner 'put'	17% (1)	put + through	11% (1)
subir 'ascend'	17% (1)	throw + away	11% (1)
Spanish 2006 (N = 5)		**English 2006 (N = 7)**	
ir 'go'	20% (1)	climb + inside	14% (1)
ir(se) rodando 'go rolling'	20% (1)	go + inside	43% (3)
mandar 'send'	20% (1)	go + out, to	28% (2)
subir 'ascend'	20% (1)	throw + into	14% (1)
tirar 'throw'	20% (1)		
Monolingual speakers (N = 52)		**Native speakers (N = 30)**	
arrojar 'throw'	3.8% (2)	climb + up	6.7% (2)
aventar 'throw'	11.5% (6)	come + down, out, up	20.0% (6)
caer 'fall'	1.9% (1)	crawl + up	3.3% (1)
entrar 'enter'	5.8% (3)	drop + down	10.0% (3)
ir(se) 'go (away)'	15.4% (8)	fall + back down, into	6.7% (2)
ir bajando 'go descending'	3.8% (2)	go + in, into, out, up up through	20.0% (6)
ir botando 'go bouncing'	1.9% (1)		
ir subiendo 'go ascending'	3.8% (2)	knock + down	3.3% (1)
meter(se) 'insert oneself, get in(to)'	13.5% (7)	put + into	3.3% (1)
regresar 'return'	1.9% (1)	roll + down, on down	16.7% (5)
sacar 'take out'	3.8% (2)	run Ø	3.3% (1)
salir(se) 'exit'	13.5% (7)	throw + down, into	6.7% (2)
salir rodando 'exit rolling'	1.9% (1)		
subir(se) 'ascend'	7.7% (4)		
tirar 'throw'	1.9% (1)		
tumbar(se) 'knock down'	1.9% (1)		
venir(se) 'come'	5.8% (3)		

[a]Prepositions of motion and expressions that conflate path and ground (Talmy, 2001) are included as satellites in this list. Instances of no satellites in the speech are indicated by Ø.

speakers do not do – English speakers' verbs are followed by satellites that express path or prepositional phrases that express path and ground (Stam, 2006a, 2008). By 2006, the learner was expressing path linguistically with a satellite 100% of the time. However, there was no change in her expression of manner. She did not use the verb *roll* in either 1997 or 2006. This differed from the native-English speakers, who all used the verb *roll* (Table 3.4).

Gesture rate

The number of gestures per clause changed in both languages between 1997 and 2006. The learner had fewer gestures per clause in Spanish than in English in 1997, whereas she had more gestures per clause in Spanish than in English in 2006 (see Table 3.5).

In Spanish, she had 1.56 gestures per clause in 1997 and 2.10 in 2006. The number of gestures per clause in 1997 was similar to the number of gestures per clause Stam (2006a) found for monolingual-Spanish speakers, who had a mean of 1.53 gestures per clause (Table 3.6). In English, she had 3.20 gestures per clause in 1997 and 1.79 in 2006. The number of gestures per clause in 2006 was more in line with the number of gestures per clause

Table 3.5 Number of gestures per clause by year

Year	Language	Gestures per clause
1997	Spanish	1.56
	English	3.20
2006	Spanish	2.10
	English	1.79

Table 3.6 Number of gestures per clause by language

Language	Group	Gestures per clause
Spanish	Participant 1997	1.56
	Participant 2006	2.10
	Monolingual speakers	1.53[a]
English	Participant 1997	3.20
	Participant 2006	1.79
	Native speakers	1.88[a]

[a]Stam (2006a: 127).

Stam (2006a) found for native-English speakers, who had a mean of 1.88 gestures per clause (Table 3.6). In other words, her gestures per clause in Spanish in 1997 followed the Spanish rate, and her gestures per clause in English in 2006 followed the English rate. This makes sense in terms of English. As the learner became more fluent in English, she gestured less per clause. The change in the rate in Spanish, however, suggests that as the learner became more fluent in English, she also became less fluent in Spanish, and in fact, the increase in gestures per clause in Spanish in 2006 was related to word retrieval problems she had in Spanish.

Speech and gesture
Path

As mentioned previously, the different patterns of thinking for speaking of native speakers of Spanish and English are also expressed gesturally. Spanish speakers' path gestures tend to co-occur with a verb or *other* (McNeill & Duncan, 2000; Stam, 2006a, 2008) and English speakers' path gestures tend to co-occur with a satellite or a verb + satellite (Kellerman & van Hoof, 2003; McNeill & Duncan, 2000; Stam, 2006a, 2006b).

The co-occurrence of path gestures with *other* in Spanish is a pattern found by Stam (2006a). She noticed that the types of *other* constituents' path gestures that co-occurred within L1 Spanish and L1 English reflected syntactic differences between the two languages as well as the principle of communicative dynamism in which new, focused or contrastive information receives prosodic emphasis and gesture (McNeill, 1992). Spanish speakers had path gestures co-occurring with many more different types of *other* constituents, such as pauses, subjects, objects of the preposition that were not ground noun phrases and indirect objects, than English speakers did. For instance, because the subject is not obligatory in Spanish, its addition in an utterance may be a point of focus and it may receive a gesture.

In 1997, the learner produced a total of five path gestures in Spanish and 22 path gestures in English. When speaking Spanish, her path gestures tended to co-occur with the verb (40%) and the ground noun phrase (40%) following the Spanish pattern (McNeill & Duncan, 2000). When speaking English, her path gestures tended to co-occur with the verb (32%) and *other* (45%) following the Spanish pattern (Stam, 2006a, 2008), but she also had some path gestures that co-occurred with the satellite (the English pattern). Her path gestures in English in 1997 were somewhere between the Spanish and English patterns (Figure 3.1a).

In 2006, the learner produced a total of 10 path gestures in Spanish and 17 path gestures in English (Figure 3.1b). Of the 10 path gestures she produced in Spanish, 30% co-occurred with the verb, 30% with more than one element, 20% with the ground noun phrase and 20% with *other*, again following the Spanish pattern even though there had been a decrease in the percentage of path gestures co-occurring with verbs (Figure 3.2).

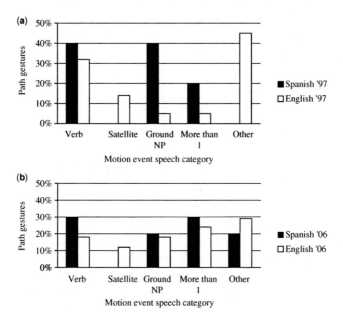

Figure 3.1 (a) Percentage of path gestures with motion event speech element Spanish and English: 1997 (b) Percentage of path gestures with motion event speech element Spanish and English: 2006

Of the 17 path gestures she produced in English in 2006, 18% co-occurred with the verb, 12% with the satellite, 18% with the ground noun phrase, 24% with more than one element and 29% with *other*. The percentage of path gestures co-occurring with the satellite remained about the same from 1997 to 2006, while both the percentages of path gestures co-occurring with the verb and *other* decreased, and the percentage co-occurring with the ground noun phrase and more than one element increased (Figure 3.3).

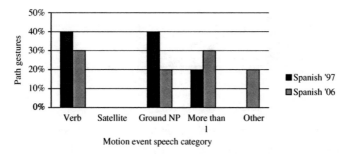

Figure 3.2 Percentage of path gestures with motion event speech element Spanish: 1997 and 2006

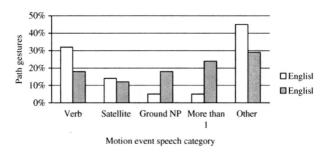

Figure 3.3 Percentage of path gestures with motion event speech element English: 1997 and 2006

Clearly, how the learner expressed path gesturally changed between 1997 and 2006, but how do these changes compare with how monolingual-Spanish and native-English speakers express path gesturally? Figures 3.4a and 3.4b compare the learner's speech and gesture results with those found by Stam (2006a) for monolingual-Spanish and native-English speakers. As can be seen by Figure 3.4a, the learner's gestural expression of path in 2006 in English has become more English-like. There also appears to be some influence of English on how the learner expresses path gesturally in Spanish in 2006 with a decrease in the percentage of path gestures

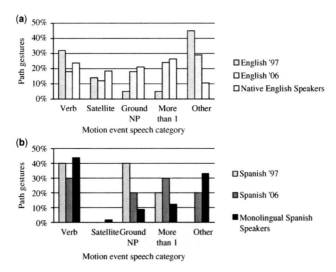

Figure 3.4 (a) Percentage of path gestures with motion event speech element – English L2 learner and native-English speakers. (b) Percentage of path gestures with motion event speech element – Spanish L2 learner and monolingual Spanish speakers

with verbs and increase in the percentage with more than one element (Figure 3.4b).

Manner

As stated previously, McNeill and Duncan (2000) found that Spanish speakers may have manner in gesture when there is none in the accompanying speech, while English speakers rarely have manner in gesture when there is none in the accompanying speech.

In Spanish, all of the learner's manner gestures co-occurred with manner in speech in 1997, whereas 50% of them co-occurred with manner in speech and 50% with no manner in speech in 2006. The 2006 results were similar to the monolingual-Spanish speakers who had 55% of their manner gestures co-occurring with manner in speech and 45% of their manner gestures co-occurring with no manner in speech (Table 3.7). In English, none of the learner's manner gestures co-occurred with manner in speech in either 1997 or 2006. This is very different from the native-English speakers who had 75% of their manner gestures co-occurring with manner in speech and 25% co-occurring with no manner in speech.

There were also differences in the types of manner gestures that were produced by the Spanish speakers and the English speakers. The Spanish speakers produced both path and manner gestures and manner gestures, whereas the English speakers produced only path and manner gestures. In Spanish the learner produced only path and manner gestures in both 1997 and 2006. In English, on the other hand, she produced path and manner and manner gestures in 1997 and only path and manner gestures in 2006 (Table 3.8). These results suggest that when it comes to manner, the learner has not yet internalized the English thinking-for-speaking pattern.

Table 3.7 Percentage of manner gestures with manner/no manner in speech

Language	*Group*	*Manner in speech*	*No manner in speech*
Spanish	Participant 1997 ($N = 1$)	100% ($N = 1$)	0%
	Participant 2006 ($N = 2$)	50% ($N = 1$)	50% ($N = 1$)
	Monolingual speakers ($N = 11$)	55% ($N = 6$)	45% ($N = 5$)
English	Participant 1997 ($N = 3$)	0%	100% ($N = 3$)
	Participant 2006 ($N = 1$)	0%	100% ($N = 1$)
	Native speakers ($N = 4$)	75% ($N = 3$)	25% ($N = 1$)

Table 3.8 Type of manner gesture

Language	Group	Path + Manner	Manner
Spanish	Participant 1997 (N = 1)	100% (N = 1)	0%
	Participant 2006 (N = 2)	100% (N = 2)	0%
	Monolingual speakers (N = 11)	82% (N = 9)	18% (N = 2)
English	Participant 1997 (N = 3)	33% (N = 1)	67% (N = 2)
	Participant 2006 (N = 1)	100% (N = 1)	0%
	Native speakers (N = 4)	100% (N = 4)	0%

Speech and gesture interaction

Let us look at how speech and gesture interact in the learner's narrations in both Spanish and English in 1997 and 2006 and how these compare with monolingual-Spanish and native-English speakers' narrations. Stam (2008: 249–250) used an example of the learner's description of Sylvester going up inside the drainpipe and Sylvester and the bowling ball coming out of the drainpipe in English from 1997 to illustrate that although the learner expressed these motion events in speech the same way that native-English speakers do, her gestures indicated that she was not thinking about motion in the same way and that she was in a state of transition.

These descriptions will be compared with examples of the learner's description of the same events in English in 2006. In addition, the learner's description of the same events in Spanish in 1997 and 2006 will be discussed and compared.

Spanish

The interaction of speech and gesture in the learner's Spanish (L1) narrations did not change much between 1997 and 2006 even though she produced more path gestures[6] in 2006. Both her speech and gesture followed a Spanish thinking-for-speaking pattern.

In describing Sylvester going up the drainpipe in 1997 [Example (1)], the learner produced only one motion event gesture – a ground one (b). This gesture emphasized the ground setting description, a characteristic of a Spanish thinking-for-speaking pattern (Berman & Slobin, 1994) and is similar to the gestures in the monolingual-Spanish narrations, where the drainpipe, the ground element, was described in detail and often had an accompanying ground gesture.

(1) (a) *después %swallow <uh> [subió otra] vez*
         afterwards %swallow <uh> he-'ascended' another time

metaphoric: right hand 'O' at lap over right leg moves up a little and to the left
down to left leg <presenting the next episode>

> (b) [*por el tubo ése donde baja el agua cuando llueve*]
>   through the tube that-one where 'descends' the water when it-rains
>   iconic: right hand C-shape moves down to waist and holds <drainpipe>
>   GROUND

When the learner narrated the cartoon in 2006, she had to be prompted
to recall the episode, which caused her to have some filled pauses in speech
[Example (2)]. She produced three motion events gestures – one ground
gesture (2a) and two path ones (path and ground, 2b and 2c), with the
path gestures co-occurring with a verb (2b) and more than one element
(2c). Her narration of the event was still within a Spanish thinking-for-
speaking pattern (Stam, 2006a, 2006b) with its emphasis on ground and
with path gestures co-occurring with verbs such as *subir* 'ascend'.

(2)   (a) <*este*> [[<*ohl*> *también otro de los pla^nes fue/#<uuh>*]
         this>   <ohl> also another of the plans was / # <uuh>
         a: iconic with superimposed beat: both hands slightly bent facing each
         other at right chest beat <drainpipe> GROUND

> (b) [/ *subi<i>r*]
>   / to 'ascend'
>   b: iconic: left hand extended, thumb slightly in at chest <pipe >; right
>   hand extended slightly bent, thumb slightly in moves in to left hand
>   <Sylvester going into the drainpipe> PATH + GROUND

> (c) [*por adentro de la canal*]]
>   through inside of the canal
>   c: iconic (enhanced): left hand extended, thumb slightly in at upper chest
>   moves down as right hand moves up to right chest <pipe >; right hand
>   extended slightly bent, thumb slightly in at right chest moves into body
>   to left hand, through left hand, up to mouth and retracts down to left
>   hand <Sylvester going into and up the drainpipe> PATH + GROUND

The learner did not describe Sylvester coming out of the drainpipe in
Spanish in 1997. She did, however, describe this event in 2006 [Example
(3)], where she produced one path gesture that covered more than one
element (verb + ground). This again was similar to the narrations of the
monolingual-Spanish speakers.

(3)   [/ *y lo manda hasta afuera //*]
         /and him sends until outside
         iconic: right hand extended slightly bent at right shoulder with elbow
         bent arches down and to the right to extreme right side toward listener
         and holds <Sylvester and bowling ball going out the drainpipe> PATH

English

The interaction of speech and gesture in the learner's English (L2) narration of Sylvester going up inside the drainpipe changed considerably between 1997 and 2006. In 1997, the learner produced more ground gestures (8), due in part to not knowing the word *pipe* but also to having a visual picture of the ground element and wanting the interlocutor to understand this element, than in 2006 when she produced only two ground gestures and knew the word *pipe*. In addition, she produced two manner only gestures in 1997, but did not produce any in 2006 (Table 3.8). Furthermore, her gestures were very segmented in 1997 – almost every grammatical constituent had its own gesture. In 2006, this was not the case. Her gestures covered more speech like native-English speakers do (Stam, 2006a, 2008). Let us look at her descriptions of Sylvester going up inside the drainpipe in 1997 [Example (4)] and 2006 [Example (5)].

(4)   RH[[he* the cat][went //][through the*][///][the<e> pipe / and * but the*]]/
       LH[[he* the cat][went //]] through the* / / / the<e> pipe / and* but the* /
          a   b   c   d   e
      a: iconic: right hand at right, left hand, 'O' at left waist <Sylvester entering the drainpipe> PATH
      b: iconic: right hand at right chest moves up to right side of face, left hand, 'O' at waist lowers to lap as right hand rises <Sylvester going up inside drainpipe> PATH
      c: iconic: right hand at right side of face moves in toward body and moves up to forehead changing hand orientation to palm toward down, fingers toward left <Sylvester going through the drainpipe> PATH
      d: iconic: right hand at nose level and moves up to top of head then retracts to nose level <pipe> GROUND
      e: iconic (reduced repetition of previous gesture) right hand at upper chest moves up in toward body to chin level and down away from body to upper chest, small circular movement, and holds <pipe> GROUND

      NB: Gestures 'd' and 'e' occur on a metalinguistic level with a word search and finding of the word, respectively (Stam, 2008: 249).

(5)   [[/ and then <uh> he* he go] [oes inside the* the* the pipe and / when]]
                 a   b
      a: beat: pre-stroke hold; left hand loose 'C' at right chest <pipe> GROUND, right hand tapered 'O' at right upper arm beats into left hand
      b: iconic: left hand 'C' at right chest <pipe >, right hand tapered 'O' at right upper arm arcs slightly down, curves up, moves up to head, holds and retracts <Sylvester going inside and up the drainpipe> PATH + GROUND

In 1997 [Example (4)], the learner produced five gestures in describing Sylvester going up through the drainpipe: three path and two ground gestures. In 2006 [Example (5)], she produced two gestures in describing the same event: a gesture that was both a beat and ground gesture (5a) on the subject, which introduces the event, and a path and ground gesture (5b) on more than one element (satellite and ground), which emphasizes the Sylvester going inside and up the drainpipe. This is much more similar to native-English speakers' speech and gesture as reported by Stam (2008: 248). The gesture emphasizes both Sylvester climbing up and the interiority of the motion event.

Similarly, the speech and gesture in the learner's description of Sylvester and the bowling ball coming out of the drainpipe was much more segmented in 1997 than in 2006. In 1997, the learner produced four gestures in describing Sylvester and the bowling ball coming out of the drainpipe: one manner, two path and one ground gestures [Example (6)]. The manner gesture (6a) co-occurred with a subordinating conjunction *when*, while the two path gestures co-occurred with the satellite *out* (6b) and part of a ground noun phrase *from the* (6c), and the ground gesture co-occurred with the remainder of the ground noun phrase *pipe*.

(6)   o[[kay **when*when** h̲][e<e> came **ou<u>t**][**from the**][<e> **pipe**]]
                  a   b   c   d
       a: iconic: both hands, right hand at lap moves up to upper left chest and makes 1½ circles in toward body and away from body, left hand moves up to upper left side <Sylvester + bowling ball rolling> MANNER
       b: iconic: both hands, right hand at left upper arm moves in toward body and down to left chest, and continues down to lap, left hand moves in toward body and down to left upper arm <Sylvester + bowling ball going down the drainpipe> PATH
       c: iconic: both hands, right hand at left chest moves down to lap, left hand at upper left side moves down to lap <Sylvester + bowling ball going down the drainpipe> PATH
       d: iconic: both hands, palms toward center, fingers toward center, joined at left lap <drainpipe> GROUND (Stam, 2008: 250)

In 2006, the learner produced a total of two gestures in describing this event, both path gestures [Example (7)]. One of the path gestures co-occurred with the verb (7a) and the other with the ground noun phrase (7b). The interaction of speech and gesture is much more similar to the speech and gesture of native speakers [Example (8)] where there is only one gesture than the speech and gesture in her 1997 description was.

(7)   [[and he **goes a<a>ll**] [out **of the pipe**]]
                  a   b
       a: iconic: right hand wrist bent at waist moves slightly to the right to lower right side <Sylvester + bowling ball going out the drainpipe> PATH
       b: iconic (reduced repetition of previous gesture): right hand wrist bent at lower right side moves to the right and slightly up <Sylvester + bowling ball going down and out the drainpipe> PATH

(8)   [and he <u>com</u>**es out the bot**<u>tom of the drain</u>pipe]

> iconic + deictic: left hand index finger extended at upper left side goes straight down, then curves toward center under right at lap and holds. <Sylvester + bowling ball going down and out the pipe> PATH

To summarize, between 1997 and 2006, the learner's linguistic expression of path remained the same in Spanish but changed in English. She consistently used satellites in 2006, something she did not do in 1997. Her gestural expression of path changed in both languages. In Spanish, there was a decrease in path gestures with verbs and ground noun phrases and an increase in path gestures with more than one element and other. Despite these changes in path gestures, her speech and gesture overall continued to follow the Spanish thinking-for-speaking pattern.

In English, there was a decrease in path gestures with verbs and *other* and an increase in path gestures with ground noun phrases and more than one element. In addition, her speech and gestures in English became less segmented, and her gestures covered more constituents in utterances like native-English speakers' gestures do. Over the nine years, her pattern of thinking for speaking about path in English became more native-like.

The learner's expression of manner did not change in either language between 1997 and 2006. She continued to express manner within a Spanish thinking-for-speaking pattern in both Spanish and English. She continued not to produce the manner verb *roll* in English like native-English speakers do, and she expressed manner only in gesture when there was none in speech.

Discussion and Conclusion

This study sought answers to three questions: how the learner expressed path and manner linguistically and gesturally in Spanish and English in 2006, how this compared with her expression of path and manner in both languages in 1997, and what implications this had for thinking for speaking in an L2.

The results show that the learner's expression of path and manner did not change linguistically in Spanish from 1997 to 2006. She expressed path with the verb and manner with a gerund following the Spanish thinking-for-speaking pattern and used the same types of motion verbs in both narrations. Her expression of path linguistically in English, however, did change. In 1997, she sometimes expressed path linguistically with a satellite following the English thinking-for-speaking pattern, but she also sometimes expressed it with just a verb following the Spanish thinking-for-speaking pattern. By 2006, her expression of path linguistically followed the English thinking-for-speaking pattern. She consistently expressed path with a satellite. However, her expression of manner did not change. She never used the manner verb *roll*.

Gesturally, there was no change in how the learner expressed manner in either language, but there was a change in how she expressed path in both languages from 1997 to 2006. In Spanish, there was an increase in path gestures with more than one element and *other* and a decrease in path gestures with verbs and ground noun phrases. It is possible that this increase in path gestures with more than one element and decrease with verbs is a result of L2 English influence on L1 Spanish. Pavlenko and Jarvis (2002) found bidirectional transfer L1 ↔ L2 in the speech of Russian L1/ English L2 speakers, and Brown (2007) found some evidence for L2 English influence on the linguistic expression of path in the speech of L1 non-monolingual Japanese speakers, but not for the gestural expression of path. At least in terms of speech, the L2 can influence the L1; however, it is not clear yet whether the L2 can additionally influence L1 gestural expression of path. The results of this study also showed that despite the increase in path gestures with more than one element and decrease with verbs, the learner's speech and gesture overall in her L1 continued to follow the Spanish thinking-for-speaking pattern. The question of whether L2 thinking for speaking can influence L1 thinking for speaking both linguistically and gesturally needs further exploration.

In English, there was an increase in path gestures with ground noun phrases and more than one element and a decrease in path gestures with verbs and *other*. In addition, the learner's speech and gestures together changed. The gestures covered more speech and were less segmented in 2006 than in 1997. These differences in the learner's gestural expression of path from 1997 to 2006 reflect a change in her L2 thinking for speaking – her thinking for speaking about path became more native-like. These results are similar to those found by Choi and Lantolf (2008) that showed that L2 learners had a shift to the L2 thinking-for-speaking pattern for the expression of path, but not for manner.

The change in the learner's expression of path both linguistically and gesturally is probably a result of her increased English proficiency and her use of the language on a daily basis in a number of situations both at work and socially. 'Acts of communication always take place in a cultural context, and cultural practices are part of the online processes that include thinking and speaking' (Slobin, 2007: 920). As the learner interacted more in English in American culture, her thinking for speaking about path became more native-like.

Why did her expression of manner not change in the same way? I think there are several possible explanations. Although manner is an important aspect of English verbs, it is path that is the most salient element in a motion event: something has to move somewhere (Slobin, 2007). Also, formal learners of English are explicitly taught two-word verbs and prepositions.

They are not exposed to manner to the same extent that native-English-speaking children are. Native-English-speaking children, who acquire manner verbs early (Berman & Slobin, 1994), are exposed to a large number of manner verbs in books, nursery rhymes and games. These are not present in the same way in L2 textbooks and materials for adults, and adults do not play the same types of games as children do. Therefore, exposure could be a factor in L2 learners' acquiring path and not acquiring manner thinking-for-speaking patterns. Another possibility is that learners focus on only one aspect of the motion event at a time, acquiring first path and then manner. Finally, perhaps manner is a pattern acquired in childhood that is resistant to change (Slobin, 1996a), and it just does not change in L2 acquisition.

Although this study showed that the learner's thinking for speaking about path in her L2 changed in the nine years, the results are limited. The study examined only one individual and her speech and gesture in only one episode of her cartoon narration. Nevertheless, that the learner's L2 thinking for speaking about path changed implies that L2 thinking for speaking is not static. It can change over time (cf. Han, 2008). That her L2 thinking for speaking about manner did not change implies that not all aspects of thinking for speaking change equally and learners' L2 thinking-for-speaking patterns reflect their interlanguage systems (cf. Han, this volume).

L2 learners who are immigrants to another country often find themselves between two cultures. They are no longer the same as they were in their home country, and they are not fully a member of the new country's culture. Their L2 thinking-for-speaking patterns may reflect not only their interlanguage systems but also their intercultural identity.

More research examining learners' L2 thinking-for-speaking patterns linguistically and gesturally in different contexts needs to be conducted. Longitudinal studies of speakers of different native languages learning various second languages, studies of individual differences, and studies that explore the role of explicit instruction of L2 thinking for speaking are all necessary for us to fully investigate to what degree learners can acquire L2 thinking-for-speaking patterns.

Notes

1. Negueruela *et al.* (2004) did not compare the speech and gesture of the Spanish learners of English and English learners of Spanish in both their L1 and L2.
2. This research was funded by a 2006–2007 faculty development grant from National-Louis University.
3. I had initially hoped to conduct a follow-up study on more than one learner. However, that was not possible as only one learner agreed to participate.

4. The learner was beyond ESOL Level 5, the last class in the former ESOL program at National-Louis University. The ESOL program (1979–2005), a semi-intensive five-level integrated skills program with a grammatically based curriculum, was designed to provide English language learners with the English necessary to succeed in undergraduate studies. Students were passed to the next level with a minimum grade of C.

5. Questions on the coding of or timing of gestures were brought to laboratory meetings at the McNeill laboratory at the University of Chicago where members of the laboratory watched the videotaped segments in question and reached a consensus on what the coding should be.

6. This increase in path gestures may have been due to more comfort with the task or a different listener. These factors warrant further exploration, but are beyond the scope of this chapter.

Chapter 4

Thinking for Speaking and Immediate Memory for Spatial Relations

KENNY R. COVENTRY, BERENICE VALDÉS and
PEDRO GUIJARRO-FUENTES

Introduction

Languages differ widely in how they talk about spatial relations, presenting a challenge for second language learners. For example, Indo-European languages, including English, employ 'projective' prepositions to describe where objects are located in space. These terms (*to the left of*, *in front of*, etc.) depend for their interpretation on the choice of reference frame adopted (Levinson, 1996). *The pram is behind the mailbox* can mean the pram is located on the opposite side of the mailbox from where the slot is (using the intrinsic/object-centered frame) or alternatively that the pram is located beside the opposite side from where the speaker and hearer are located (using the relative/viewer-centered frame). In contrast, languages such as Arandic, Guugu Yimithirr and Tzeltal use the absolute frame to describe such relations (equivalents of *The pram is North/West/uphill/downhill of the mailbox*). This has led some researchers to ask whether there are corresponding differences in speakers' non-linguistic abilities. Moreover, if one assumes that such differences are present in first language (L1) speakers, one can ask whether second language learners acquire conceptual differences corresponding to the new distinctions made in the second language (L2), and at what point such differences emerge (see Odlin, 2008a, for a discussion).

In a program of work examining the L1 and L2 acquisition of spatial prepositions in English and Spanish, our primary goal was to examine whether L2 learners at different levels of proficiency exhibit conceptual shifts in their understanding of support and containment relations (as well as other relations) as a function of language spoken. While English has two separate words for containment and support relations (*in* and *on*, respectively), Spanish has a single term (*en*) that applies to both containment and support relations. This difference between English and Spanish seemed to be a good candidate to examine any conceptual shifts as a function of language level. However, as we report below, we were unable to pursue the issue of conceptual shifts associated with these spatial relations as initial studies run with native speakers of English and Spanish question whether such a conceptual difference occurs even for L1 speakers of these languages.

Does space structure language or does language structure space?

There has been much work in recent years examining the issue of whether the language one speaks affects one's ability to make non-linguistic judgments. The three semantic categories that have received the most attention with regard to this debate have been color terms (see e.g. Regier *et al.*, 2005; Roberson *et al.*, 2005), number terms (e.g. Gelman & Butterworth, 2005; Gordon, 2004; Pica *et al.*, 2004) and spatial terms (reviewed below). With regard to color and number terms the jury is still out on the extent to which language affects non-linguistic judgments. The data for spatial categories are similarly equivocal. For example, Pederson *et al.* (1998) tested speakers across a range of languages with varying reference frame use and found a correspondence between reference frame use in language and reference frame use in a range of 'non-linguistic' tasks. In one task, participants first saw a card with a large dot and a small dot on it placed on a table (Figure 4.1). Each participant was then turned 180° and had to select the card placed on a second table in front of him/her that was the same as the card seen on the first table. Speakers of languages that use the absolute frame predominantly chose the card with the dots in the same location in the absolute frame (i.e. the card furthest away from the participant in Figure 4.1, right), whereas speakers of languages such as Dutch and English predominantly chose the card with the dots in the same location within the relative frame (the nearest card to the participant, Figure 4.1, right).

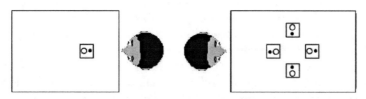

Stage 1. Participant looks at card on table.

Stage 2. Participant is rotated 180 degrees and has to choose the card seen in Stage 1.

Figure 4.1 Schematic representation of one of the tasks used by Pederson *et al.* (1998)

While some have taken these results as clear evidence for linguistic relativity (e.g. Levinson, 2003b; Pederson *et al.*, 1998), the interpretation of the results remains controversial (see e.g. Gallistel, 2002; Li & Gleitman, 2002). Certainly, the results from the tasks used by Pederson *et al.* are consistent with Slobin's thinking-for-speaking hypothesis, namely that language directs attention to some aspects of a visual scene while diminishing attention to other aspects, a weak version of the Whorfian hypothesis (Slobin, 1996a).

The other side of the coin regarding the relation between language and spatial concepts is the extent to which linguistic spatial distinctions follow from basic pre-linguistic spatial categorization. In other words, does space structure language, or does language structure space? An elegant series of experiments comparing Korean and English speakers' understanding of containment and support events suggest that both space structures language and language structures space. Choi and Bowerman (1991) initially tested whether the first language children learn (English versus Korean) affects spatial conceptualization and categorization. These languages differ in the way in which they express path; English is a 'satellite' language, where path is expressed by a constituent that is separate from the main verb (e.g. a particle or preposition), while Korean is a 'verb-frame' language where path is expressed in the verb itself (cf. Talmy, 1985; see also Cadierno, this volume; Hasko, 2009). So, in English, *a video cassette is put in a video case, a lid is put on a kettle, a pear is put in a bowl* and *a glass is put on a table*, but in Korean the verb *kkita* is used for tight-fit path events (e.g. put video cassette in video case/put lid on kettle), *nehta* is used for loose-fit containment relations (e.g. put pear in bowl), and *nohta* is used for loose-fit support relations (e.g. put glass on table) (Bowerman, 1996a). Therefore, Korean carves up the spatial world according to degrees of fit between objects, while English differentiates the spatial world according to spatial notions of containment versus support. Given this difference, Choi and Bowerman (1991) tested whether children learning English and Korean, respectively, extend meanings of terms according to the semantic structure of their input language. English children produced *in* for paths into both tight- and loose-fit containers and extended their use of *in* accordingly, whereas Korean children produced *kkita* for putting objects into tight places, *nehta* for putting objects into loose containers, and extended their use accordingly. Moreover, Choi *et al.* (1999) used a preferential looking task to assess the generalizations made by children learning either English or Korean. By the age of one-and-a-half to two years, the children in both cases spent more time looking at the language appropriate aspects of spatial relations; English children looked more at containment scenes than non-containment scenes on hearing *in*, whereas Korean children looked more at tight-fit scenes than loose-fit scenes when hearing *kkita*. However, testing even younger children, McDonough *et al.* (2003; see also

Hespos & Spelke, 2004) provide evidence that both Korean and English infants have conceptual readiness for learning tight-fit/loose-fit relations at an earlier age. Testing 9–14-month-old Korean and English infants, they found that both groups categorized both tight and loose containment and tight and loose support.

Overall, the data indicate that, prior to the acquisition of L1, pre-linguistic infants make spatial distinctions in the same way, but that the process of language learning means that the language learned structures how semantic categories are formed (e.g. Bowerman & Choi, 2001). So, space structures language and language structures space.

More recently, there is some evidence within the same language for the effect of language on spatial understanding and spatial memory. Feist and Gentner (2007; see also Loewenstein & Gentner, 2005) report evidence that spatial language presented with spatial scenes affects memory for spatial scenes in L1 English adults. Participants were shown pictures displaying spatial relations (e.g. a picture of a block perched on the edge of the roof of a building) with or without sentences describing the spatial relations (e.g. *The block is on the building*). In a picture recognition task participants saw the original pictures, pictures displaying a stronger version of the spatial relation originally seen (e.g. a picture of a block properly on top of the roof rather than perched on the edge of it) or a weaker version of the spatial relation (e.g. a picture of a block to the right of the roof not in contact with it at all). Feist and Gentner found that participants falsely recognized the stronger version of the spatial relations, but only when the sentences at encoding included a spatial preposition, suggesting that spatial language interacted with perceptual information during encoding. This study provides the impetus for a more detailed examination of possible conceptual differences between Spanish and English vis-à-vis containment and support spatial relations.

Spatial language learning and linguistic relativity

Taking the Feist and Gentner (2007) study as a starting point, we set out to test whether the manipulation of language during the encoding of a visual image may prime the false recognition of visual features that correspond with the linguistic features encoded previously. Studies with speakers in L1 were intended to establish an initial difference between L1 speakers of Spanish and English in order to provide a suitable baseline to then test L2 speakers of English and Spanish at varying levels of proficiency using a more online task than those used previously in the spatial domain. We expected that English L1 speakers, with their language distinguishing between support (*on*) and containment (*in*), would be more sensitive to changes in these spatial relations (as a function of the preposition used initially to describe the relation) than Spanish L1 speakers who have a single lexical item (*en*) for both of these spatial relations. Moreover, some researchers have claimed that learning a second language involves mapping between L1 and L2 (language transfer), while others have argued that the language to be learned structures spatial categories without interference from L1 (Carroll, 1997; Ellis, 2006; Ijaz, 1986; Jarvis & Odlin, 2000, amongst others). From this it follows that there could be potential conceptual change as a function of the language being learned. If a difference in perceptual judgments with regard to changes in *linguistic descriptions* of containment/support for English versus Spanish L1 speakers occurs, it is of great interest to establish whether such a difference occurs in L2 English, and at what point a conceptual change occurs. In the remainder of this chapter we fail to find conceptual differences associated with linguistic differences in L1 for containment/support relations, challenging more extreme versions of linguistic relativity, and undermining the rationale for testing for conceptual differences for these relations in second language learners.

Programme of Experiments

In three experiments reported below with L1 speakers of English and Spanish, we tested whether differences in the way in which these languages 'carve up' containment and support are associated with differences in perceptual judgments regarding changes in these relations. For example, in Figure 4.2 the dogs can be described as being *in the hand* or *on the hand* in English, where *in* conceptualizes the hand as a container and *on* conceptualizes the hand as a supporting surface. In Spanish, however, *en* is used for both sets of relations; thus the use of *en* does not indicate whether a containment or support relation is intended. We predicted that the encoding of pictures (primes) accompanied by sentences that include spatial prepositions (*in/on*) in English would affect similarity judgments (same/different) on a second scene (probe) with the same or different levels of containment/support.

The methodology we chose to adopt was much finer grained than most studies have used previously to test whether differences between languages are associated with non-linguistic differences. For example, in the

Figure 4.2 Example of one of the images used in Experiments 1a and 1b

Pederson *et al.* studies discussed above, participants could use language as a tool at encoding and then on retrieval to remember the card previously presented, entailing differences in choice of card that do not necessarily provide evidence of differing conceptual representations. It is therefore desirable to adopt a methodology involving a shorter time course where language is less likely to be used explicitly as a memory tool to perform the task.

Implicit memory effects have been studied with priming procedures where the occurrence of an event (prime) facilitates the recognition of a second event (probe) when they are identical or related in perceptual or semantic properties (e.g. Schacter & Badgaiyan, 2001; Tulving & Schacter, 1990). The methodology we chose to adopt employed a picture priming procedure in which prime encoding was manipulated with spatial language. Following Feist and Gentner (2007), the main rationale was that spatial language presented with the prime scene would influence perceptual memory processes producing a bias in the recognition of non-identical pictures that were compatible with the linguistic properties encoded. Moreover, the rapid Stimulus Onset Asynchrony (SOA; time between prime and probe stimuli) employed in this study allowed us to explore implicit memory effects that do not rely on the active maintenance of the linguistic material. Participants were first asked whether a sentence containing a spatial preposition presented with a picture matched that picture (prime trials). A second picture was then presented (without an accompanying sentence) that either displayed the same, less or more containment than the first (prime) picture. Participants were asked to indicate whether the pictures were the same or different.

Previous studies (e.g. Coventry & Garrod, 2004; Coventry & Prat-Sala, 2001; Feist & Gentner, 1998) have shown that the use of the spatial prepositions *in* and *on* is determined by the level of containment of the located object in the ground object. For example, with regard to Figure 4.3, increasing concavity of the reference object increases a preference for *in*, while decreasing concavity increases a preference for *on*.

In order to select the appropriate materials for the experiments, it was necessary to first conduct a pilot experiment to determine *standard* prime images and their non-identical probes (plus and minus containment variants). Participants were shown a set of eight scenes depicting spatial relations of containment between objects (e.g. dogs in hand, ants in grass, angels in clouds, etc.). Different pictures of these scenes systematically varied in degrees of containment (see Figure 4.3). Participants had to indicate using a Likert scale (from 1 to 11) how appropriate the use of *in* and *on* were to describe these scenes. We employed eight different scenes with 10 levels for containment, resulting in a total of 80 pictures. Sixty-five students from Northumbria University voluntarily participated in this study (written informed consent was obtained). Each participant completed a

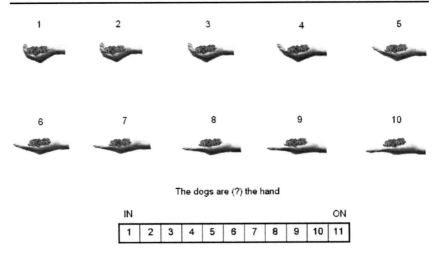

Figure 4.3 Example of containment variants (in sequence) used for one of the scenes in the pilot experiment and the type of questions participants had to answer for each picture. The order of the Likert scale was balanced across participants so that for half of the participants *in* was in the low extreme and vice versa for the other half

set with 10 pictures from the same scene but with 10 different levels of containment, presented in random order.

Table 4.1 shows the mean ratings obtained for all the scenes and their variations. Scores were adjusted to one direction: the lower the score the more appropriate *in* is, and the higher the score the more appropriate *on* is. Numbers in bold and underlined indicate the image selected as standard and its variations toward less (*on*) and more (*in*) containment.

The pictures selected for prime pictures in the experiments below were those pictures that obtained the closest value to the mean rating value of 6. Plus and minus containment pictures were selected as far as possible with equal increases/decreases in ratings from the standard (see Table 4.1).

After selecting the main three pictures for each scene in terms of containment, variations of number of objects were also introduced. The rationale for this was to match the number of linguistic distinctions and materials between languages. Just as Spanish and English differ in lexicalization of containment and support relations, Spanish and English also differ in the number of verbs used to describe locations of events versus location of groups of objects. With respect to Figure 4.2, in English one can say that 'The dogs are in the hand' or that 'The game is in the hand', but in Spanish the verb *estar* is used to describe locations of objects, while *ser* is used to describe locations of events (Bosque & Demonte, 1999; Butt & Benjamin, 2000; Sera *et al.*, 1999). So, in addition to varying the level of concavity of reference objects in scenes, we also varied the number of

Table 4.1 Mean ratings obtained for each of the 10 variants of the pictures for each scene (pilot study)

Containment	In									On
Pictures	*1*	*2*	*3*	*4*	*5*	*6*	*7*	*8*	*9*	*10*
The dogs are (?) the hand	2.55	3.27	3.55	**4.36**	**6.91**	**8.00**	8.36	10.18	9.91	10.36
The boats are (?) the water	1.00	1.00	2.00	2.00	3.60	**4.20**	**5.60**	**8.00**	7.80	10.80
The boars are (?) the sand	2.25	2.25	2.25	3.00	**4.00**	**6.25**	**8.25**	9.50	10.25	11.00
The birds are (?) the race	2.00	1.50	1.75	1.75	2.50	**5.25**	**6.00**	7.50	**8.50**	10.75
The flamingos are (?) the mud	1.20	2.40	2.80	**4.60**	**6.20**	**7.00**	7.20	10.20	10.60	10.60
The angels are (?) the clouds	1.50	1.75	3.50	3.25	4.25	**4.75**	**8.00**	9.25	**10.50**	10.75
The clowns are (?) the hammock	2.67	2.17	1.50	2.33	2.67	3.50	**4.17**	**6.17**	**7.67**	10.33
The ants are (?) the grass	1.50	2.00	3.40	4.10	**4.60**	**7.10**	**8.00**	8.20	10.10	10.50

Note: Numbers in bold and underlined are the mean ratings of the pictures that were selected as standard, plus and minus containment variants.

objects located. We hypothesized that the use of *ser* versus *estar* might mean that Spanish speakers would be more likely than English speakers to false alarm to number variations of the probe display in accordance with the verb encoded in the prime display.

Standard pictures had between four and eight located objects, depending on the type of scene, and we created plus and minus variants by adding or taking away a single object. There were therefore a total of nine pictures per scene (3 for containment × 3 for number). These variations were created to be the *probe* pictures where only one out of nine was identical and the rest were different either in number, concavity or both (Figure 4.4).

Experiment 1a (English)

This experiment tested whether sentences containing *in* or *on* presented during prime picture encoding would affect the recognition of similar pictures with increased/decreased levels of containment. We predicted

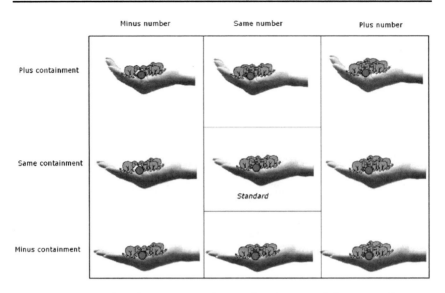

Figure 4.4 Examples of pictures used as probes for one of the material sets in Experiments 1a and 1b

that presentation of *in* with a prime scene would lead to increased likelihood of falsely recognizing a scene with more concavity than has been presented before, and conversely that presentation of *on* at prime would lead to the increased likelihood of falsely recognizing a scene with less concavity than has been presented before.

Participants

Twenty-four students from Northumbria University received payment for their participation. All participants were native-English speakers with poor or no knowledge of other languages.

Design and procedure

Each participant completed a 2 (sentence match/mismatch) × 2 (preposition: *in/on*) × 3 (containment: minus, plus, same) × 3 (number: minus, plus, same) computer-based picture priming experiment.

Participants were asked to perform two tasks. First, they had to indicate whether a sentence presented with a (prime) picture matched the picture or not. Prime displays contained only standard images with a sentence below that correctly described the picture (match trials) or not (mismatch trials). Mismatch trials were created using non-matching sentences for control purposes and were not included in the analyses. Probe displays consisted of a picture of one of the nine variants (e.g. see Figure 4.4) and in this second task participants were asked to indicate if the picture was the same or different from the picture just shown (prime scene).

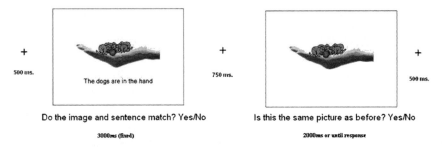

Figure 4.5 Trial sequence: example showing a repetition trial (same level of containment, same number)

Participants were asked to use the C and M keys to respond using their dominant hand to indicate YES (match/same) and the other hand to indicate NO (mismatch/different).

Figure 4.5 displays an example trial in the experiment. Each trial started with a fixation point (+) for 500 ms. This was replaced by the prime display, which was present for 3 s. After this time, another fixation cross was present for 750 ms, followed by the probe display, which remained on the screen for 2 s, or until a response was made. The probe display was then replaced by another fixation (+) for 500 ms. The prime–probe SOA was 3750 ms.

If language affects encoding of visual scenes as Feist and Gentner (2007) suggest, then English speakers should false alarm more to the stronger containment probes than to the weaker containment probes when *in* is presented in the prime sentence, and conversely, they should false alarm more to the weaker containment scenes when *on* is presented with the prime sentence.

Results

Two types of analyses were performed on the data. First, we consider the error data for participants, and then we report the reaction time data for responses.

Accuracy analyses

Table 4.2 shows mean percentages of 'SAME' responses in all conditions in Experiment 1a. A 2 (preposition: *in/on*) × 3 (containment: minus, plus, same) × 3 (number: minus, plus, same) analysis of variance (ANOVA) on percentage of 'SAME' probe display responses showed significant main effects of number, $F(2,46) = 408.2$, MSE = 513.9, $p < 0.01$, and containment, $F(2,46) = 24.18$, MSE = 24.1809, $p < 0.01$. Post-hoc analyses using Fisher's least significant difference (LSD) tests revealed, as expected, that probes that shared the same level of containment as the prime showed a significantly higher percentage of 'SAME' responses (44.19%) than those with less (36%) or more containment (33.7%).

Table 4.2 Mean percentages of 'SAME' responses for probe task in Experiment 1a

	MCMN	MCPN	MCSN	PCMN	PCPN	PCSN	SCMN	SCPN	SAME
In	7.89	18.87	83.61	8.63	17.72	77.54	21.07	24.49	88.42
On	9.15	17.63	78.79	9.14	15.82	73.12	17.49	24.37	89.34
Mean	8.52	18.25	81.20	8.89	16.77	75.33	19.28	24.43	88.88

Note: M = minus, P = plus, S = same, N = number and C = containment.

Also, as expected, LSD analyses showed that the percentage of 'SAME' responses was significantly higher for variants with the same number of objects (81.8%), followed by probes containing a greater number of objects (19.82%), and finally those containing a lesser number of objects (12.22%). Differences between all levels of number were significant, $p < 0.05$.

Variations of number were considerably easier to discriminate than variations of containment. Nevertheless, participants were also sensitive to containment as reflected by the significantly higher amount of 'SAME' responses for the same containment variants (see Table 4.2).

There were no other significant main effects or interactions, indicating that the preposition presented as prime does *not* affect the frequency of false alarms. Critically, the interaction between preposition at prime and level of containment of probe was not significant $F(2,46) = 0.08$, $p = 0.92$.

Reaction time analyses

Reaction time (RT) analysis was performed only for those variants with the same number as the standard. Probes with variations of number were too easy to discriminate and the amount of false alarms is below 50% with not enough RT data to analyse. Table 4.3 shows mean RTs obtained for the same number conditions.

A 2 (preposition: *in/on*) × 3 (containment: minus, plus, same) ANOVA on RT for 'SAME' responses showed a significant main effect of containment, $F(2,46) = 4.25$, MSE = 10,807, $p < 0.01$. LSD analyses showed that RTs were significantly slower ($p < 0.05$) for false alarms of variants that had the same number but less concavity (1041.4 ms) than for the other variants while those variants with the same number and greater concavity were not

Table 4.3 Mean RTs (ms) for probes with the 'same number condition' in Experiment 1a

	MC	PC	SAME
In	1043.87	964.23	986.93
On	1038.91	1009.71	990.48

Note: M = minus, P = plus and C = containment.

significantly faster or slower than the identical, same number–same containment, pairs (986.97 and 988.70 ms, respectively).

There were no other significant main effects or interactions, indicating that the preposition presented in prime sentences does not affect response times.

Experiment 1b (Spanish)

This experiment was designed as a language control for Experiment 1a with respect to the effect of spatial language at encoding on the prime–probe matching judgment task. Additionally, the experiment tested whether *ser* versus *estar* presented with primes would affect false alarm rates to probes. In Spanish, the location of an event is normally described with the verb *ser* (e.g. 'La fiesta *es* en mi casa/The party *is* in my house'), while the location of objects is described using the verb *estar* (e.g. 'Los niños están en mi casa/The children are in my house'). This distinction allowed us to describe the same group of objects as singular (an event) or as plural (a group of objects). We thought that manipulation in the encoding of stimuli as events (*ser*; singular) or objects (*estar*; plural) may give rise to different biases in the recognition of probes with more or less levels of number for Spanish, in contrast to the expectation that there would be no effect of spatial language for Spanish on recognition of concavity changes (given that Spanish only has a single term for support/containment relations, *en*).

Participants

Thirteen Psychology students from the National Autonomous University of Mexico (UNAM) were paid for their participation. All participants were native-Spanish speakers with poor or no knowledge of English.

Design and procedure

Each participant completed a 2 (sentence match/mismatch) × 2 (verb: *es/estan*) × 3 (containment: minus, plus, same) × 3 (number: minus, plus, same) computer-based priming experiment.

Results

Two types of analyses were performed on the data. First, we consider the error data for participants, and then we report the RT data for responses.

Accuracy analyses

Table 4.4 shows the mean percentage of 'SAME' responses in Experiment 1b. A 2 (verb: *ser/estar*) × 3 (containment) × 3 (number) ANOVA on percentage of 'SAME' responses revealed significant main effects of

Table 4.4 Mean percentage of 'SAME' responses for all conditions of the probe task in Experiment 1b

	MCMN	MCPN	MCSN	PCMN	PCPN	PCSN	SAME	SCMN	SCPN
ES	10.90	18.59	63.60	6.62	18.70	60.16	82.13	19.51	22.13
ESTAN	14.42	18.41	67.58	7.59	16.35	59.81	85.36	17.17	23.06

Note: M = minus, P = plus, S = same, N = number and C = containment.

containment, $F(2,24) = 13.92$, MSE = 262.8, $p < 0.01$ and number, $F(2,24) = 206.29$, MSE = 367.3, $p < 0.01$, and a significant containment × number interaction, $F(4,48) = 6.12$, MSE = 111.2, $p < 0.01$. LSD analyses revealed that, overall, as in English, the percentage of 'SAME' responses was significantly higher for variants with the same level of containment (41.56%) than for those with less containment (32.3%) or more containment (28.2%). LSD analyses also showed that the amount of SAME responses was significantly higher for probes containing the same number of objects (69.8%) followed by probes containing more objects (19.54%) and finally those containing fewer objects (12.7%). All number variants were significantly different from each other, $p < 0.05$.

Analyses of the containment × number interaction revealed that differences between minus and plus variants for number were only significant for plus containment probes. There was no main effect of verb or interaction between verb and number or containment.

RT analyses

Mean RTs for the 'same number' conditions of probe task are shown in Table 4.5. A 2 (verb: *ser/estar*) × 3 (containment: minus, plus, same) ANOVA on RT for 'SAME' responses showed a significant main effect of containment, $F(2,24) = 3.49$, MSE = 10,462, $p < 0.05$. LSD analyses showed that mean RT was significantly slower for false alarms for variants that had the same number but less containment (949.36 ms) than for the other variants, while those variants with the same number and more containment were not different from the identical, same number–same containment pairs (883 and 886 ms, respectively).

Table 4.5 Mean RTs (ms) for the probe task in the 'same number' conditions in Experiment 1b

	MCSN	PCSN	SAME
ES	922.79	895.16	896.25
ESTAN	975.93	870.35	876.21
	949.36	882.76	886.23

Note: M = minus, S = same, P = plus and N = number.

Discussion

Contrary to the thinking-for-speaking hypothesis, implicit recognition of spatial relations seems to be not affected either by the use of spatial prepositions in English (Experiment 1a) or by the use of verbs in Spanish (Experiment 1b).

In both experiments, participants showed a tendency to false alarm more to those items with different levels of containment as long as they shared the same number of elements as the standard (prime) picture. In addition to this, it seems clear that minus number variants were easier to discriminate overall. This was probably due to the fact that the perceptual saliency of an added object was not balanced in terms of position and size with the minus number displays.

Despite number being the main variable to discriminate between identical and different pairs, participants seem to be also sensitive to containment manipulations as reflected in the advantage of 'SAME' responses for identical pairs (repetition condition) both in Spanish and in English.

RT also showed a consistent pattern of effects in both groups, characterized by a slower RT for false alarms with the same number but minus containment. Perhaps more surprising is the fact that RTs for false alarms to the plus containment–same number variant were not different from the RTs for accurately detected identical pairs (repetition condition).

The results of these experiments across two languages do not provide support for the view that there are conceptual differences in spatial relations or number judgments associated with differences in spatial language and verbs between languages. However, it is possible that the salience of the number manipulation overall may have masked any effects of the spatial relation manipulation. To explore this possibility, in Experiment 2 we removed the number variable and included more subtle levels of containment as well as a non-preposition (further control) condition in English L1.

Experiment 2 (English)

Stimuli

Pictures used for Experiments 1a and 1b were further manipulated deleting multiple objects so that only one located object was depicted for each reference object. In addition, two more levels of containment were created for each set of materials increasing or decreasing the degree of containment between the standard and the minus and plus containment variants, therefore adding a second level of difficulty of containment discrimination (Figure 4.6).

Sentences in English used in Experiments 1a and 1b were modified for single objects (e.g. *The duck is in/on the dish*). Additionally, a non-preposition (control) condition was added using a conjunction (e.g. *Duck and dish*).

Minus containment   Standard   Plus containment

Figure 4.6 Example of pictures with five levels of containment employed

Participants
Nineteen students from Northumbria University participated voluntarily or received payment for their participation. All participants were native-English speakers with poor or no knowledge of other languages.

Design and procedure
Each participant completed a 2 (sentence match/mismatch) × 3 (language: *in/on/and*) × 5 (containment: minus1, minus2, plus1, plus2 and same) computer-based priming experiment.

The experimental procedure was exactly as in Experiments 1a and 1b, but due to elimination of the number variable, the number of variants was reduced from nine to five, and one level of the language variable was added.

Results

As in Experiments 1a and 1b, mismatch trials were only used as controls and were not analyzed. We report the results of error and RT analyses separately.

Accuracy analyses
Table 4.6 shows mean percentage of 'SAME' responses for all types of probes.

A 3 (language: *in/on/and*) × 5 (containment: minus1, minus2, plus1, plus2 and same) ANOVA for percentage of 'SAME' responses revealed a significant main effect of containment, $F(4,72) = 43.7$, $MSE = 472$, $p < 0.01$, but none of the other main effects or interactions were significant.

LSD post-hoc analyses of containment showed that, as in Experiments 1a and 1b, probes with the same containment as the prime (repeated condition) showed a higher percentage of 'SAME' responses. The lowest

Table 4.6 Mean percentages of 'SAME' responses for all types of probes in Experiment 2

	MINUS2	*MINUS1*	*SAME*	*PLUS1*	*PLUS2*
And	42.92	68.50	89.22	50.94	45.96
In	43.89	67.01	89.40	57.05	45.13
On	42.23	67.50	88.57	56.33	43.52

Table 4.7 Mean RT (ms) for 'SAME' responses on the probe display in Experiment 2

	Minus1	*Plus1*	*Same*
And	795.6	846.5	755.7
In	775.9	775.1	777.4
On	842.9	779.3	757.8
	804.8	800.3	763.6

percentage of false alarms was obtained for variants that were in the extremes (minus2 and plus2), and were not significantly different from one another (both below 50%). Finally, plus containment variants (plus1) showed this time significantly fewer false alarms (54.8%) than minus containment variants (minus1; 67.7%).

RT analyses

Table 4.7 shows mean RT obtained for the probe task in all conditions of Experiment 2 with more than 50% of false alarms.

A 3 (language: in/on/and) × 3 (containment: minus1, plus1 and same) ANOVA over RT of 'SAME' responses produced no significant effect of any variable or interactions.

Discussion

In the second experiment, again with native-English speakers, we eliminated the number manipulation and introduced two additional gradations of containment in the images in order to give language effects more of a chance to be detected should they be present. However, the results of this experiment failed to find any effect of the language presented with the prime on either the percentage of false alarms or RTs to make false alarms.

General Discussion

We set out to test L1 speakers of English and Spanish on their ability to detect changes in levels of concavity (and number), given that these languages differ in their lexicalization patterns for spatial prepositions and verbs. Our intention was to use differences emerging from L1 speakers between languages as a baseline with which to go on to test L2 speakers at different levels of proficiency in these languages. Surprisingly, in the experiments reported, we failed to find any evidence for an effect of language on immediate recognition of spatial relations, undermining the rationale to look for conceptual shifts in containment/support relations in second language learners.

The methodology we adopted allowed us to control the mapping between spatial language and spatial scenes very carefully; *in* and *on* were both appropriate to describe the prime scenes. The time course of the study was also shorter than in studies that have found evidence for thinking for speaking. These differences may be critical in an explanation of why we failed to find language effects while others have found such effects.

The Pederson *et al.* (1998) studies examining the correspondence between reference frame use in language and reference frame use on non-linguistic spatial tasks allowed participants time to process the stimuli at encoding. Thus, participants had time to verbally encode the scenes, and later retrieve language as a means of facilitating non-linguistic choice for a later scene.

More similar to the present studies are the experiments reported by Feist and Gentner (2007) in which they presented sentences with spatial prepositions together with pictures at encoding and found a pattern of false alarms at later recognition toward the relation denoted by the sentence. However, there are two key differences in the methodology used in our studies and that used by Feist and Gentner. First, in their experiments, the (standard) scenes at encoding involved a weak version of the relation depicted by the preposition in the sentence. For instance, an object touching the edge of a supporting surface is not a very good *on* relation, although *on* is still the best spatial preposition to describe that relation. So, the sentence 'The block is on the building' is a facilitative description of the spatial scene. In contrast, in the present studies, *in* and *on* were equally good descriptions of each probe scene, so the sentence is not in itself a unique facilitator for memory for the scene.

The second (more compelling) difference between the Feist and Gentner experiments and the present studies relates to the time course of the task. The recognition test used by Feist and Gentner employed an 'old' versus 'new' paradigm where the prime pictures and recognition task pictures were presented in blocks. So, like the Pederson *et al.* (1998) tasks, participants may be advantaged by employing a linguistic encoding strategy as a means of remembering the scenes. In the present experiments, although participants made a language judgment about the prime scene, arguably there is no time to use language as a memory facilitator. Indeed if this difference is key for the present studies, the failure to find language effects does not discount thinking-for-speaking effects (as there was no time for those effects here), but does cast doubt on the plausibility of any stronger claims regarding linguistic determinism.

There are implications of these results regarding conceptual transfer as applied to second language learning. There may well be a point during L2 acquisition where learners are able to use the linguistic encoding in the L2 sufficiently well to produce non-linguistic behavior on a task similar to that produced by L1 speakers on the same task. However, one needs to be cautious with regard to the claim that such results entail that either L1 or advanced L2 speakers of that language have a differing non-linguistic representation of the domain in question. Language may be used as a tool to help future behavior, rather than as a means of nurturing some conceptual distinctions while disregarding others.

In summary, the experiments with L1 speakers we have reported have failed to find effects of language on visual discrimination. However, the methodology adopted allows easy manipulation of the time between prime and probe. This may establish when (if at all) thinking-for-speaking effects come into play, and if so, when differences between Spanish and English speakers may emerge. We are currently investigating these possibilities.

Acknowledgements

We are indebted to the Arts and Humanities Research Council for funding this research (grant awarded to the first and third authors). We also thank Shelli Feist for helpful discussions and the Autonomous National University of Mexico for facilitating recruitment and testing of participants.

Chapter 5
The Gloss Trap

DAVID STRINGER

Introduction

Comparative syntactic studies of the world's languages are greatly facilitated by the use of glosses, which allow for a closer analysis than is possible through conventional translation. However, the creation of glosses can be misleading if the elements given as lexical analogues differ from language to language, to the extent that the meanings of words determine possible syntactic environments. In fact, it is extremely difficult to find true matches in the open-class lexicons of any two languages, and this is certainly the case for closed-class items, whose syntactic properties are inevitably language-particular (Emonds, 1985: 165–170, 2000: 115). Such differences in lexicalization across languages appear to be so ubiquitous as to be indicative of a fundamental organizing principle in the mental lexicon. I draw on observations by Saussure (1983 [1916]) to argue for a principle of lexical relativity, according to which lexical concepts are determined relative to other items in the lexicon, with the result that no two languages lexicalize concepts in the same way. This does not necessarily lead to a radical Whorfian approach, as the semantic machinery used to build lexical items contains elements of meaning that are plausibly universal, and mental construals of the world are not only constructed through language; however, it does support an approach in which the particular language we speak determines linguistically mediated construals of events, states and objects, in line with Slobin's (1996a) proposal of Thinking for Speaking. For the present purposes, discussion is restricted to encoded aspects of lexical meaning, rather than aspects of meaning that may change according to context, on the assumption that encoding and inference are independent systems of interpretation (Sperber & Wilson, 1995 [1986]). For example, the English verb *spray*, regardless of context, encodes the interpretation of the moving object in the event as a three-dimensional (3D) aggregate of psychologically dimensionless points; *smear* requires that the moving object be a 3D semisolid substance; and the verb *wrap* specifies that the moving object be a two-dimensional (2D) flexible solid (see Pinker, 1989: Chapter 5 for discussion). Such semantic specifications not only hold across normal contexts, but are also robust even in counter-intuitive scenarios. One does not usually spray deck chairs onto a public lawn, but if one spoke of a machine that did just that, the spraying would still involve a 3D aggregate of psychologically dimensionless points. Meaning in context is a necessary part of interpretation, but the current focus of investigation is inherent lexical semantics.

Although most linguists recognize that glosses are an imperfect tool, cases continually surface in which syntactic generalizations are made on the basis of assumed equivalence in a given context between lexical analogues whose properties differ in significant ways. Syntactic comparison in such cases often relies on a notion of lexical equivalence at the level of the gloss: a morpheme glossed as 'walk' is assumed to correspond in relevant respects to the English verb *walk*; a morpheme glossed as 'into' is assumed to correspond in relevant respects to the English preposition *into*. If one language allows a phrase such as *walk into the house*, while another language prohibits the supposedly equivalent combination, this may be held to be a syntactic difference between the two languages. In this chapter, I consider a flaw in this type of analysis, which surfaces with some regularity in studies of comparative syntax and second language acquisition, and point to a solution in terms of fine-grained lexical semantic decomposition. I examine two instances of the gloss trap in the domain of motion events, and argue that proposed language-particular lexicalization patterns unravel on closer inspection of the syntax and semantics of the predicates involved. In each case, the differences are shown to lie in lexical items, not in whole languages. In the following section, I briefly review some of the evidence suggesting that lexical items do not reflect a universal set of concepts, but rather package concepts in different ways in different languages. I then consider the two aforementioned generalizations from the perspective of lexical relativity and second language acquisition: (i) that verbs expressing Manner (of motion) in so-called 'verb-framed' languages cannot take directional complements (Hohenstein *et al.*, 2004; Inagaki, 2001, 2002; Jackendoff, 1990); and (ii) that English verb classes underlying syntactic alternations (locative, dative, causative, etc.) exist as classes with 'equivalent' verbs in other languages, thus creating problems for L2 acquisition when the syntactic settings of such classes fail to coincide (Bley-Vroman & Joo, 2001; Juffs, 1996; Schwartz *et al.*, 2003). In the final section, the implications of lexical relativity for second language acquisition are drawn out. Comparative syntactic analysis of predicates is argued to be feasible through their decomposition into grammatically relevant semantic components. In the light of the lexicalist approach to such issues, it is suggested that the gloss trap may be avoided in studying the L2 acquisition of argument structure by means of *a priori* contrastive analyses at the level of lexical semantics. Viewing acquisition of the L2 lexicon as, in part, a reanalysis of the lexical semantics of the L1 lexicon (Sprouse, 2006) makes it possible to predict exactly where many problems for learners are likely to lie.

Lexical Relativity and the Gloss Trap

The reality of lexical relativity

Despite the fact that lexical non-equivalence across languages is intuitively apparent to most translators, language teachers and linguists (see the collected papers in VanPatten *et al.*, 2004), the opposite idea has also been posited in the literature: that open-class lexical items in the world's languages are drawn from a universal lexicon that labels a universal and innate set of concepts. For example, Chomsky (1995: 131) writes: 'If substantive elements (verbs, nouns, etc.) are drawn from a universal vocabulary, then only functional elements will be parameterized'. The idea that the only important differences between languages are encoded in the functional lexicon has also been pursued in the work of Fukui (1993, 1995). The more general notion of the open-class lexicon as a repository of universal concepts is in line with the 'semantic atomism' proposed by Fodor (1998), who claims that we should never find that a lexical item in one language is broken down into constituent meaning parts in another language.

The myth of lexical equivalence soon dissipates on consideration of research that has specifically focused on comparing any two lexicons in detail. When Apreszjan and Pàll (1982) compiled their Russian–Hungarian dictionary, they opted to eliminate the problem of giving inevitably false equivalents by doing away with definitions altogether, relying instead on descriptions with examples of typically co-occurring elements, and translations of the example sentences. Even in the absence of definitions, the entries are very long (the Russian verb *brat* 'take' takes ten pages) and, according to Mel'čuk (1985), remain incomplete. When Adjemian (1983) compared lexical acquisition by English learners of French and French learners of English, he found that the syntax associated with L1 verbs was subject to transfer, so that native French speakers incorrectly made English verbs reflexive when the French analogues had this property (e.g. *se retirer* – REFL retire – 'retire'), and English learners of French used strictly intransitive verbs in causative contexts (e.g. **marcher les chats* 'walk the cats'). One of the most striking examples of this kind of comparative analysis is Wierzbicka's (1985) attempt to provide complete semantic descriptions of common English words, reminiscent in its boldness and optimism of a grand medieval quest, ultimately quixotic. The point to note here is that none of these words could be exactly matched by Wierzbicka to their analogues in Polish: something is lost even when translating such commonplace objects as *cup* or *shirt*.

More recent work on the L2 acquisition of argument structure serves to strengthen the idea that lexical relativity is fundamental to our understanding of both the initial state of learners and their subsequent paths of development. In the case of locatives, Kim (1999) shows that Korean analogues of ground-oriented English locatives often alternate, unlike in English (*fill the glass with water / *fill the water into the glass*). The reanalysis by Schwartz *et al.* (2003) of the results obtained by Joo (2000) shows that this difference in meaning and syntax transfers: Korean learners of English assume lexical equivalence and wrongly allow the alternation. If the findings of Dekydtspotter *et al.* (2008) are generalizable, these learners eventually come to have native-like judgements, despite an absence of evidence in the input to force them to a more restrictive grammar. This parallels the problem in the first language acquisition of such alternation patterns, as children also overgeneralize and then retreat to a more restrictive grammar in the absence of negative evidence (Pinker, 1989). This learnability conundrum remains without a convincing explanation, and highlights the need for more fine-grained theories of both first and second language acquisition of the lexicon.

In sum, the idea of a universal open-class vocabulary is wholly undermined by the abundant evidence for lexical relativity, which appears to be fundamental for our understanding of the nature and development of the mental lexicon.

The scope of lexical relativity

The degree to which lexical relativity characterizes human languages remains an open question. One might ask if, rather than lexical mismatches simply being commonplace, they systematically fall out of the design template of natural languages. I adopt the position that lexical equivalence is virtually non-existent due largely to the fact that both the denotational and syntactic properties of words are constrained by those of other words in the same combinatorial system. This point was made eloquently and influentially by Saussure (1983 [1916]: 112–120), who argued that the 'sense' of a word can be thought of as a linguistic 'value'. Just as the value of a coin can be determined by its relation to something dissimilar that can be exchanged for the coin (e.g. bread), and by its relation to something similar that can be compared with it (e.g. other coins in the same currency, or a coin in a different currency), a word can be substituted for something dissimilar (i.e. an idea) and can be compared with something similar (i.e. other words). To follow through with this metaphor, the semantic value of a word is determined not only by its relationship with an associated concept, but also by its relationship to other words in the same linguistic system. Saussure illustrates this point with several well-known examples. The French word *mouton* corresponds both to English *sheep* and *mutton*, that is it refers both to the animal and to the meat. In this comparative light, the scope of the meaning of English *sheep* can be seen to be partly determined by the existence of the term *mutton* (Saussure, 1983 [1916]: 114). Saussure argued that this is also true in respect of closed-class morphology. In Sanskrit, the equivalents of the French *mes yeux, mes oreilles, mes bras, mes jambes* ('my eyes, my ears, my arms, my legs') are not plural, but dual. Thus the semantic value of the French plural morpheme does not correspond exactly to that of the Sanskrit plural: the meaning of the latter is determined relative to the existence of the dual.

One important part of Saussure's (1983 [1916]) account of lexical relativity that must be re-evaluated is his insistence on relative differences in a single lexicon as the only source of meaning: for him, words may be defined *only* in contrast with one another: '... although in general a difference presupposes positive terms between which the difference holds, in a language there are only differences, *and no positive terms*' (1983 [1916]: 118, italics in the original). Only when the semantic and phonological values are arbitrarily linked does the 'sign' as a whole take on a positive aspect (1983 [1916]: 118–119). However, as Bloom (2000: 73) notes, opposition in and of itself is insufficient to characterize lexical meaning. While words in a given relational set may be characterized with reference to one another, the opposition between totally unrelated lexical items does not contribute to our understanding of the meaning or syntactic behaviour of either item. To take a further example from Saussure, French verbs such as *redouter* 'to dread', *craindre* 'to fear' and *avoir peur* 'to be afraid' have particular meaning only in contrast with other members of the set; if one of these lexical items did not exist, its nuances would be shared out among the other members (Saussure, 1983 [1916]: 114). Nevertheless, these words are not defined in contrast with all the other words in the lexicon. If the contrasts in question are all between closely related items, we need to be able to say how the items are related as well as what distinguishes them, and it is unclear how such groupings could be made without reference to positive aspects of meaning. Stringer (2005: 90) defines lexical relativity as follows:

(1) *The Lexical Relativity Hypothesis*: When comparing lexical analogues in different languages, the meaning of any lexical item [LI] is relative to its ambient lexicon.

An articulate theory of what constitutes the 'ambient lexicon' (the other lexical entries to which the meaning of the item is relative) is beyond the scope of the current chapter; suffice it to say that it is conceptually necessary.

The relative nature of lexical meaning with a single language carries with it a fundamental implication for the debate on linguistic relativity: the lexicalization of concepts necessarily differs between languages. This affects not only the referential properties of vocabulary items, but also any aspects of syntax that are lexically determined. For example, as verb meanings are representations of events, specifying roles and properties of participants, the particular verb we use determines how we conceptualize the event as we speak (to others or ourselves). This does not rule out alternative, non-linguistic means of event construal, but it does imply that 'thinking for speaking' is true at least in respect of the syntax of argument structure, on the assumption that this is lexically derived (Jackendoff, 1990; Levin, 1993; Pinker, 1989, 2007). Even very subtle differences in conceptualization can affect syntax, and conversely, subtle differences in syntax can reveal conceptual disparity. As Levin and Rappaport Hovav (2005: 19) argue, 'When alternate construals are possible and involve different grammatically relevant aspects of meaning, the result can be pairs of near synonyms within or across languages showing different argument realization options'. Lexical relativity therefore has important implications for syntactic variation.

The forms of lexical relativity

Recasting lexical relativity in positive terms, two kinds of conceptual variation may be considered: firstly, those inherent conceptual elements that play no role in syntax; and secondly, those semantic elements that do have syntactic effects, whether they be inherent to predicates or contextually required in their arguments.

The first type of variation is a typical rather than exceptional characteristic of open-class lexicons. Conceptual elements that play no role in syntax may be readily observed on close examination of most pairs of corresponding open-class lexical items, even when it seems most counterintuitive from a monolingual perspective. Surely modern inventions must be labelled with equivalent vocabulary, one might suppose. Yet the English noun *television* has no exact equivalent in German: *der Fernseher* refers to the machine, while *das Fernsehen* refers to the medium.[1] Other common nouns splinter in a similar fashion in translation: English *rice* corresponds to both Japanese *kome* (uncooked rice) and *gohan* (cooked rice); English *sink* corresponds to both French *évier* (for washing dishes) and *lavabo* (for washing hands); French *noix*, which generally corresponds to English *nut*, is also the specific French term for *walnut*, rendering ambiguous a term such as *huile de noix* 'nut/walnut oil'. Such mismatches are not restricted to the nominal domain, but are found with activities and states that one might expect to be expressed with the same types of verbs. A universal human activity such as drinking seems likely to be expressed with universal semantics. However, the English verb *drink* is used only of liquids. In

Turkish, one may 'drink' smoke as well as liquids; in Japanese, one may 'drink' medicinal pills or powders with or without water, as long as they are orally ingested; in Kazak, the verb 'drink' is used for both liquids and solids, in contexts where English would require the verb *eat*. Such examples may oversimplify the mapping from one lexical item into another language, which is rarely a case of one-to-two correspondence: the relations are often much more complicated. Sometimes there is a lexical gap, such that no word may be analogous, and the concept must be expressed periphrastically. Thus, while Japanese has two verbs meaning 'go under', *moguru* meaning 'go under and stay there' and *kuguru* meaning 'go under and out the other side', English has no single verb meaning 'go-under'. In other cases, rather than there being a lexical gap, there are a number of different verbs corresponding (often inexactly) to various senses of a single term. For example, the English verb *put* has multiple translations in Korean, each incorporating other aspects of meaning, none having lexical equivalents in English:

(2)   (a) *pwuchita* ≈ 'juxtapose surfaces' (e.g. put a magnet on a refrigerator)
      (b) *nohta* ≈ 'put on a horizontal surface' (e.g. put a cup onto a table)
      (c) *ssuta* ≈ 'put clothing on head' (e.g. put a hat on)
      (d) *kkita* ≈ 'fit tightly' (e.g. put a ring on a finger, or a videocassette in a case)
      (e) *nehta* ≈ 'put loosely around' (e.g. put an apple in a bowl, or a book in a bag)
                                        (adapted from Bowerman & Choi, 2001)

Thus it is nonsensical to ask how the verb *put* differs in English and Korean in terms of its semantic features or its argument structure, or if the stages of acquisition of *put* are similar for English and Korean children, or if the syntax of *put* transfers from Korean to English in second language acquisition. All such questions have a hidden presupposition: that there is a verb 'put' in both languages (and presumably in all languages). To gloss one of the above Korean verbs as *put*, which may be reasonable in the context of a particular analysis, leaves one in danger of falling into the gloss trap if syntactic generalizations are based on such a correspondence.

Such examples can easily be multiplied, and in each case, the folk reaction is one of surprise. English-speaking learners of Japanese are inevitably bewildered as they realize that the body parts *foot* and *leg* are expressed with the same term in Japanese (*ashi*). Yet, despite having relative complexity in some lexical entries, and relative simplicity in others, speakers of all languages seem to have enough lexical resources to communicate perfectly well. As such, tradeoffs in complexity in the lexicon parallel those in syntax and phonology.

The second type of lexical mismatch involves what I have elsewhere called 'computational semantic features' (Stringer, 2005: 101): those elements of lexical meaning that play a role in syntax, which are either inherent to predicates or selected by predicates and inherent to their arguments. Such semantic components play an important role in most lexicalist theories, and are variously referred to as 'interpretable syntactic features' (Emonds, 2000); 'ontological categories' or 'conceptual functions' (Jackendoff, 1990); 'meaning components' (Levin, 1993); or the 'grammatically relevant semantic subsystem' (Pinker, 1989). Copious evidence for the existence of inherent semantic features with grammatical import is given by Levin (1993), drawing on resource materials from the MIT Lexicon Project in the 1980s. Levin (1993) shows how variation in syntactic argument structure can be used to discover which meaning elements in predicates might have syntactic effects. For example, the verbs (a) *cut*, (b) *crack*, (c) *stroke* and (d) *whack* may seem conceptually similar at first glance, but detailed analysis reveals that *crack* and *stroke* may not be used in the 'conative' construction (e.g. *Harry cut at the pastry*), *crack* may not be used in the 'body-part ascension' construction (e.g. *Sally cut Harry on the arm*), and *stroke* and *whack* may not be used in the 'middle' construction (e.g. *This surface cuts easily*), while *cut* is grammatical in all three environments (Levin, 1993: 6–7). The semantic elements that appear relevant to this distribution appear to be conflated as follows.

(3) (a) *cut*:   [CAUSE, CHANGE OF STATE, CONTACT, MOTION]
    (b) *crack*:   [CAUSE, CHANGE OF STATE]
    (c) *stroke*:   [CONTACT]
    (d) *whack*:   [CONTACT, MOTION]

If this analysis is correct, then predictions can be made as to the syntax of verbs that share the same semantic features. Such predictions are borne out with the syntactic distribution of (a) *cut*-type verbs (*scratch, hack, slash,* etc.); (b) *crack*-type verbs (*rip, break, snap,* etc.); (c) *stroke*-type verbs (*tickle, pat, touch,* etc.); and (d) *whack*-type verbs (*kick, hit, tap,* etc.), leading to the conclusion that lexical semantic features do play a determining role in the syntax of argument structure.

Such meaning components may well be universal in languages, or at least universally available to language learners. However, they are packaged differently in different languages, resulting in lexical mismatches. Thus the English verb *drown* encodes CHANGE: there is a change of state such that death must certainly ensue. In contrast, the Japanese verb *oboreru* can be used in contexts in which a person may 'drown' for five minutes and then be rescued; a change of state may be inferred in certain contexts, but it is not encoded in the verb. Similarly, the English preposition *on* encodes CONTACT, while the Japanese analogous expression *no ue de* – GEN top LocP – 'on' may be used whether there is contact or not. The Japanese sentence below is always semantically ambiguous in respect of the bird's contact with the tree.

(4)   Tori wa eda no ue de utatteiru.
       bird TOP branch GEN top at sing-PROG
       'A bird is singing {on/above} the branch'.

Correspondingly, the element CAUSE may be lexically encoded in an English verb such as *roll* or *break*, but requires extra morphology for its expression in Turkish (Montrul, 2001: 4, 5).

(5)   (a) Gemi bat-miş.
            ship sink-past
            'The ship sank'.
       (b) Dü_man gemi-yi bat -*ir*-miş.
            enemy ship-acc. sink-CAUSE-past
            'The enemy sank the ship/made the ship sink'.

Such mismatches between lexical analogues across languages are found not only for the lexical semantic elements CHANGE, CONTACT and CAUSE, but also for every grammatically relevant semantic component in the language faculty. As seen in the work of Levin (1993), such differences in lexicalization invariably cause domino effects in syntax, which leads us to predict that lexical transfer in second language acquisition leads to non-target-like patterns of interlanguage syntax.

Manner Verbs and Directional Complements

Talmy's typology revisited

One crosslinguistic generalization that has been made partly on the basis of loose glosses is the widely accepted assumption that verbs expressing manner of motion in certain languages cannot take directional complements. The constraint in question is drawn from Talmy's (1985, 1991) observation that 'verb-framed' languages, such as those in the Romance, Altaic, Semitic and Polynesian families, usually express 'paths' (or 'trajectories') in verbs, while 'satellite-framed' languages, such as those in the Indo-European family, do so in adpositions, affixes or particles, as exemplified below in the verb-framed French example and its satellite-framed English translation (for brief reviews, see also Cadierno, this volume; Hasko, 2009; Stam, this volume).

(6)   Le petit cochon est entré dans la maison en courant.   (PATH in verb)
       the little pig AUX entered in the house by running
       'The little pig ran into the house'.   (PATH in adposition)

It should be noted at the outset that Talmy (1985, 1991) does not posit this dichotomy in the world's languages as a formal constraint. Rather, a verb-framed language is so by virtue of the above means of expression being a 'characteristic lexicalization type', in other words: '(i) it is *colloquial* in style, rather than literary, stilted, etc.; (ii) it is *frequent* in occurrence in speech, rather than only occasional; (iii) it is *pervasive*, rather than limited, that is, a wide range of semantic notions are associated with this type' (Talmy, 1985: 62; italics in the original). Nevertheless, a number of researchers have advanced the idea that Talmy's typology concerns more than characteristic expression, and might be stated in terms of either a formal principle or constraint operative at the whole-language level, for example Levin and Rapoport's (1988) principle of 'lexical subordination'; Jackendoff's (1990) GO-adjunct rule; Snyder's (1995) positing of a null telic morpheme in this type of English structure, linked to a more general 'compounding parameter'; and Inagaki's (2001, 2002) hypothesis of parameterized PATH conflation. Such accounts take as significant the observation that if, when translating into a verb-framed language, we substitute lexical analogues for a given English MANNER verb and a given English directional preposition and then combine them, the result may be ungrammatical. However, I maintain that once the lexical semantics of both verbs and adpositions are taken into consideration, the argumentation underlying these approaches can be seen to unravel.

English prepositions and the gloss trap

The problem can be illustrated by taking a look at some contrasts between two adpositions, French *à* and Japanese *ni*, and their common English glosses. The French preposition *à* as found in motion events is usually glossed as either 'at' or 'to', depending on whether the interpretation is locational or directional, as shown below. I follow Emonds (2000) in assigning to this adposition the general spatial feature LOCATION, which subsumes interpretations of PLACE and PATH.

(7) Gilda était à la gare.   PLACE
     Gilda was at the station
     'Gilda was at the station'.
(8) Gilda est allé à la gare.   PATH
     Gilda AUX gone to the station
     'Gilda went to the station'.

However, while glossing *à* as 'at' or 'to' in such a context may be appropriate for a particular level of analysis, it would be inaccurate to assume that it is equivalent to either English preposition. Such assumptions may lead to the following type of misanalysis.

The wrong rationale:

Step 1: In English, one can say:
(9)   Gilda waded to the sandbank.

Step 2: In French, one cannot say:
(10)   *Gilda a pataugé au banc de sable.
        Gilda AUX waded to-the bank of sand
        'Gilda waded to the sandbank'.

Step 3: In French, one must express this with a PATH verb:
(11)   Gilda est allé au banc de sable en pataugeant.
        Gilda AUX went to-the bank of sand by wading
        'Gilda waded to the sandbank'.

Step 4: Therefore French and English syntax differ in this respect.

The reason this analysis falters is the gloss in Step 2, which holds *à* and *to* as 'equivalent' (i.e. having the same lexical properties and syntactic effects). While English *at* is strictly and inherently locational,[2] and English *to* is strictly and inherently directional, French *à* is a more general spatial preposition that is locational by default and is directional only in the appropriate syntactic environment, that is when it is the complement of a directional verb. French *patauger* 'wade' is not such a verb.[3] If the example in Step 2 contained a *bona fide* directional preposition such as *vers* 'towards', the 'English' pattern would be perfectly possible:[4]

(12) Gilda a pataugé vers le banc de sable.
     Gilda AUX waded towards the bank of sand
     'Gilda waded towards the sandbank'.

From this perspective, the difference between French and English in the above examples appears to be lexically determined rather than the product of a language-wide parameter setting.

Similar argumentation holds for glosses of Japanese *ni*, which is likewise ambiguous between locational and directional interpretations:

(13) Hiro wa gakko ni imashita.   PLACE
     Hiro TOP school at was
     'Hiro was at school'.

(14) Hiro wa gakko ni itta.   PATH
     Hiro TOP school to went
     'Hiro went to school'.

English glosses of *ni* exhibit even more variation than French *à*, due to a relatively impoverished inventory of directional adpositions in Japanese. Both French à and Japanese *ni* indicate location conceptualized as a zero-dimensional point in space, or arrival at that point. However, if a French speaker conceptualizes the location not as a point but as a 3D interior space, or as a 2D surface, the prepositions *dans* 'in' and *sur* 'on' are, respectively, more appropriate.

(15) Gilda était {dans la mer/sur le toit}.   PLACE
     Gilda was {in the sea/on the roof}
     'Gilda was {in the sea/on the roof}'.

(16) Gilda {a sauté dans la mer/a grimpé sur le toit}.   PATH
     Gilda {AUX jumped in(to) the sea/AUX climbed on(to) the roof}
     'Gilda {jumped into the sea/climbed onto the roof}'.

Japanese *ni* serves as an all-purpose locative postposition in such cases, as shown below.

(17) Hiro wa {umi ni/yane ni} imashita.   PLACE
     Hiro TOP {sea in/roof on} was
     'Hiro was {in the room/on the roof}.

(18) Hiro wa {umi ni jampu shita/yane ni nobotta}.   PATH
     Hiro TOP {sea in(to) jump did/roof on(to) climbed}
     'Hiro {jumped into the sea/climbed onto the roof}'.

The assumption that the multiple glosses of *ni* have a theoretical status could lead not only to the PATH/PLACE confusion we saw above with French *à*, but also to further misanalysis if geometric properties are taken into account, as follows:

The wrong rationale:

Step 1: In English, one can say:
(19)   Mika danced into the room.

Step 2: In Japanese, one cannot say:
(20)   *Mika wa heya ni odotta.
        Mika-TOP room in(to) danced
        'Mika danced into the room'.

Step 3: In Japanese, one must express this with a PATH verb:
(21)   Mika wa heya ni odotte haitta.
        Mika-TOP room into dancing entered
        'Mika danced into the room'.

Step 4: Therefore Japanese and English syntax differ in this respect.

Again, the reason why this analysis falters is the gloss in Step 2, which holds *ni* and *into* as equivalent. In parallel to the French examples above, *ni* is unlike English *into* in that it is not inherently directional. The directional reading is only possible when *ni* is the complement of a directional verb. Japanese *odoru* 'dance' is not such a verb. Moreover, as shown above, while sometimes found in the same surface environment, Japanese *ni* is unlike English *in* and French *dans* in that it has no geometric specifications in any case (thus French *sauter dans* – 'jump in' is not equivalent to Japanese *ni jampu suru* – 'LOCATIVE jump-do'). Again, the differences prove to be due to lexical aspects of the adposition: English *into* specifies a 3D interior and is unambiguously directional, while Japanese *ni* neither specifies a 3D interior nor is unambiguously directional. It is a general locative adposition, which can only support a directional interpretation if merged with an appropriate verb.

The above examples show that sublexical features with grammatical import, such as LOCATION, PATH and PLACE, may vary in the representations of lexical analogues, making it difficult to assume that *at, to* or *into* can serve as adequate English glosses for either French *à* or Japanese *ni* in any linguistic example in which the preposition plays an important role.

Such a use of literal translation to facilitate comparative syntactic analysis can be seen in the treatment of Talmy's typology by Hohenstein *et al.* (2004: 572) with reference to the following English and Spanish examples:

(22) (a) The children ran
     (b) The children ran into the room.

(23) (a) Las niñas corrieron.
     (b) *Las niñas corrieron hacia adentro del cuarto.

Example (23b) is an attempt to literally translate Example (22b), for the purpose of showing that Spanish grammar does not allow directional phrases such as *into the room* to merge with manner verbs such as *run*. These examples are used to support a claim for language-specific syntax: '... The issue with Spanish is that it lacks the requisite rule, so that Spanish manner verbs cannot always appear with the same directional phrases' (Hohenstein *et al.*, 2004: 572). It is here assumed that English *into* finds its lexical equivalent in the Spanish phrase *hacia adentro de* (towards inside of). However, the assembly of this latter phrase does not take into account the lexical properties of its parts, which I shall briefly examine in turn. *Hacia* 'towards' shares several properties with its English counterpart (it is an unbounded, transitive preposition, and can, in fact be merged with a MANNER verb), for example,

(24) Las niñas corrieron hacia el cuarto.
     the girls ran towards the room
     'The girls ran towards the room'.

Adentro 'inside', on the other hand, is an intransitive preposition (or verb particle, or satellite, depending on the analysis), which also may be used with satellite-framed syntax. Thus Example (25a) is possible, but Example (25b) is impossible.

(25) (a) Las niñas corrieron adentro.
     the girls ran inside
     'The girls ran inside'.

(b)   *Las niñas corrieron adentro el cuarto
      the girls ran inside the room
      'The girls ran inside the room'.

Presumably, the grammatical preposition *de* is added to *adentro* to make it resemble the locative P *dentro* (*de*), which is legitimately transitive, as shown below.

(26) Las niñas estaban dentro del cuarto.
      the girls were inside of-the room
      'The girls were inside the room'.

Irrespective of theoretical assumptions, it seems clear that the Spanish combination *hacia adentro de*, invented by these authors, cannot be considered a lexical equivalent of English *into*, and thus its impossibility cannot serve as the basis for the claim that Spanish grammar lacks a 'requisite rule'. The fact of the matter is that English *into* has no lexical equivalent in Spanish.

The question remains as to whether Manner V may merge with locational P on a directional interpretation in such languages if features *do* match either side of the V–PP merger. In a series of experiments eliciting descriptions of motion events from Japanese and French children and adults, Stringer (2005) documented productive use of such combinations. As long as the Manner V is PATH-incorporating (e.g. 'run', 'swim', 'fly', *'dance', *'float', *'walk'), the so-called satellite-framed pattern is possible, as exemplified below for Japanese and French (the child examples were later judged to be grammatical in the given directional context by five native informants).

(27) <soto   e hashitta>   (Jap, 3 yrs)
      outside to ran
      'He ran outside'.

(28) <yama   no ue   kara korogatta>   (Jap, 6 yrs)
      mountain GEN top from rolled
      'He rolled from the top of the mountain'.

(29) <ishi no ue   ni jampu shi-yō to   shiteru   no>   (Jap, 5 yrs)
      stone GEN top P_{LOC} jump do-INT COMP do.TE.PROG PART
      'He's trying to jump onto the rock'.

(30) <il a   roulé en bas   de la montagne>   (Fr, adult)
      he AUX rolled P_{LOC} bottom of the mountain
      'He rolled down the mountain'.

(31) <il continue à le poursuivre, il court dans la caverne>   (Fr, 7yrs)
      he continues to him pursue, he runs in the cave
      'He keeps chasing him, he runs into the cave'.

(32) <il nage de l'autre côté>   (Fr, 7 yrs)
      he swims P_{LOC} the other side
      'He swims across'.

Previous research on whether Manner V–LocP combinations are allowed in verb-framed languages has invoked boundedness as the determining factor, in an attempt to explain those counterexamples to Talmy's generalization involving unbounded P such as Spanish *hacia* 'towards', and French *autour de* 'around' (Aske, 1989; Stringer, 2002). However, this approach must be re-evaluated in the light of the above examples, which show that such combinations in Japanese and French are not restricted to unbounded (atelic) contexts. Both Japanese and French clearly allow combinations of Manner V and LocP with a bounded (telic) interpretation if the verb belongs to the subclass of Manner V that incorporates PATH.

Setting aside the issue of what speakers usually do in particular discourse contexts, it is clear that variation between languages in terms of grammatical possibilities in the expression of motion events resides not in a language-specific 'principle' (Levin & Rapoport, 1988) or 'rule' (Jackendoff, 1990) or 'parameter' (Inagaki, 2001, 2002), but in the lexical resources available to the syntax.

Verb Classes And Syntactic Alternations

A further area in which potential gloss traps abound is in the study of syntactic alternations. The first in-depth, theoretically sophisticated examination of this domain from the perspective of second language acquisition is arguably found in the pioneering work of Juffs (1996). He develops a modified version of Pinker's (1989) semantic structure theory to examine the representation and second language acquisition of locatives, causatives and psych verbs by Chinese learners of English. While Juffs (1996) provides a very careful analysis of his data, pointing out exceptions and providing insightful glosses, his whole-language approach is undermined by the evidence, and the linguistic examples given have led others into the gloss trap. He proposes the following lexicalization parameter:

(33) (a) English-type languages allow the conflation of causation and change of state in roots:
+[ACT(+effect) [GO [STATE]]]
   (b) Chinese-type languages do not:
–[ACT(+effect) [GO [STATE]]]

Simplifying the semantic representation, this parameter may be expressed as follows:

(34) (a) English-type: +[CAUSE [CHANGE]]
   (b) Chinese-type: –[CAUSE [CHANGE]]

The generalization can be seen in the following examples (Juffs, 1996: 117 [my italics]), all involving a Figure (or moving object) and a Ground (a location with reference to which the object is moved). When the verb *gai*, sometimes glossed as 'cover', is in the bare form, the Figure (the blanket) is selected as the direct object, but not the Ground (the bed).

(35) (a) *Zhang San yong tanzi *gai* le chuang.
Zhang San use blanket cover ASP bed
'John covered the bed with a blanket'.
(b) Zhang San wang chuang *gai* le tanzi.
Zhang San to bed on cover ASP blanket
*'John covered a blanket onto the bed'.

This verb, therefore, does not correspond to English *cover*, which has the opposite pattern: one can *cover a bed with a blanket*, but not *a blanket onto a bed*. However, if the CHANGE morpheme *zhu* is added, it selects the Ground as direct object, but not the Figure (Juffs, 1996: 87 [my italics]).

(36) (a) Zhang San yong tanzi ba chuang *gaizhu* le.
Zhang San use blanket OBJ-bed cover-'stop' ASP
'John covered the bed with a blanket'.
(b) *Zhang San wang chuang shang ba tanzi *gaizhu* le.
Zhang San to bed on OBJ-blanket cover-'stop' ASP
*'John covered a blanket onto the bed'

Juffs (1996) argues that when overt verbal morphology in Chinese corresponds to the proposed abstract meaning components in English, we see shared syntax. This certainly does appear to be the case, bolstering the idea of universal mappings between lexical semantics and syntax (Gropen *et al.*, 1991).

Chinese learners of English may be misled by mismatches of the type exemplified above. Juffs (1996) found that L1 mappings were subject to transfer, generating forms such as *The man covered the cloth onto the table* in an elicited production task. Advanced speakers produced significantly fewer of these forms, indicating that the underlying grammar of such L2 forms is, in fact, learnable. The interpretation of Juffs (1996) is that these interlanguage mappings are the result of transfer of 'lexical parameters' that can be reset during the course of L2 development. However, the numerous exceptions to the generalization suggest that conflation patterns are at the level of lexical items, not the whole language. True alternators include *mô* 'smear/spread', *tu* 'paint/spread' and *sa* 'sprinkle'. Examples with the verb *pen* 'spray' are given below (Juffs, 1996: 84 [my italics]):

(37) (a) Nongmin wang guoshu shang *pen* le nongyao
peasant to fruit-tree on spray ASP pesticide
'The peasant sprayed pesticide onto the tree'.
(b) Nongmin yong nongyao *pen* le guoshu
peasant use pesticide spray ASP fruit-tree
'The peasant sprayed the fruit-tree with pesticide'.

Such verbs violate the proposed generalization in Chinese, and call into question the language-specific restriction on the [CAUSE [CHANGE]] configuration. This conflation is indeed possible in root morphemes. Juffs (1996: 98) is aware of these exceptions, and admits, '... it is hard to argue conclusively that parametric variation across all members of verb classes exists'. This weakens the proposal of a formal parameter, and suggests the pattern found with many Chinese verbs is simply a lexicalization tendency. The only way forward on the lexical parameterization approach is to say that such parameters are not categorical settings but statements of tendency, and this appears to be Juff's solution: '... a parameter is a strong statement of a cross-linguistic bias' (1996: 98). This, in turn, leads to a cline problem: How strong must the bias be before one can claim a particular setting of the ±[CAUSE [CHANGE]] parameter?

The subtleties of Chinese morphology articulated in Juffs' (1996) examples have on occasion been lost as these examples are cited elsewhere, with the result that generalizations are made on the basis of simplified and inaccurate glosses. A commonplace in the literature on the locative alternation is to ask whether container-oriented verbs such as *fill*, which do not alternate in English (*He filled the glass with water*; **He filled water into the glass*), do so in East Asian languages such as Chinese, Korean and Japanese. For example, Schwartz *et al.* (2003: 251), following Kim (1999), claim that 'there is no cross-linguistic variation for *pour*-class verbs; such verbs are not allowed in Ground frame', and go on to argue that 'English alternating change-of-state verbs like *stuff* and *cram* [the *fill* class] allow both Ground frame and Figure frame, but in Chinese and Thai, they allow only the Figure frame, even though the meaning of these verbs is change-of-state'. In contrast, Hirschbuhler (2004) claims that 'fill-type verbs' do alternate in Chinese. A common assumption here is that an equivalent verb to English *fill* can be identified in Chinese and its syntactic behaviour compared with its English counterpart. However, as shown earlier with reference to Korean analogues of English *put*, such mappings are often less than straightforward. To ask whether or not the verb *fill* alternates in Chinese is to fall into the gloss trap: there is no verb 'fill' in Chinese, as Juffs (1996) recognizes.[5] Consider the following examples, taken from Juffs (1996: 86 [my italics]).

(38) (a) Zhang San zai beizi li *dao* le shui
　　　　Zhang San at cup in pour ASP water
　　(b) Zhang San ba shui *daojin* le beizi
　　　　Zhang San OBJ-water pour-in ASP cup
　　(c) *Zhang San yong shui ba beizi *daojin* le
　　　　Zhang San use water OBJ-cup pour-in ASP
　　(d) *Zhang San ba shui *daoman* le beizi
　　　　Zhang San OBJ-water pour-full ASP cup
　　(e) Zhang San yong shui ba beizi *daoman* le
　　　　Zhang San use water OBJ-cup pour-full ASP

The verb *dao* is approximately analogous to English *pour*. It may host the morpheme *jin*, roughly translatable as *in*,[6] in which case it selects the Figure as direct object, or it may host the morpheme *man*, here glossed as *full*, in which case it takes the Ground as direct object. Although *daoman* may be rendered as English *fill* for the purposes of translation, it can in no way be considered equivalent; it cannot be used of filling events that do not involve pouring (scooping water into a cup from a bowl, filling a bucket with rainwater, etc.) and it derives its CHANGE semantics entirely from the morpheme *man*. Closer examination of other locative verbs uncovers the kind of extreme relativity mismatches discussed earlier. For example, that the verb *zhuangshi* 'decorate' does not select Ground objects in Chinese is unsurprising when we realize that it is not semantically equivalent to 'decorate': it can be glossed as 'put-ornament', something you can do in a room but not to a room.

The implication for L1 transfer in the course of second language acquisition is clear. That Chinese learners of English produce utterances such as *The man covered the cloth onto the table* is not due to transfer of a parameter setting, as maintained by Juffs (1996), but the result of lexical transfer. This conclusion may be applied to non-target-like forms arising from the kinds of lexical mismatches discussed in the previous section: if predicate–argument structure is represented in the lexicon, rather than stated in the form of language-specific principles, transfer will take place item by item.

Modelling Second Language Acquisition of the Lexicon

Reinterpreting previous investigations of the L2 acquisition of argument structure

In the face of the counterevidence for parameterization of PATH conflation and [CAUSE [CHANGE]] conflation discussed above, the findings of Inagaki (2001, 2002) and Juffs (1996) must be re-evaluated in order to explain the interlanguage patterns found. On Inagaki's (2001) account, the primitive semantic notions PATH and PLACE are realized as distinct nodes in the syntax, and the relevant difference between English and Japanese may be stated in terms of patterns of incorporation (Baker, 1988). More specifically, English incorporates a Place head into a Path head, as in Example (39), while Japanese incorporates a Path head into V, as in Example (40), thus preventing a Manner V from being generated in the main predicate slot. Examples are given in English for ease of comparison.

(39) [V [PATH [PLACE [NP]]]   e.g. [go [into [t [the room]]]]

(40) [V [PATH [PLACE [NP]]]   e.g. [enter [t [in [the room]]]]

However, as shown earlier in Examples (27–29), Japanese does allow both conflation types, so this cannot be a case of parametric transfer. An alternative account is needed to explain why English learners of Japanese incorrectly allow verbs such as *aruku* 'walk' to merge with a locational PP on a directional interpretation as in the example below.

(41) *Sam wa ie no naka ni aruita.
  Sam TOP house GEN inside LocP walked
  'Sam walked into the house'.

At least two lexicalist accounts of this are possible. Either (i) learners overgeneralize on the basis of L2 input, as verbs such as *hashiru* 'run', *oyogu* 'swim', *korogaru* 'roll' and *suberu* 'slide' do permit this conflation type (Stringer, 2005), or (ii) there is transfer of the syntax and semantics of the English lexical item *walk* to its analogue in the interlanguage. These hypotheses are not mutually exclusive. On either account, further investigation requires a more detailed lexical semantic analysis of particular verbs and adpositions, rather than couching the acquisition problem in terms of general syntactic frames (for further discussion, see Stringer, 2007).

The conclusions of Juffs (1996) may also be straightforwardly restated in lexicalist terms. Juffs (1996: 230) claims that the evidence indicates that (i) '... L1 semantics–syntax correspondences are transferred from the L1 to the L2 grammar' (i.e. *there is full lexical transfer*), (ii) '... lexical parameters can be reset' (i.e. *lexical acquisition is possible*) and (iii) '... semantic structures which require pre-emption are those which learners have most difficulty with' (i.e. *lexical mismatches create problems for acquisition*).

The debate over the locative alternation in interlanguage development conducted in the wake of Juff's (1996) initiatory work may be subjected to a similar lexicalist reanalysis. Bley-Vroman and Joo (2001) argue that Korean learners of English allow the verb *pour* to alternate, thus violating a universal mapping principle that MANNER verbs with no CHANGE component select themes as direct objects. They assume that the phonological label /pɔɹ/ has been associated with the meaning of a Korean equivalent *pwutta*, but that the L2 learners' behaviour concords with neither English nor Korean, as L2 learners are not bound by this mapping principle of Universal Grammar. However, what *pour* means for these learners is by no means certain. In various contexts where *pour* would be used in English, the verb *chaywuta* 'fill' might be used in Korean, as in the following example.

(42) Juhi-ka mul-ul cep-ey chaywu-ess-ta.
  Juhi-NOM water-ACC cup-Loc fill-PAST-DECL
  '*Yumi filled water into the glass'.

Given multiple verb-to-verb mappings across languages of the type discussed earlier, for each interlanguage verb there may be several possible mappings; moreover, one particular mapping may not be chosen in exclusion to others. Furthermore, the representation may not be stable, but subject to alternations in the course of development before a given representation becomes established. This is, after all, what happens in first language acquisition, where English verbs such as *pour* and *fill* may alternate until children are about eight years old. Pinker (1989) draws on Bowerman (1981, 1982) to provide examples like the following:

(43) Pour, pour, pour. Mommy, I poured you.
[Waving empty container near mother.]
Mother: You poured me?
Yeah, with water. (E: age 2;11)
(44) Can I fill some salt into the bear?
[fill a bear-shaped salt shaker with some salt]. (E: age 5;0)
(adapted from Pinker, 1989: 26)

The critique of Bley-Vroman and Joo (2001) by Schwartz *et al.* (2003) is more compatible with the approach set forth here. While Bley-Vroman and Joo (2001) claim that locative verbs in the interlanguage are not finely differentiated and should pattern the same with regard to syntactic alternations, Schwartz *et al.* (2003) predict variation in the behaviour of individual verbs, and 'do not necessarily expect the precise verb classes of English to characterize Korean-English Interlanguage' (Schwartz *et al.*, 2003: 259). Their approach is nevertheless coloured by the underlying assumption that verb classes have psychological reality. The position adopted here, in line with Levin and Rappaport Hovav (2005), is that the association of particular meaning components with a particular lexical entry is fundamental; verbs classes are epiphenomena.

Avoiding the gloss trap: L2 lexical acquisition as relexification

The lexicalist approach to the L2 acquisition of argument structure is commensurate with the model of acquisition advocated by Sprouse (2006), who suggests that Lefebvre's (1998) model of Relexification, which she uses to explain creole genesis, may be suitable as a model of L2 acquisition more generally. This can be seen as an extension of the influential Full Transfer/Full Access model of Schwartz and Sprouse (1994, 1996). In stating the stronger version of his hypothesis, Sprouse (2006: 170) goes so far as to say that 'Full Transfer can be restated in terms of Relexification, and that Relexification is at the core of the Second Language Instinct, accounting both for the L2 initial state and for the frequent failure of failure-driven (UG-constrained) revision ('learning') to effect convergence on the Target Language'. On this account, transfer of L1 knowledge to the interlanguage does not actually involve transfer from one set of lexical representations to another: L1 lexical representations do not go anywhere. The L1 lexicon is itself the initial state for L2 lexical acquisition; lexical entries initially maintain their syntactic and semantic packaging, and are simply relabelled with perceived L2 phonology, as illustrated below.

(45)

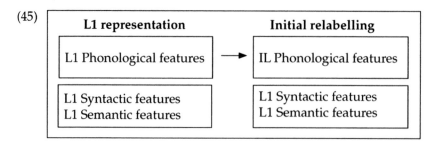

Thus a Korean learner of English will start the process of acquisition of a verb such as *pour* by simply relabelling the perceived L1 analogue given the context in which the input is made available: that is the syntax and semantics of *pwutta* or *chaywuta* (as discussed earlier) will remain initially, and only be subsequently revised if there is sufficient and appropriate input made available for failure-driven reanalysis. Similarly, a Korean learner of English will first associate the L2 label *put* with one or more of a range of L1 verbs including *pwuchita*, *nohta*, *ssuta*, *kkita* and *nehta*. This interlanguage representation may be subject to change given continued input, and at particular stages of its development will not necessarily resemble either the L2 target or one of the L1 analogues in terms of the semantic features that determine participation in particular syntactic alternations.

Given the ubiquity of lexical relativity, it is necessary to have a heightened awareness of the gloss trap in investigations of L2 syntax. One strategy that might be employed in such investigations is as follows. First, a descriptive metalanguage can be developed in terms of shared, syntactically relevant concepts, either as part of the syntax (Inagaki, 2001) or the semantics (Juffs, 1996) of lexical representations. Every such description carries theoretical assumptions. Crosslinguistic analysis of this type must be consciously theory-driven, as the semantic components invoked provide the very platform for comparison. Second, lexical items in both the native language and the target language can be decomposed to reveal those elements of meaning that are grammatically relevant. An analysis of one or two verbs generalized to a verb class in one language does not presuppose the same grouping of analogous verbs in another language. Third, just as in syntax and phonology, the 'comparative fallacy' (Bley-Vroman, 1983) must be scrupulously avoided in the study of lexical acquisition: it is always possible that learners will draw on aspects of the language faculty that are manifested in neither the L1 nor the L2, so an *a priori* contrastive analysis at the level of lexical semantics must also be supplemented by knowledge of semantic elements and possible conflation patterns in human language more generally.

Conclusion

Lexical relativity is a fundamental organizing principle of the mental lexicon, implying that when we conceptualize events, states and things at the lexical level, such construals are to some degree language-specific. It follows that we must tread carefully when making crosslinguistic syntactic generalizations on the basis of supposedly equivalent glosses. Two avenues of research into the syntax of motion events were examined here, both of which are characterized by crosslinguistic generalizations which unravel on closer inspection of the predicates involved. First, a comparative analysis of spatial adpositions was used to question the widely accepted generalization that verbs expressing manner-of-motion in verb-framed languages cannot take directional complements (e.g. Inagaki, 2002; Talmy, 1991). Second, a comparative analysis of syntactic alternation patterns showed that generalizations based on the behaviour of 'equivalent' verbs (e.g. Juffs, 1996) are likely to be misleading in the absence of an item-by-item lexical semantic analysis. Hypotheses elaborated in both domains rest on the assumption of equivalence between lexical items, which are, in fact, syntactically unique. The implications for our understanding of L2 argument structure are clear: neither parameter-resetting at the whole-language level nor redundancy rules across verb classes can serve as theoretical models in this domain; rather, a lexicalist account is required in which L1 semantic representations form the initial state of the interlanguage lexicon.

Glosses remain an integral and undeniably useful part of linguistic research, but they remain a rough guide: they can prove to be as much of a hindrance as a help if one assumes that a close lexical equivalent is reflective of the properties of the original lexical item. On the approach advocated here, a lexical item may be viewed as a particular combination of meaning components, which corresponds, in inexact fashion, to an analogous combination in another language. These sublexical features not only contribute to the precise meaning but also determine the combinatorial possibilities of the lexical item. For this reason, semantic decomposition is a prerequisite for comparative syntactic analysis in the domain of argument structure. On a final note, although lexical items differ across languages, the grammatically relevant semantic components that they contain appear to be drawn from a universal set of meaning elements, involving notions of space, time, matter and causality, as discussed earlier. Thus, the crosslinguistic study of words not only helps us understand variation, but also provides insight into universals of language and cognition.

Acknowledgements

Appreciation is due for valuable comments on these ideas by the reviewers, as well as to Robert Bley-Vroman, Kamil Ud Deen, Joe Emonds and Bonnie Schwartz, and to those who gave feedback at AAAL 2007 in Costa Mesa and EuroSLA 2007 in Newcastle, especially Heidi Byrnes and Alan Juffs. Special thanks are also due to my fellow acquisitionists at the Department of Second Language Studies, Indiana University, for insightful discussions and critique. The usual disclaimers apply.

Notes

1. Thanks to Rex Sprouse for this observation.
2. Other than in the 'conative' and 'directive force' senses, for example *He cut at the rope/They ran at the enemy*. Note the impossibility of a simple directional sense in, for example **She walked at her friend/*We drove at our destination*.
3. Indeed, *patauger* also fails to map exactly onto the meaning of its English 'equivalent', *wade*. While an appropriate translation in examples such as (9–11), in its intransitive use *patauger* may have a playful, non-directional sense, more aptly translated as 'splash about'.
4. That the relevant feature is PATH rather than boundedness (*contra* Aske, 1989; Stringer, 2002) is discussed below.
5. A reviewer suggests that *guan* might be closer to *fill* than *dao*. However, *guan* is also usually translated as *pour*, usually implying more physical effort; more importantly, it patterns exactly like *dao* in Example (37), being ungrammatical in the (c) and (d) examples. Thus the argument holds for either verb.
6. This gloss may be controversial, as *jin* can also be used as a main verb or in serial-verb constructions, in which case it is often translated as *enter*. However, I accept Juff's (1996) assertion that it approximates to the English morpheme *in* when used in the relevant locative contexts.

Chapter 6

Linguistic Effects on Thinking for Writing: The Case of Articles in L2 English

MONIKA EKIERT

Introduction

Much of the current understanding of second language (L2) learning is driven by the assumption that adult L2 acquisition is a cognitive process of establishing form–meaning connections (cf. Robinson & Ellis, 2008; VanPatten *et al.*, 2004). This comes after years of the field's preoccupation with providing evidence for the emergence of specific linguistic forms (e.g. grammatical morphemes or syntactic constructions) independent of the meanings they express. In cases where the form–meaning connections were the focal point, too often only target language (TL) forms and TL meanings were scrutinized (cf. Bley-Vroman, 1983). Linguistic meaning has only recently been identified as a likely suspect in causing difficulty in adult language acquisition. Indeed, it has been shown that L2 learners are capable of building language systems of their own by using L2 structures with meanings that are not L2-like (Han, 2008; Han & Larsen-Freeman, 2005; Jarvis & Pavlenko, 2008; von Stutterheim, 2003; Selinker, 2006; VanPatten *et al.*, 2004).

Cognitive semantics provides a fruitful basis for the investigation of form–meaning connections and linguistic meanings. Yet, only a handful of studies have attempted to show the influence that language-specific meanings play in the acquisition of L2 form–meaning connections (see, e.g. Bardovi-Harlig, 2000; Cadierno, 2007; Cadierno & Lund, 2004; Han, 2008; von Stutterheim, 2003; von Stutterheim & Klein, 1987). The range of semantic concepts and the corresponding meanings studied in the field of L2 acquisition has been limited (e.g. temporality, space, motion) and must be expanded if a fuller understanding of L2 acquisition difficulty is to be obtained (cf. Han, this volume).

L2 researchers and teachers have long recognized that the semantics of English articles is one of the most difficult aspects of the English language for L2 learners to master. As recently pointed out by Ellis, 'the fuzziness and complexity of these mappings surely goes a long way to making ESL article acquisition so difficult' (Ellis, 2008: 377). Indeed, the English article system causes even the most advanced language users to make errors, even when other elements of the language seem to have been mastered to near-native levels. Although there exists a sizeable body of research on the L2 acquisition of English articles, conducted both from psycholinguistic (Butler, 2002; Chaudron & Parker, 1990; Jarvis, 2002; Liu & Gleason, 2002; Thomas, 1989; Young, 1996) and generative (Ionin *et al.*, 2008; Lardiere, 2004, 2007; Leung, 2001; Robertson, 2000; Trenkic, 2002, 2007, 2008; White, 2003) perspectives, few empirical studies have investigated the relationship between L1-driven conceptual systems and their relation to the use of English articles by L2 learners.

In this chapter, an attempt is made to help fill this gap by asking how L1 Polish participants used articles in L2 English and what kinds of meanings contributed to their uses of English articles. Focusing on a relatively understudied L1–L2 combination of languages in article research, the current small-scale, exploratory study aims to address the intended form–meaning mappings in L2 English article use. In the following sections, I first briefly review the relevant theoretical and empirical research that served as the background for the study and then describe and discuss the results of the study.

Theoretical Background

Language and cognition

Viewing language as an integral facet of cognition, cognitive linguistics posits that 'grammatical constructs have conceptual import' (Langacker, 1998: 2). Theories of cognitive grammar view meaning as the dynamic activity of human minds interacting with their environment. The meaningfulness of grammatical elements emphasizes the human capacity for construing the same situation in alternate ways (Jackendoff, 1990). Under this view, meaning construction is a dynamic process whereby linguistic units (words and grammatical constructions) serve as partial prompts for an array of conceptual operations.

One way of uncovering the conceptual structure in language is by investigating a limited and privileged inventory of grammatically expressible concepts that, according to Talmy (1985, 2000a, 2008), form a closed-class language subsystem. These closed-class elements provide a skeletal structure or scaffold for the conceptual material and have accordingly been held to be the fundamental concept-structuring system of language. As Pinker (1989) points out, 'one's language does determine how one must conceptualize reality when one has to talk about it' (Pinker, 1989: 360). The language-specific preferences in constituting meaning can be traced back to meanings that are grammaticized via the closed-class forms in the respective languages.

Obligatory grammatical distinctions, the so-called grammaticizable notions, play a critical role in both the acquisition and processing of language and have been said to reveal the meaningful nature of grammar. They cluster around nouns and verbs constituting a peculiarly limited and apparently universal set of meanings that are, in some sense, prespecified for language (Talmy, 2000a, 2008; see also Stringer, this volume, for a discussion). For example, nouns can be grammatically marked for various types of class membership (e.g. gender and/or animacy), number and discourse perspective (e.g. definiteness), and verbs can be grammatically marked for tense, grounds of evidence, relations of discourse participants, direction of movement and type of moving figure. It has been proposed that distinctions that are encoded grammatically, such as gender or definiteness, should probably have little or no effect on tasks that have no linguistic basis. This particular proposition has been popularized in language acquisition studies by Slobin (1987, 1993a, 1996a, 2000, 2003), who suggested that language influences the expression of thought while in the process of formulating or interpreting verbal messages, in what he termed *thinking for speaking*. The thinking-for-speaking hypothesis, despite its limiting label, embraces all forms of linguistic production (speaking, writing, signing) and reception (listening, reading, viewing) as well as a range of mental processes (understanding, imagining, remembering). Under this view, language will influence a language user's processing of an event when talking about it because language forces a segmentation of the event compatible with the devices the language has for expressing the event.

Semantic dimensions underlying morphological choices come to structure the L1 learner's space of grammaticized notions orienting the learner to language-specific encoding of certain discourse features. By way of illustration, the extent and manner to which a language encodes referent identifiability was shown to affect the course of development of this essential discourse-pragmatic function in L1 speakers of languages with and without an article system (Dasinger, 1995). The study found that, overall, early development in children learning L1 Finnish, a language lacking articles, parallels that of children learning article-bearing languages until the age of five when referential expressions used by child learners are tied to the extralinguistic context. After age five, when intralinguistic means gradually become available to children, Finnish-speaking children were found to be less successful in tasks requiring definite reference to one of a group of identical objects, although lexical items that express the notion of identifiability are readily available in their L1. Dasinger suggested that 'the apparent lack of the Finnish-speaking child's realization of the necessity of explicitly marking intralinguistic relationships in certain situations may very well be the result of the absence of the obligatory expression of definiteness in the language' (1995: 283). In other words, the repeated grammatical marking of a particular contrast – as in the use of definite and indefinite articles in English – may orient the L1 learner to the conceptual or discourse dimensions underlying that contrast. By the same token, the lack of that overt marking may leave L1 learners insensitive to certain aspects of experience.

Using multiple language data that included elicited narratives, natural discourse, creative fiction, and translation work, Slobin (1987, 1993a, 1996a, 2000, 2003) illustrated how speakers of different languages are predisposed to attend to the dimensions of experience that are coded in obligatory grammatical categories. This is so because the language that we speak has trained us to pay different kinds of attention to particular details of events and situations when talking about them. As pointed out by Slobin, this training carried out in childhood could be exceptionally resistant to restructuring in adult second language acquisition. He asserted:

> For the child, the construction of the grammar and the construction of semantic/pragmatic concepts go hand-in-hand. For the adult, construction of the grammar often requires a revision of semantic/pragmatic concepts, along with what may well be a more difficult task of perceptual identification of the relevant morphological elements. (Slobin, 1993a: 242)

Slobin also hypothesized that typological differences between languages lead their speakers to prepare information for expression in different ways. In other words, different native languages lead L2 speakers to prioritize different aspects of events when formulating messages in an L2 due to the presence or absence of obligatory grammatical constructions or lexical selections in the L1 (Slobin, 2003).

Cognitively oriented SLA researchers (cf. Robinson & Ellis, 2008) have recently taken up the issues involved in understanding how different languages map conceptualizations to grammatical categories. One of the issues of interest concerns the extent to which these differences may require the learner to *rethink* for L2 speaking in making these mappings. The implications of cognitive linguistics and, in particular, Slobin's work for the field of SLA have been recognized by a number of researchers. The current empirical work includes investigations of a number of semantic domains, such as motion events in satellite- and verb-framed languages (Cadierno, 2007; Cadierno & Lund, 2004), temporality and event-time structures (von Stutterheim, 2003; von Stutterheim & Klein, 1987), time and aspect expression (Bardovi-Harlig, 2000), and plurality and cognitive categorization (Athanasopoulos, 2006, 2007). Clearly, further research encompassing more grammatical categories and corresponding semantic domains needs to be done in future.

Articles as expressions of definiteness

The field of theoretical linguistics offers a wealth of analyses on the nature of definiteness as expressed in English by articles (cf. Lyons, 1999). Unlike in research with pedagogical orientation, in linguistic analyses, articles and the notion of definiteness that they express have been treated as separate from noun classes and their properties. One commonality among the different contemporary accounts of definiteness is the rejection of the traditional binary distinction between the definite and the indefinite. Syntactic, semantic, and pragmatic constructs of definiteness have been advanced instead, each accentuating a different aspect of the meanings that articles may encode. One of the most recent attempts at synthesis is Lyons' (1999) model, in which definiteness is a morphosyntactic category that grammaticalizes the universal pragmatic category of identifiability. Lyons argues that definiteness is a grammaticalized category 'on par with tense, mood, number, gender, etc. ... Like these, it is the grammaticalization (that is, the representation of grammar) of some category of meaning. ... The correspondence between a grammatical category and the category of meaning it is based on is never one-to-one' (1999: 275).

Definiteness is thought of as one of a number of categories that serve to guide the hearer in working out how the discourse is structured and how entities referred to fit into it (Lyons, 1999). Article use in discourse is multifunctional. The model adopted in the current study (Bickerton, 1981; Huebner, 1983; Maratsos, 1976) accounts for article distribution in English in terms of two binary features, [+/− specific reference (SR)] and [+/− assumed hearer's knowledge (HK)]. Taking an external and analytic perspective on article use by English speakers, linguists propose that the language user must conceptualize, on the one hand, the abstract distinction between specific and nonspecific reference to members of a class, and, on the other, the shared knowledge of the speaker and the hearer. Maratsos (1976) offers a useful framework of visualizing the interaction of discourse variables such as the hearer's likely knowledge of particular referents (summarized in Table 6.1).

In Table 6.1, the speaker- and hearer-specific quadrant corresponds to instances of referential definites in which the speaker has in mind a particular member of the class and is confident that the hearer will be able to understand the expression he uses as referring to the same unique member of that class. The speaker-specific and hearer-non-specific quadrant represents the case in which the reference is specific for the speaker, but not for the hearer. In this case, as pointed out by Maratsos, the speaker must defer to the hearer's lack of knowledge and refer with an indefinite expression. The speaker- and hearer-non-specific quadrant exemplifies the case in which reference is specific for neither speaker nor hearer – any member of the class may be intended or the referent may be nonexistent (nonreferential indefinites).

Table 6.1 The relation between definite and nondefinite forms and specific and nonspecific in speaker and listener

	Speaker specific	*Speaker nonspecific*
Hearer specific	Referential definites [+SR, +HK]	
	Where should we put the <u>table</u>?	
	<u>The engine</u> began to make a funny noise.	
Hearer nonspecific	Referential indefinites [+SR, –HK]	Nonreferential indefinites [–SR, –HK]
	<u>A dog</u> bit me.	*Draw <u>a horse</u>.*
	There's <u>a table</u> over there.	*I don' have <u>a car</u>.*

Source: Adapted from Maratsos (1976).

In English, the coding for referential indefinites remains identical as the coding for nonreferential indefinites – in both cases, the morpheme *a* is employed. A complementary account by Fodor and Sag (1982) distinguishes between *definiteness* and *specificity* as they relate to the knowledge of the speaker and the hearer. Following Fodor and Sag, definiteness reflects the state of knowledge of both the speaker and hearer, while specificity reflects the state of knowledge of the speaker only.[1]

Commenting on the complex nature of articles, Samuda and Bygate (2008) note that a study on the use of all semantic types of articles 'could generate a mixed bag, with no particular types of use sufficiently frequent for the results to be informative' (2008: 243). Therefore, in the current study, only referential ([+SR, –HK] and [+SR, +HK]) uses of *the* and *a* were considered. Finer-grained classifications of referential definites (Hawkins, 1978; Liu & Gleason, 2002; Lyons, 1999) describe the applications of *the* as, broadly speaking, anaphoric, situational, and general knowledge uses. The current study adopted Liu and Gleason's (2002) taxonomy of referential uses of *the* that will be referred to as: (a) textual, (b) structural and (c) situational types.[2] These three uses of *the* are explained as follows:

(1) Textual uses, also known as anaphoric, refer to situations where *the* is used with a noun that has been previously referred to or is related to a previously mentioned noun (e.g. *Jane bought a ring and a necklace for her mother's birthday. Her mother loved the ring but hated the necklace*).

(2) Structural uses are those where *the* is used with a first-mention noun that has a modifier (e.g. *The horse I bet on is still in front*).

(3) Situational uses of *the* involve visible situations when the person makes use of information readily available within one's sensory reach (e.g. *Pass me the salt*), immediate situation when the person makes use of information readily available, but not available within one's sensory reach (e.g. *Don't go there. The dog will bite you*), or larger situation

uses relying on specific knowledge available to the local community (e.g. people from the same neighborhood talking about *the church, the post office, the pub*).

Some linguists (e.g. Lyons, 1999) distinguish between textual and structural uses of *the*, on the one hand, and the remaining uses of *the* (such as immediate or larger situation uses), on the other. Lyons argues that these two broad classes should be treated as distinct subcategories of definiteness, which simply happen to have the same encoding in English. According to him, the textual and structural definites stand apart from the others in that the context within which the referent is to be found is linguistic (i.e. the discourse). The other groups of uses relate to the extralinguistic context, exploiting encyclopedic knowledge or knowledge of the immediate or wider situation.

Crosslinguistically, languages can be categorized into two groups: those that have articles and those that do not have them. The question arises whether articleless ([-ART]) languages utilize the concepts of definiteness and indefiniteness, and if yes, to what extent. As Lyons (1999) notes, all languages have demonstratives and personal pronouns, which, arguably, are inherently definite. Based on that fact alone, many claim that definiteness is a universal concept. However, linguists who consider definiteness a grammatical category (overtly marked by a definite article of some kind) reject its universality (cf. Lyons, 1999; Trenkic, 2002). Instead, they propose *identifiability* to be a true universal category. Identifiability is an element of interpretation in all languages, even though in many it is not grammaticalized. In English, identifiability, alongside abstract properties of uniqueness, familiarity, and specificity, is claimed to be the essence of definiteness (Abbott, 2005). From a crosslinguistic perspective, it is important to determine whether the referent identifiability expressed by articles is in any way similar to the identifiability conveyed by other types of structures available in [-ART] languages.

The accepted view on [-ART] languages (see e.g. Celce-Murcia & Larsen-Freeman, 1999; Korchmaros, 1983; Kryk, 1987) is that they possess certain grammatical and discoursal elements that may have the function of expressing definiteness. Polish, unlike English, has no articles and thus has no equivalent way of expressing definiteness. Instead, deictic categories such as demonstratives and possessives, word order, verbal aspects, and case marking have been said to signal definiteness and indefiniteness in certain contexts. This view, however, is not corroborated by work conducted on typological universals (Kramsky, 1972), cognitive universals (Trenkic, 2002), or definiteness in English (Chesterman, 1991; Lyons, 1999). For example, Trenkic (2002), using a corpus analysis of Internet newspaper resources in Serbian (a Slavic language with an NP structure similar to Polish) and English, offered an empirical verification that demonstratives, possessives, or quantifiers are no more frequent in Serbian than in English. Similarly, Smoczynska (1985) writes that in Polish, possessive pronouns are used less frequently than in English. Terms such as body parts or kinship terms are usually used without possessive pronouns, unless the possessor happens not to be identical with the agent. It appears then that demonstratives, possessives and quantifiers in [-ART] languages can be translation equivalents of English demonstratives, possessives and quantifiers, and not of the articles *the* and *a*.

Comparing article-bearing languages with nonarticle languages, Trenkic (2002) proposes that, instead of looking for syntactic equivalents of English articles in Slavic languages that do not employ them, it is of more use to assume that semantic definiteness, which in English is conventionally implicated with the presence of the definite article, in Serbian (and by the same token in Polish) is conversationally implicated through relevant context and the speakers' general knowledge of the world. In addition to that, Trenkic makes an important crosslinguistic observation that in the process of establishing the definiteness status of referents in meaningful communication, the task of *a speaker* in a language with grammatical definiteness (i.e. with a system of articles) is in many aspects similar to the task of *a hearer* in a language without articles, in the sense that both have to decide what the definiteness status of a referent is supposed to be: 'the former in order to adequately mark it grammatically, the latter in order to adequately interpret the message' (Trenkic, 2002: 124). This is a crucial point in understanding what type of crosslinguistic difficulty L1 Polish learners of English face. Since in Polish, marking and semantically interpreting nominals for definiteness are not driven by syntax, L1 Polish learners of L2 English can be said to not be equipped with a morphosyntactic code for encoding definiteness.

Research questions

In light of the considerations outlined above, the following research questions were addressed in the present study:

(1) How did L1 Polish learners apply articles in L2 English?
(2) What kinds of meanings determined L1 Polish learners' application of articles in L2 English?

Method

Participants

The participants were three advanced adult ESL learners enrolled in a language program in New York City. The two female participants, Ulla and Bogna, and one male, Patryk, ranged in age from 35 to 45 years and spoke Polish as their L1. Their level of proficiency was determined by an in-house placement test. At the onset of the study, each participant had lived in the United States for more than two years and used English daily. In addition, two native speakers of American English and one native speaker of Polish served to provide the baseline data.

Instruments

The study employed narrative tasks to elicit production of written discourse, following Loschky and Bley-Vroman's (1993) recommendation that 'in creating tasks for developing knowledge of articles, the task designer ... [should] consider using narrative tasks for the definite/indefinite distinction' (1993: 133). Three tasks were utilized in the study: a narrative task, a missing article task, and a stimulated recall task.

Narrative task

The narrative task was designed to assess the participants' use of articles at the sentential and suprasentential levels in a free production task. In this task, participants were asked to retell, in writing, a movie-based story after being shown a silent five-minute clip from the sitcom 'Frasier' in which a man, waiting for his date on Valentine's Day, decides to iron his pants, and a series of disastrous events ensues (see Appendix A for the task prompt, sample clips and a sample target narrative).

Missing article task

The missing article task was used to assess the participants' understanding of form–meaning connections involved in the application of articles in discourse. Seven Aesop's fables[3] were chosen for this task as they provided genre consistency as well as natural contexts for use of the target forms (Loschky & Bley-Vroman, 1993). The fables selected were equivalent in terms of length and content. Using the Flesch Reading Ease test, the difficulty of selected fables was calculated to range from 70 to 80, indicating that they were fairly easy to read and equivalent in difficulty. To provide relative comparability of task conditions, fables were accompanied by a set of illustrations (see Appendix B for a sample fable and illustration).

Target uses of articles were deleted in the texts selected to serve as stimuli. No blanks were provided for the missing obligatory uses of the articles based on Liu and Gleason's (2002) argument that if blanks were included, learners might fill every blank with *a* or *the*, making the data very unreliable. A summary of types of articles tested in this task is presented in Table 6.2. Thirty-six obligatory contexts were identified in Set 1, 54 in Set 2 and 34 in Set 3.

Stimulated recall task

Stimulated recall sessions were conducted to investigate what kinds of meanings determined L1 Polish learners' use of articles in L2 English. A

Table 6.2 Types of articles in the missing article task

Referential *a* and *the*	Set 1	Set 2	Set 3
First mention *a*	14	14	10
Textual *the* (second mention)	14	33	20
Situational *the*	3	5	0
Structural *the*	5	2	4
Total	36	54	34

major advantage in the use of verbal reports is that the researcher can often gain access to processes that are unavailable by other means. The stimulated recall task allows for an exploration of learners' internal perspective on the function(s) of articles used by them in the task. A limitation in the use of stimulated recall, however, is that participants may not be aware of their own thought processes and/or may not wish or be able to reveal them (Mackey & Gass, 2005). The stimulus used for the immediate recall sessions was the missing article task with learners' insertions.

Procedures

Elicited and introspective data were collected at three points in time, over a period of three months, with four weeks separating each data collection point. Table 6.3 shows the data collection schedule.

Written narratives were collected in the beginning and at the end of the data collection period. On both occasions, the participants were shown the same clip. The same clip was used to control for task differences that could potentially affect performance 'leaving unanswered the question of whether the subject has control over the language resources or not' (Larsen-Freeman, 2006: 595). The viewing was uninterrupted[4] and the participants had 30 minutes to complete the task. Only uncorrected first drafts were collected for analysis.

At three data collection points, the participants took the missing article task. Each time, different sets of fable-based narratives were administered, as follows. First, the participants were asked to look at illustrations accom-

Table 6.3 Data collection schedule

Time 1	Time 2	Time 3
Narrative task		Narrative task
Missing article task (Set 1)	Missing article task (Set 2)	Missing article task (Set 3)
Stimulated recall	Stimulated recall	Stimulated recall

panying the fables. Next, the picture stimuli were replaced by the equivalent written stimuli in English. Then, the participants were asked to insert articles wherever they deemed necessary. Thirty minutes was allotted for this task in order to provide participants with sufficient time to read the fables and insert articles.

Immediately after completing each missing article task, the participants were asked to provide the researcher with reason(s) for their article choices. In other words, the focus of the recall sessions was on the use and misuse of articles. Nonuse was not probed in the stimulated recall task. The immediate recall sessions were conducted in the participants' L1 in the hope that the use of their native language would allow the participants to express their thoughts fully. Initially, the participants found the technique surprising, and some training was provided to help them get used to the introspective nature of the task.

Analyses

Participants' original hand-written narratives were retyped by the researcher. Two native-speaking judges were asked to mark any unnecessary uses of articles in the data and to insert any obligatory articles that were missing in the participants' production. Inter-rater agreement on the written texts was 93%. Disagreements were resolved by discussion, and the cases where the intended meaning of the writer was ambiguous were discarded.

All instances of articles in the learner corpus were coded for their semantic types by two experienced raters (the researcher and her colleague), and inter-rater agreement was 96%. Differences were discussed and reconciled.

Both quantitative and qualitative analyses were performed on the data. Instances of use, misuse and omissions of English articles were examined through discourse analysis, which considered the notion of definiteness as expressed via the semantic features of specificity and hearer knowledge. In order to establish the function(s) performed by the articles and the patterning in the participants' use of the form, frequency scores for each semantic function realized by the article forms were obtained, including omission and misuse of articles. Next, percentage scores of correct and incorrect suppliance were calculated for the use of *a* and *the* as the ratio of the number of article forms to the number of obligatory environments. Finally, the discourse contexts for the overused tokens were identified.

Following Han (2008), assessment of article accuracy was not confined to morpheme accuracy; 'rather, it [was] carried out within a larger linguistic and discourse context, including constructions that might not specifically involve the morphemes' (2008: 72). For example, the narrative task elicited a large number of situational uses of *the* in prepositional phrases. In order to look more closely at contexts that may systematically influence the production of target uses of articles by L2 learners, situational uses of *the* in prepositional phrases (P + *the* + N) were isolated into a subcategory of situational uses.[5] Moreover, other types of determiners, such as possessives, demonstratives and quantifiers, were analyzed. As expected, the two elicitation tasks created a variety of referential indefinite and definite contexts. However, the tasks were also uniquely different in that some of the uses of the referential *the* appeared in one task, but not in the other (e.g. structural uses of *the* were entirely absent from the narrative task).

Using Butler's (2002) coding scheme, reasons for article use provided by the participants were first classified as particular (i.e. the participant was able to identify reasons for selecting the article, including rules of grammar), or nonparticular (i.e. the learner could not identify any specific reasons for his/her article choice). These reasons were then analyzed qualitatively.

Results

Narrative task

Table 6.4 summarizes the patterns of noun reference employed by the three participants at Times 1 and 3. The environments where articles were used and misused as well as other determiner types employed by the writers were identified and compared. Arraying the data in this way shows how learners used their linguistic resources at one time and whether those resources were employed systematically over time. The length of the participants' narratives ranged from 173 to 325 words at Time 1, and from 130 to 260 words at Time 3. On average, the narratives written at Time 3 were shorter than the narratives written at Time 1 by 30–50 words. In comparison, the L1 American English participants, whose narratives constituted baseline data in this study, wrote responses ranging from 260 to 400 words (see Appendix A for a sample narrative). The L1 Polish narrator produced a response of 370 words.

In the American English narratives, between 4 and 11 noun phrases were newly introduced and marked by the referential *a*, and between 2 and 11 textual uses of *the* were employed. The task elicited 18–29 uses of the situational *the*, including a large number of situational uses of *the* in prepositional phrases (between 6 and 14). The first writer employed possessive pronouns quite frequently (11 uses) compared to the second writer (four uses), resulting in an almost 1:2 ratio of possessive pronouns versus articles for the former, and a 1:12 ratio for the latter participant. Content-wise, the nouns marked by possessive pronouns were similar for both writers as they referred to body parts (*his face, his finger, his tooth*) or possessions (*his pants*). Neither quantifiers nor demonstratives were used by the American English writers. By comparison, a similar narrative in

Table 6.4 Overview of determiner types in the narrative task

Time	Time 1			Time 3		
Category	Use	Overuse and misuse	Omission	Use	Overuse and misuse	Omission
	n	*n*	*n*	*n*	*n*	*n*
Ulla						
Word count	253	N/A	N/A	225	N/A	N/A
Articles	12	1	6	28	1	1
Possessives	11	0	0	4	0	0
Quantifiers	1	1	0	0	0	0
Demonstratives	0	1	0	1	0	0
Patryk						
Word count	325	N/A	N/A	260	N/A	N/A
Articles	4	0	22	21	1	14
Possessives	11	0	2	7	0	1
Quantifiers	0	0	0	1	0	0
Demonstratives	5	0	0	2	0	0
Bogna						
Word count	173	N/A	N/A	130	N/A	N/A
Articles	10	1	19	13	1	3
Possessives	3	0	4	3	0	0
Quantifiers	0	0	0	0	0	0
Demonstratives	0	0	0	1	0	0

Note: *n* = number of tokens.

Polish had only two possessive pronouns that were used with NPs describing states (*his look*, *his movements*) and no demonstratives or quantifiers.

Table 6.5 summarizes the semantic environments in which articles were used, misused, and omitted by the three participants at Times 1 and 3.

In terms of reference tracking, Ulla appeared to rely very heavily on possessives in her first narrative, limiting their use in the second narrative (i.e. 1:1 ratio of possessives to articles at Time 1, and 1:7 at Time 3). In her first narrative, Ulla used inherently definite possessive pronouns in reference to body parts as in *my blood*, *my injured finger* and *his finger*, or possessions as

Table 6.5 Article use, misuse and omission in the narrative task

Time	Time 1			Time 3		
Category and target article	the n (%)	a n (%)	Omission n (%)	the n (%)	a n (%)	Omission n (%)
Ulla						
First mention *a*	1 (33.3)	0	2 (66.7)	0	6 (100)	0
Textual *the* (second mention)	2 (40.0)	0	3 (60.0)	10 (100)	0	0
Situational *the*	2 (66.7)	0	1 (33.3)	5 (83.3)	0	1(16.7)
Situational *the* in PP (Prep + *the* + N)	8 (100)	0	0	8 (100)	0	0
Patryk						
First mention *a*	0	0	5 (100)	0	5 (71.5)	2 (28.5)
Textual *the* (second mention)	0	0	7 (100)	12 (85.7)	0	2 (14.3)
Situational *the*	0	0	6 (100)	0	0	8 (100)
Situational *the* in PP (Prep + *the* + N)	4 (50.0)	0	4 (50.0)	4 (57.1)	1 (14.3)	2 (28.6)
Bogna						
First mention *a*	1 (16.7)	1 (16.7)	4 (66.6)	1 (50.0)	1 (50.0)	0
Textual *the* (second mention)	4 (44.4)	0	5 (55.6)	2 (100)	0	0
Situational *the*	4 (66.6)	0	2 (33.4)	5 (71.5)	0	2 (28.5)
Situational *the* in PP (Prep + *the* + N)	1 (11.1)	0	8 (88.9)	5 (83.3)	0	1 (16.7)

in *my pants, my apartment* (her first narrative was written in the first person), *his dog* and *his couch*. Ulla also employed the textual *the* (second and subsequent mention) and the situational *the* (where the referent of a first mention noun can be sensed directly or indirectly by the inter-locutors), albeit inconsistently. For example, the first situational use of *the oil* was marked by the article. However, the subsequent mention of it was bare. On the other hand, Ulla was very consistent in her use of *the* in prepositional phrases such as *on the couch, in the kitchen, into the cabinet.* Those uses amounted to eight target-like instances out of eight obligatory contexts. Ulla never used *a* in her first narrative. Instead, when marking first mention nouns, she employed a numeral *one* as in *I saw one thread*, and the quantifier *any* as misused in the sentence *I found any can of oil.* She also misused *the* in the first mention context.

In Ulla's second narrative, first mention referents were introduced with referential *a*, including a case of a noncount item (*a scissor*). She then consistently maintained reference to the same items throughout the narrative. For instance, she introduced the main character first as *a man*, and then referred to the main character with the textual *the* eight times. Similarly, after introducing *an iron*, she reintroduced it two more times as *the iron*. There were 10 obligatory textual uses of *the* and she applied *the* in all. She missed one situational use of *the* in the second narrative.

Patryk's strategies with regard to reference tracking in discourse were somewhat similar to Ulla's, as he heavily relied on possessive pronouns (e.g. *his girlfriend, his pants, his dog, his head, his finger*), but dissimilar in that he employed demonstratives in his narratives (e.g. *this method, this water, this moment*) and had high rates of article omission. In his narratives, the ratio of possessives and demonstratives to articles was a high 4:1 in the first narrative and a much lower 1:2 in the second narrative. In Patryk's first narrative, articles were used only in prepositional phrases (PP). Nonetheless, they were equally frequently omitted in PP environments. There was no misuse or overuse of articles at Time 1. In his second narrative, *the* was used not only in PP contexts, but also in second mention environments. In addition, *a* served to express the referential indefinite function in the second narrative. For example, Patryk introduced five first mention nouns with a target-like article and was able to maintain reference to those nouns with a textual *the* (e.g. he referred to *a dog* and then *the dog*, *a room* and then three more times to *the room*). He still omitted textual uses of *a* (first mention) and *the* (second mention) on two occasions, but on a much smaller scale than situational uses of *the*. For the latter category, the rate of omission was high and virtually unchanged in both of Patryk's narratives.

Compared to Ulla and Patryk, Bogna produced the shortest narratives, but had the most target-like ratios of possessive pronoun versus article use, 1:2 in the first narrative and 1:3 in the second narrative, respectively. In addition, in her narratives first mention nouns favored the use of *a* and second mention nouns the use of *the* (e.g. at Time 1 she referred to *an ironing desk* and then *the desk* and at Time 3 she wrote about *an iron* and employed two subsequent mentions of *the iron*). However, Bogna's omission rates were very high in the first narrative (across all uses of *a* and *the*) and much lower, but still present, in the second narrative.

To summarize, several trends in reference tracking can be identified in the three learners' narratives. First, possessives and demonstratives played an equal and sometimes bigger role than articles as far as referent identifiability is concerned in these L2 writers' narratives. Second, there was improvement, over time, in the learners' accuracy on textual uses (first and second mention) of *a* and *the*. Third, situational uses of *the*, even though they have shown improvement, remained variable throughout the data collection period for all three learners, with a relatively higher ratio of accuracy on situational uses of *the* in prepositional contexts.

Missing article task

Unlike the narrative task, the missing article task created obligatory contexts for referential uses of *a* and *the*, thus providing a complementary picture of the participants' knowledge of English articles. Given in Table 6.6 are percentages of target-like uses of the indefinite article *a* in first mention referential contexts, contrasted with the uses of the definite article *the* in three referential environments: textual, situational and structural. As evidenced by the percentages of above 50 on almost all article types, omission of articles was the dominant trend for all three participants across the data collection points. By Time 3, omissions dropped below 50% for two of the three participants. With regard to target-like application of articles, the highest observed accuracy was noted on the first mention indefinite *a* as well as on the second and subsequent mention of *the*. These two referential environments elicited both the highest rates of article overuse as well as the lowest rates of omission, suggesting that these particular environments were recognized by the participants as requiring some form of overt (in)definite marking in English. The other two types of *the*, situational and structural, remained variable throughout the data collection period for all participants.

In order to establish if there was any pattern in the participants' application of articles, all uses, both target-like and non-target-like, of *a* and *the*, were tabulated according to their role in discourse as well as syntactic environments. An analysis of article environments in this task indicated that: (1) textual uses of *a* and *the* in the ART + Noun environments (first and subsequent mention nouns) comprised the largest category in the data, and (2) the remaining uses of articles mostly occurred in the Pre + ART + Noun prepositional-phrase constructions (note that unlike in the narrative task, in the missing article task those uses were not limited to just situational uses). These tendencies are displayed in Figure 6.1 for all three participants over time.

Stimulated recall

Participants' stimulated recalls revealed that they developed various hypotheses about the English article system, which, following Butler (2002),

Table 6.6 Article use, misuse and omission in the missing article task

Category and target article	Ulla			Patryk			Bogna		
	the n (%)	*a* n (%)	Omission n (%)	*the* n (%)	*a* n (%)	Omission n (%)	*the* n (%)	*a* n (%)	Omission n (%)
Time					*Time 1*				
First mention *a*	1 (7)	5 (35)	8 (58)	1 (7)	5 (35)	8 (58)	1 (7)	4 (28)	9 (65)
Textual *the* (second mention)	1 (7)	0	13 (93)	5 (35)	0	9 (65)	3 (21)	1 (7)	10 (72)
Situational *the*	0	0	3 (100)	0	33	2 (77)	0	1 (33)	2 (77)
Structural *the*	1 (20)	0	4 (80)	0	0	5 (100)	1 (20)	0	4 (80)
Time					*Time 2*				
First mention *a*	4 (28)	2 (14)	8 (58)	2 (14)	4 (28)	8 (58)	3 (21)	2 (14)	9 (65)
Textual *the* (second mention)	7 (21)	0	26 (79)	20 (60)	4 (12)	9 (28)	20 (60)	3 (9)	10 (31)
Situational *the*	2 (40)	0	3 (60)	0	2 (40)	3 (60)	0	0	5 (100)
Structural *the*	0	0	2 (100)	1 (50)	0	1 (50)	0	0	2 (100)
Time					*Time 3*				
First mention *a*	2 (20)	7 (70)	1 (10)	1 (10)	5 (50)	4 (40)	1 (10)	4 (40)	5 (50)
Textual *the* (second mention)	19 (95)	0	1 (5)	19 (95)	0	1 (5)	12 (60)	1 (5)	7 (35)
Situational *the*	N/A	N/A	N/A	N/A	N/A	N/A	N/A	N/A	N/A
Structural *the*	3 (75)	0	1 (25)	0	0	4 (100)	2 (50)	0	2 (50)

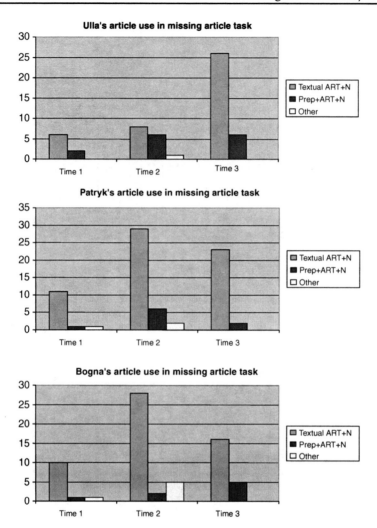

Figure 6.1 Frequencies of article types in the missing article task

could be characterized as context-insensitive and context-sensitive. Among the context-insensitive, a few independent rules were identified by the learners, such as (a) use *a* in the beginning of a story (Ulla), (b) use *the* at the beginning of a new sentence (Bogna), (c) use *a* with singular nouns (Patryk, Bogna), (d) use articles with every noun (Bogna) and (e) use *a* with nouns introduced for the first time, but *the* when the same noun is mentioned for the second time (Ulla, Patryk).

The formulation of context-sensitive hypotheses appeared to have been influenced by the dimensions of (a) textuality, (b) specificity, (c) familiarity, (d) number and (e) topical information. It is necessary to point out that these dimensions may or may not have overlapped with target-like concepts. Participants' meanings and specific examples of article applications will be presented in what follows, first in an overview of common reasons behind the intended meanings and then with a qualitative description of recalls.

Generally, target-like and non-target-like uses of *a* were, in part, motivated by certain qualities of the nouns as identified by the participants and related to: referent nonspecificity expressed by a lexical modifier *jakiś*, which roughly corresponds to *some* in English; referent unfamiliarity defined as *little is known about this person or object*; referent singularity as in *there is just one person or object here*; the *one-of-many* quality of the referents; and fable-related topical information about the referents as in *this is the first time this character encounters the other character*. In contrast, target-like and non-target-like uses of *the* were ascribed by the learners to: referent familiarity defined as *something is known about this person or object*; referent specificity as in *this is specifically defined*; referent uniqueness as in *there is just one item like this*; and fable-related topical information about the referents as in *the other character knows a lot about this character from their common activities*.

Ulla, the most rule-oriented of the three, was very much concerned with marking the referents appearing in the story openings with *a* as in (1), (2) and (3):

(1) *One day* <u>*a countryman*</u> ...
(2) *There was* <u>*a shepherd boy*</u> ...
(3) <u>*A wolf*</u> *was eating its dinner one day.*

She also often referred to the first mention rule when explaining her target-like applications of *a*. One of the recalls at Time 2 showed that Ulla entertained several working hypotheses at a given time. When asked to explain her target-like application of *an* in Example (4):

(4) *One day later, the fox received* <u>*an invitation*</u> *from the stork*

Ulla first said she used *an* because of the indefinite quality of the referent (i.e. *jakieś tam zaproszenie = some invitation*), then withdrew that explanation claiming that actually the invitation in the fable was indeed very specific as it came from a known source (i.e. the stork) and, finally, settled on the first mention rule to explain her choice of *an* in this case. One may claim that in citing the first mention rule, Ulla combined the notion of specificity and lack of hearer's knowledge (HK), arriving at target-like use of the article. However, it is very likely that the rule was exercised independently without the learner having a clear understanding of the binary nature of the rule (+SR, −HK).

Indeed, this episode shows that for Ulla the notion of (in)definiteness as expressed by articles appears to be lined up with the notion of (non) specificity. Noteworthy is the fact that the learner adheres to her own interpretation of specificity as the above and the following examples show. Again at Time 2 in the missing article task, Ulla substituted *the* for *a* in Example (5):

(5)   *The stork served dinner in *the tall pot with *the narrow mouth.*

She explained that the pot and the pot's mouth, even though mentioned for the first time in the narrative, were specific as they were described in detail by adjectives *tall* and *narrow*. At Time 3, however, she marked referents in similar environments (Adjective + Noun) with the indefinite *a*, once again, supporting her choices with the first mention rule (e.g. *a fine breakfast*, *a hungry fox*).

A similar pattern of blending of (in)definiteness and (non)specificity could be ascribed to the meanings that drove Patryk's use of articles. At Time 2, he was asked to provide recall on his article use in the following passage:

(6)   *The fox cooked *delicious soup* (first mention) . . .. *It served *a soup* (second mention) . . .. *Meanwhile, the fox quickly lapped up *a soup* (third mention) *with its tongue.*

Commenting on Example (6), Patryk explained that in all of these mentions of the soup, the referent is *underspecified as we don't know what kind it was – was it tomato, chicken?* On the same occasion, he overused *the* in a first mention context:

(7)   **The man, his donkey, and a dog were travelling.*

Referring to Example (7), Patryk explained that *man* in this story is made specific by the fact that the character is travelling with his donkey. On the other hand, *dog* was marked with a target-like *a* and, in recall, Patryk explained that it was *some dog (jakiś)* indicating its indefiniteness.

In Patryk's case, the reasons for target-like and non-target-like use of *a* and *the* in the narratives oscillated between explicitly cited dimensions of (non)specificity and (un)familiarity. Patryk's references to the first and subsequent mention rules, although present, were relatively rare. Again, worthy of note is the fact that the learner's interpretation of the notions of specificity and familiarity does not necessarily coincide with the TL notions of the same concepts as described earlier in the 'Articles as expressions of definiteness' section. For instance, when speaking of (un)familiarity, Patryk did not make a distinction between the speaker's and the hearer's perspectives. When providing comments on his insertions, he always used the plural *we know this referent* or *he is known to us* conflating the speaker and the hearer. The learner was not probed on the meaning of *we* or *us* in this study.

Bogna needed the most training with the stimulated recall task and only by Time 3 was she accustomed to the introspective nature of the task.

After she declared herself unable to give any reasons for her use of articles, she was not pressed for answers at Times 1 and 2. From the little that is available from Bogna, certain similarities between her and the other two participants emerge. Like Ulla, she was very rule-oriented declaring that articles in English are needed before nouns, that noun singularity or plurality is an important factor in rule application and that the application of *the* should be considered at the beginning of a new sentence. Like Patryk, she explicitly cited the dimensions of (non)specificity and (un)familiarity as playing roles in her choices. At Time 3, she was asked to comment on her use of *a* in the second mention context in the following passage:

(8) *A wolf was eating its dinner one day, when *piece of bone got stuck in its throat …. The crane found *a piece of bone* (second mention) *and carefully removed it.*

Commenting on Example (8), Bogna stated that the second mention of *piece of bone* is *unspecified as we still don't know what kind of piece of bone the crane was able to retrieve*, most likely evidencing crosslinguistic difference in construal of specificity. As pointed out by one of the reviewers, the learner's meaning is akin to the hearer's perspective vis-à-vis specificity. In this study, no comments were elicited on article nonuse in the first mention context.

Omission was rarely explained by any of the three learners, but when specifically asked at Time 3 why they stopped to use *the* with certain subsequent uses of the same referent, Ulla said she had used too many articles already, Bogna declared she intuitively felt it as stylistic overuse, and Patryk had no opinion.

Discussion and Conclusion

The current study investigated how three L1 Polish speakers used articles in their L2 English and what kinds of meanings contributed to it. The data for this study included elicited and introspective data. The participants were shown to be sensitive to the distinction between indefinite and definite referents and to have a repertoire of different linguistic devices that they used to express definiteness in L2 English. They also developed various hypotheses about the English article system and used articles meaningfully. The findings, as they pertain to each of the two research questions, will be discussed in turn.

Omission of articles was the dominant trend for the three participants on both tasks and across all data collection points. The native language of the participants was, most likely, the major influence and the reason behind the omission patterns of the referential indefinites and definites. As noted earlier in the literature review section, the lack of corresponding forms in the native language may explain why speakers of articleless languages fail to realize the need to mark nominals in languages where this category is grammatically realized (e.g. Trenkic, 2002). In fact, two participants, Bogna and Ulla, expressed a certain stylistic dissatisfaction with what they perceived as an excessive number of articles in the missing article task, allowing for an interpretation that, for learners like them, overt markers of (in)definiteness are not crucial in establishing the identifiability status of referents in discourse and, therefore, may be used selectively. A passage from Patryk's first written narrative is a case in point:

(9)   *Mr. X waiting for someone, probably <u>his girlfriend</u>. He doesn't feel comfortable because he knows <u>his pants</u> need ironing. He set up <u>*ironing set</u>. During <u>this time</u>, <u>his dog</u> still watching what is going on. When <u>*iron</u> is ready, he starts ironing <u>his pants</u>. Suddenly, he sees <u>*thread</u>. He tries to remove it. Unfortunately, <u>this method</u> doesn't work.*

In Example (9), all obligatory uses of articles were omitted. Upon a closer inspection, however, it appears that the referent status of the bare NPs in question is already established by means of the word position. Two of the referents, both missing the indefinite article (e.g. *ironing set* and *thread*) appear in sentence-final positions indicating new information, whereas one missing the definite article (i.e. *iron*) appears in the sentence-initial position signalling given information. Newness of information has been strongly associated by linguists (see, e.g. Chafe, 1976) with referent unidentifiability (and, by some, with indefiniteness), while givenness has been associated with referent identifiability (hence, definiteness). From a pragmatic point of view, additional marking of these contexts for identifiability may be sensed as redundant as the referents' status vis-à-vis definiteness has already been established through pragmatic means, a pattern found in many languages, including Patryk's L1, Polish.

For example, the Polish and English sentences in Example (10) are translation equivalents:

(10) Do sklepu wszedł mężczyzna.
     to   store   entered man
     A   man   entered the store.

In English, 'man' is [+SR, −HK] by virtue of the indefinite article. In Polish, however, it is required that new information be positioned toward the end of the sentence, and the clause-final position of *mężczyzna* implies that it is nonspecific. This example is contrasted with sentence (11), in which *man* is marked as specific by the definite article in English:

(11) Mężczyzna wszedł do sklepu.
     man   entered to store
     The man entered the store.

In Polish, the first element in a sentence carries little new information. Instead, it functions to signal given information, and thus *mężczyzna* is specific. Since Polish nouns are fully inflected for case, word order is not necessary for case assignment. In consequence, word order in Polish can take on some pragmatic functions for which articles are used in English, but is not employed consistently to signal or preserve the indefinite/definite contrast.

An example from Ulla's first narrative shows a similar propensity via the same 'strategy' (i.e. word position, as well as possessive pronouns and demonstratives) to identify referents in discourse:

(12) *I decided to iron <u>my pants</u>. I took <u>*iron and ironing board</u> and started doing it. I saw <u>*that one thread</u> and wanted to cut it.*

In Example (12), the first mention of *iron and ironing board* again occupies a sentence-final slot, which establishes the referent's status in the narrative. As described earlier in the literature review section, word order in Polish can take on some pragmatic functions for which articles are used in English, and may be employed, although inconsistently, to signal or preserve the indefinite/definite contrast. The patterns of article omission revealed in Examples (9) and (10) suggest strong thinking-for-writing effects (Slobin, 1987, 1993a, 1996a, 2000, 2003), where 'in the evanescent time frame of constructing utterances in discourse, one fits one's thoughts into *available linguistic forms* [italics added]' (Slobin, 1987: 435). Following Slobin, the patterns found in Examples (9) and (10) illustrate how the participants were predisposed to attend to certain aspects of the reference tracking in the narrative due to obligatory categories in their native grammar that were readily available to them, such as word order.

It must be noted that, even though improvement has been noted for textual uses of *a* and *the* over time, the application of articles in the textual semantic domain remained variable. In Ulla's second narrative, target-like and non-target-like applications of first mention *a* coexist, as in Examples (13) and (14):

(13) *<u>The man</u> went to the kitchen and brought <u>an iron</u> and <u>a desk</u>.*
(14) *When he saw it, he run for <u>*fire extinguisher</u>.*

A similar pattern of intra-learner variability is found both in Patryk's second narrative as evidenced in Examples (15) and (16),

(15) *Suddenly, the man saw <u>*thread</u> on his pants and tried to remove it.*
(16) *He dropped <u>a can with liquid</u> on the couch.*

and in Bogna's second narrative as evidenced in Examples (17) and (18):

(17) *<u>The man</u> put in <u>an iron desk</u> and started ironing.*
(18) *<u>*Sofa</u> was broken.*

In addition to articles, certain linguistic markers such as demonstratives were found among the overt 'building materials' (Han, 2008) used by the participants to ensure referent identifiability in written narratives. A good starting point for the discussion of the demonstrative use in this study is the simultaneous use of *that* and *one* in Ulla's passage in Example (10). The two mark the same referent (i.e. *thread*) and contribute to a vague indefinite/definite interpretation of that referent in English. It was reported in the literature (e.g. Huang, 1999; Robertson, 2000) that Chinese learners of English were using demonstratives, particularly *this*, and the numeral *one* as markers of definiteness and indefiniteness, respectively (see also Han, this volume). In the current study, the two markers appear simultaneously and in reference to one and the same object (i.e. *thread*). Their use, however, appears to have little to do with establishing referents' definiteness.

Examples of demonstrative use found not only in Example (10), but also in Example (9), exemplify the point made by Trenkic (2002) that the primary role of demonstratives in all languages, both with and without articles, is 'not to make clear that the reference is definite, but ... to make an already ... identifiable reference *absolutely* [italics added] clear' (2002: 120). Remarking on the same point, Lyons (1999) explained that with demonstratives 'the work of referent identification is being done for the hearer by the speaker, for example, by pointing' (1999: 21). In other words, while demonstratives' function is to point, articles do not point to the referents (Trenkic, 2002). Indeed, in Examples (9) and (10), the demonstratives (i.e. *this time* and *this method* in Patryk's writing, and *that one thread* in Ulla's writing) serve that very pointing function; therefore, from Ulla's point of view, it may have been perfectly acceptable to combine the two, *that* and *one*, in one phrase in order to point to the hanging thread.

Turning to the issue of how articles, when applied, were used by the participants, the study found evidence that indefinite *a* and definite *the* were employed by the participants with mixed success. By Time 3, and with regard to target-like application of articles, the highest observed accuracy was noted for the textual uses of articles, that is the first mention of indefinite *a* and the second and subsequent mention of *the*. These two environments also elicited the highest rates of substitution of articles, *a* for *the* and vice versa, as well as the lowest rates of omission, suggesting that these particular environments were recognized by the participants as requiring some form of overt (in)definite marking in English. It appears, then, that the TL influenced the way in which articles were applied by the participants.

In addition, there was improvement, over time, in the participants' accuracy on textual uses of *a* and *the*. Task repetition, ongoing classroom instruction, and repeated participation in recall sessions with the researcher may have influenced the participants' increased attention to language form, hence, the improved accuracy. Textual uses, being categorical and rule-dependent, may have also been most amenable to change. In fact, the rules of first and second mention were cited by the participants as reasons for many instances of article use. Of the two, *a* and *the*, the textual *the* had a higher improvement rate on both tasks for all three participants. In contrast, situational uses of *the* remained relatively more variable. Situational *the* was also more frequently omitted throughout the data collection period by all three participants, with considerably more accurate application of situational *the* in prepositional contexts present in the written narratives than in bare situational NPs. On that account, it is worth recalling Lyons's (1999) argument that textual uses of *the* and situational uses of *the* should be treated as distinct subcategories of definiteness, which simply happen to assume the same form in English. In other words, textual *the* and situational *the* are two different morphemes (i.e. the referents of textual uses of *the* are found in the linguistic context, whereas the referents of situational uses of *the* are found in the extralinguistic context). One possible explanation why these participants were more sensitive to textual clues may lie in L1-determined reference tracking preferences.

The preference for the inclusion of articles in certain semantic environments, such as in textual contexts, and for their omission in other environments, such as in situational contexts, could be explained by the *grammar of narrative* as described by Berman and Slobin (1994), who note that 'the [learner's] task in acquiring 'the grammar of narrative' would be to identify the foreground or the main plot line of the story (the semantic task) and to acquire the necessary syntactic forms for mapping this foreground onto linguistic expressions (the formal task)' (1994: 7). It could be hypothesized, then, that the participants in the current study might have been highlighting the main story elements, such as continuous references to the main character and certain recurring objects in the story, with textual uses of *the* in order to disambiguate the main plot line. This predilection can be, once again, explained by the L1 of the participants. Polish, an articleless language, does not obligatorily mark nominals for definiteness with any grammatical devices. Rather, when communicating in Polish, interlocutors infer referent identifiability; that is many referential interpretations in Polish are left to the hearer, who relies on the pragmatics of the context (Trenkic, 2002). The speaker of Polish will then use an overt marking of (in)definiteness when the need for expressing the identifiability of the referent has been registered at the conceptual level (Trenkic, 2007). This is a crucial point in understanding what type of crosslinguistic difficulty an L2 learner of English may face, but also in interpreting the variable and inconsistent use of articles by the participants in this study, and specifically, their tendency to mark textual contexts with articles.

When the participants were probed to reveal what kinds of underlying meanings governed their use of English articles, evidence was found that indefinite *a* and definite *the* were employed to express somewhat different concepts, but also that article use in English was determined, in part, by the L1-influenced conceptual system. As discussed earlier, target-like use of English articles is motivated by the interaction of two features in discourse: specificity of the referent and shared knowledge between both speaker and hearer. The participants in this study were shown to be sensitive to these two abstract features of definiteness. However, these features, when unpacked, appeared to be distinctly different from the TL conceptions. Definiteness seemed to be blended in with specificity. In the earlier cited Example (7) found in Patryk's missing article task (i.e. *The man, his donkey, and a dog were travelling*), the participant interpreted the referents *man* and *dog* as specific and nonspecific using the fable's content (i.e. Patryk explained that *man* in this story was made specific by the fact that the character was travelling with his donkey, whereas *dog* was not specified at all). As pointed out by Fodor and Sag (1982), specificity reflects the state of knowledge of the speaker only, while for definiteness to be encoded in English, the state of knowledge of both speaker and hearer must be taken into account.[6] Polish has the lexical and grammatical means for encoding specificity (e.g. demonstratives or possessive pronouns), but it lacks a means for encoding the HK. Nor is such encoding necessary for adequate message interpretation. In other words, the hearer's state of knowledge is not accounted for, as pointed out by Trenkic (2002). It appears, then, that the L1 provided the impetus for the correct and incorrect use of *a* and *the* in Example (7).

In conclusion, findings from the study described in this chapter revealed some thinking-for-writing effects (Slobin, 1987, 1993a, 1996a, 2000, 2003) at the level of referent identifiability conceptualization. As Han (2008) notes, the acquisition of distributional restrictions of a new form by an adult L2 learner presents a challenge 'for it requires the restructuring of a primarily L1-based conceptual system' (2008: 74). The overall premise of this study, namely that article errors should not be exclusively attributed to inadequate acquisition of the forms of the TL, was shown to be correct. L2 acquisition appears to be hindered by a limited, L1-motivated set of options (i.e. forms) for the grammatical encodings of characteristics of objects and events, but also by the lack of an equivalent conceptual system (i.e. meanings). As pointed out by Jarvis and Pavlenko (2008), learning a new language involves learning how to make new attributions to familiar objects and events, in this case, assigning definiteness to referents in discourse.

As mentioned at the outset of the study, this has been an exploratory study with a number of shortcomings. Even though a few of them have been alluded to throughout the paper, some need to be spelled out explicitly. The first limitation of the study lies in the relatively small scope of article uses considered here. Only nonidiomatic and nongeneric uses of *a* and *the* were elicited and analyzed, naturally limiting the findings. A second shortcoming has to do with just one genre used in the elicitation tasks, that is the narrative genre. For the current study, it was deemed important that the genre does not become a source of variability in article use; however, the choice of the narrative genre limited the findings to referential cases of articles only. Similarly, due to the written mode adopted in the study, little can be said about the participants' oral performance. A diversification of data types may shed light on genre- and mode-related variability in L2 production. A third limitation is the narrow linguistic focus as far as the notion of definiteness is concerned. In light of the fact that, in addition to articles, multiple linguistic devices other than determiners may have been used by the participants to ensure reference tracking, a follow-up study could focus on a variety of structures involved in determining referent identifiability in L2 English, such as, on the one hand, pronouns and adjectives (cf. Trenkic, 2007) and, on the other hand, universal discourse context, that is current, known and new reference to topics (cf. Chaudron & Parker, 1990). Fourth, task repetition and the lack of masking of the researcher's interest in articles throughout the period of data collection make for relatively mixed results with regard to improvement of certain patterns in article use by the participants. Finally, with so few participants and a short timeframe, the study has limited generalizability. Investigating participants at different stages of development would allow for a better understanding of conceptual changes that accompany adult L2 acquisition. Despite these limitations, the current study begins to shed light on the ways in which L1 Polish learners of English handle conceptual distinctions such as definiteness and its basic instantiation in the form of articles.

Acknowledgements

I thank the editors of this volume for their detailed comments and feedback as well as the anonymous referees for comments. I also thank Kristen di Gennaro, Phil Choong, Andrea Révész, Catherine Box, Sarah Creider, Marta Baffy and Andrew Lamb for their invaluable help at different stages of this project. Any remaining mistakes are my own.

Notes

1. According to Lyons (1999), English operates on a [+/− definite] basis rather than on a [+/− specific basis] (like Samoan). Ionin *et al.* (2008) hypothesized that L1 speakers of [-ART] languages, when acquiring L2 English, have full access to the two options of the parameters, and, as a result, will overgeneralize the use of *the* to [−definite, +specific] contexts and the use of *a* to [+definite, −specific] contexts. Ionin and her colleagues hypothesized that article omission will occur mainly in singular [−definite] contexts 'because the indefinite article *a* is less informative' (2008: 226). Their findings confirmed the hypothesis suggesting that L2 learners gravitate between the systems organized around definiteness and specificity.

2. This classification was itself based on Hawkins' (1978) Location Theory.
3. The fables used in this study came from a selection of *Story Cards: Aesop's Fables* by R. J. Clark (1995).
4. Jarvis (2002) reported that interrupting the story stimulus had an effect on his participants' use of articles.
5. Trenkic (2007) advocates that instead of looking at overall levels of accuracy rates, research on articles ought to look more closely at well-defined patterns of asymmetries. She argues that, 'L2ers [users] do not produce functional forms equally poorly or equally well in all contexts' (2007: 291). According to Trenkic, the contexts offer a way of looking into the underlying cause of article misuse. In her own research, she focused on adjectivally premodified contexts in which articles occur.
6. As pointed out by one of the reviewers, instructed intake might have led to the mixed use of *the man* and *a dog*.

Appendix A

Narrative task

Prompt: You will be shown a five-minute clip from the NBC sitcom *Frasier*. Please watch the clip and then write a narrative description of the events that took place on Valentine's Day in this Seattle apartment. You will have 30 minutes to write the story. You may take notes while watching the clip.

Sample clips:

Sample native speaker response:

A man in a very well appointed, high-rise apartment had a series of accidents. It seems that while he was ironing his pants, he absentmindedly set the hot iron on top of the pants while he got distracted with other things. The ironing board was set up in the living room, next to the couch, lounge chair and dining room table. One of the things he was distracted by was a loose thread on his pants. In attempting to cut the thread, he cut himself. The sight of the blood made him faint and he fell on the couch. When he came to, he realized he had gotten a spot of blood on the couch, so he got some stain remover to get the blood spot out. He soon spilled some of the spot remover onto the couch. He went back to the kitchen, thinking he smelled something funny. He checked all of the pots and determined that the smell was not coming from the kitchen. He went back into the living room and finally saw the iron on his pants. By this time, the pants were aflame. He tried to put the fire out by folding the pants onto themselves but instead, he ended up hurling the pants, accidentally, onto the couch. What with some of the spot remover on the couch, the cushions on the couch were immediately engulfed in flames. He rushed to the back of the house to get a fire extinguisher. Once he'd pulled the pin, he got the extinguisher to work but could not aim it – it seemed to have some kind of kickback, like a rifle, and he was aiming the thing everywhere but where it was needed. When he finally got it under control, and aimed it at the fire, the extinguisher was empty. He ran back to the kitchen to get the pots of food from the stove and used them to douse the fire. With the fire out he attempted to air out the apartment by opening and closing the front door quickly and repeatedly. While doing this he again noticed his bleeding finger and fainted.

Appendix B

Missing article task

Sample fable: A man, his donkey, and a dog were travelling. The man decided to take a break, and he fell asleep under a tree by the side of the road. The donkey wandered out into the field, feeding on the grass. As soon as they were some distance away from the man, the dog said quietly to the donkey: 'You're having a nice lunch, but I'm quite hungry. If you would only lie down for a moment or two, I could reach into the pack that you're carrying and have a bite or two of food'. The donkey was not interested in helping the dog. 'You'll have to wait until the master wakes up. He'll give you some food'. Suddenly, a wolf sprang out from behind a tree and grabbed the donkey by the neck. 'Help! Help!' cried the donkey to the dog. The dog, however, would not move. 'You'll have to wait until the master wakes up. He'll help you', said the dog.

Sample illustration:

Chapter 7

Grammatical Morpheme Inadequacy as a Function of Linguistic Relativity: A Longitudinal Case Study

ZHAOHONG HAN

Introduction

Grammatical morphemes and functors, such as nominal and verbal inflections and determiners, are notoriously difficult for adult L2 acquisition across the board (passim the second language acquisition [SLA] literature). They have continuously drawn attention from researchers of all quarters. For example, L2 acquisition of English articles has been investigated under a range of theoretical approaches, from generative linguistic, to cognitive linguistic and to miscellaneous others, using a variety of designs and methods (e.g. Butler, 2002; Huebner, 1983; Liu & Gleason, 2002; Robertson, 2000; Thomas, 1989; White, 2003). Consequently, the literature has made available myriad explications regarding the nature and source of the morphological problem. However, conceptual and methodological problems render the existing proposals inadequate. Because the proposals are mostly based on studies that are non-longitudinal, that utilize pooled data, that treat grammatical morphemes as isolated, purely formal entities, and last but not least, that are target-centric (Larsen-Freeman, 2006), a number of key issues have remained poorly understood. One such issue is that of inter-learner variability. Learners from some L1 backgrounds apparently are, overall, more successful than those from other backgrounds in acquiring grammatical morphemes (Jarvis, 2002). Another paramount issue is intra-learner variability: Individual L2 learners display selectivity vis-à-vis grammatical morphemes such that they are able to fully acquire some but only partially acquire others (Franceschina, 2005). Additionally, the issue of *persistent*, *variable* use of certain grammatical morphemes (Lardiere, 1998; White, 2003) has not been adequately investigated.

This chapter seeks to contribute to the understanding of the last two issues, intra-learner variability and persistence. It brings longitudinal evidence to bear on, and provides an alternative to extant conceptions of, the morphological problem, in particular, as it relates to the English plural –*s* and articles. I will, heretofore, proceed as follows: first I will provide the theoretical background, highlighting the need to assume, in lieu of the existing perspectives, the perspective of linguistic relativism, more specifically, the thinking-for-speaking/writing hypothesis (Slobin, 1996a), in investigating the morphological difficulty. After that, the design of the study will be described and the results reported and discussed.

Grammatical morphemes

The term 'grammatical morphemes' is used broadly in this chapter to refer to inflectional morphemes and functors. Thus, in English, it covers plural –*s*, articles and possessive –*s* for noun phrases (NPs); -*ing*, past tense marking, third person singular –*s* for verb phrases and auxiliaries such as contractible copula (e.g. *He's a student*) and contractor auxiliary (e.g. *He's taken a shower*). These morphemes, researchers have long noticed, are 'unequal' (cf. Goldschneider & DeKeyer, 2001). The lack of equality is manifested, firstly, in a pronounced universal order that both first, and some second, language learners appear to follow in acquiring the morphemes (see, e.g. Brown, 1973; Dulay & Burt, 1974), the order suggesting that the morphemes pose differential difficulty for acquisition. For example, the plural –*s* is generally acquired before, and hence is considered easier than, articles (see, e.g. R. Ellis, 2003, 2005). Acquisition therein is directly linked to accuracy. As R. Ellis notes, 'the more accurately a morpheme was used, the earlier it must have been acquired' (Ellis, 1994: 91). A second notable facet of the unequal character is that second language learners from certain L1 backgrounds may derail from the universal trajectory for *select* morphemes, to the effect that a learner may append or skip a stage vis-à-vis the universal, developmental sequence or may experience a delay in proceeding through the stages (e.g. Kwon & Han, 2008; Schumann, 1978; Zobl, 1982).

Grammatical morphemes as a whole are a great obstacle in L2 acquisition. They appear both to be the first thing eluding incipient learners (Klein & Dittmar, 1979; Perdue, 1993) and one of the last things to plague end-state users who are otherwise native-like (DeKeyser, 2000; Johnson & Newport, 1989; White, 2003). Consider the following two excerpts.

[1] Beginning L2 English learner

I from Japan. My husband is student. ... My husband school in Columbia. My husband is study in Columbia. He everyday study study. I not understand English. My English not good. In Japan student English junior high school start. But many year ago I forget English. Sometimes I watch TV or listen radio. Newscaster, newscaster is very fast to speak English. I can't do correctly. Why you ask many question for me? (Japanese L1/English TL, Wei, 2000: 113)

[2] End-state L2 English user

Frequently discussed issue in conceptual/semantic transfer is the definition of concepts as opposed to semantics. ... most SLA research with linguistic relativity framework use thinking for speaking framework and have learners produce narratives. ... conceptual transfer framework involves identifying learners' I-concepts – concepts that represent thoughts, notions, or mental representations in minds – through an examination of learners' (non)linguistic performance.

Excerpt [1] has nothing but the 'bare bone' of a message: nouns, verbs, etc., devoid almost of any grammatical morphemes, with the most notable absences pertaining to plurals and articles. By contrast, Excerpt [2] has almost everything, with most of the needed grammatical morphemes in place but nonetheless with systematic underuse of articles.

The difficulty with grammatical morphemes and its multiple facets have been amply exposed by researchers from a variety of perspectives. For instance, from a psycholinguistic perspective, Jiang (2004) conducted three experiments with native speakers and non-native speakers (L1 Chinese), comparing their processing of grammatical and agrammatical sentences featuring anomalous number agreement (e.g. *The bridge to the island were about ten miles away*), and the results consistently indicated L2 learners' lack of processing of the number morpheme:

L2 learners were found to show no difference in reading time between number agreement and number disagreement sentences. Unlike native speakers, nonnative speakers' processing time was not affected by number disagreement. (Jiang, 2004: 603)

Examining learners' perception of interactional feedback, Mackey *et al.* (2000) reported that 'learners were relatively accurate in their perceptions about lexical, semantic, and phonological feedback. However, morphosyntactic feedback was generally not perceived as such' (Mackey *et al.*, 2000: 471–472). Strikingly similar findings were reported by Kim and Han (2007) investigating English as a foreign language (EFL) learners' and teachers' perceptions of interactional feedback, wherein morphosyntactic feedback, while overriding other types of interactional feedback in terms of frequency, elicited the least amount of noticing and recognition from learners. The studies thereby point out the recalcitrant nature of L2 learners' immunity to input on grammatical morphemes. Of note, in particular, is that pedagogical input, although otherwise helpful, may lose its influence over learners when it comes to grammatical morphemes.

Not only may the morphological problem be resistant to external intervention, but it can also be persistent, as shown by Lardiere (1998, 2007) and White (2003), among others. On a generative linguistic approach, Lardiere's (1998, 2000, 2007) longitudinal case study – by far the longest spanning investigation of L2 morphosyntactic acquisition – yields the finding that her subject's 'suppliance of past tense in obligatory past finite contexts remains stable and very low at approximately 34 percent over the entire eight-and-a-half year time span' (2000: 118). From a similar theoretical perspective, White's study focused on a particular persistent phenomenon, namely, *variable* use of grammatical morphemes. 'Such variability ... is pervasive during the course of acquisition', as White (2003: 129) notes, and is found even in the end state. White further observes that 'bilingual speakers who are fluent in the L2, who use it frequently, and who have had ample exposure to L2 input over an extended period of time, may nevertheless "fail" in this particular domain', concluding that 'fossilization is involved' (White, 2003: 129; cf. Hawkins, 2000; Lardiere, 2000).

Commensurate with the large amount of attention paid to the morphological problem, explanations are profuse. One of the most cited is VanPatten's (1996) meaning primacy hypothesis, according to which L2 learners perform biased processing of input such that they attend to meaningful elements and ignore meaningless ones. More specifically, the hypothesis predicts that elements of high communicative value,[1] such as content words, are processed over grammatical forms, and in turn, that inflectional morphemes of communicative value (e.g. *-ing*) are processed over those of little such value (e.g. third person singular *–s*).

Corroborating this conception, Wei (2000) differentiates between conceptually motivated and non-conceptually motivated system morphemes, contending that the former are acquired earlier than the latter. Conceptually motivated system morphemes (e.g. plural *–s* in English), according to Wei, are the grammatical morphemes that are activated for the sake of fleshing out content morphemes such as nouns and verbs; in contrast, non-conceptually motivated morphemes (e.g. third person *–s* in English) are structurally assigned only to satisfy grammatical requirement.

In a similar vein, Clahsen and Felser (2006) propose a shallow processing hypothesis, stating that 'adult L2 processing is restricted to shallow computations, utilizing largely nonlinguistic, pragmatic, and lexical information at the exclusion of morphosyntactic information' (Clahsen & Felser, 2006: 35). Hence, all three proposals put the blame, so to speak, on the learner whose preoccupation with meaning was considered a chief source of morphological inadequacy, a point to which I will return shortly.

Other explanations for the morphological problem include 'lack of salience' (Bardovi-Harlig, 1987; DeKeyser, 2005), 'ambiguous interpretation' (Ellis, 2006), 'lack of negotiation' (Mackey *et al.*, 2000), 'lack of sensitivity' (Carroll, 2005; Jiang, 2004; Long, 1996, 2003), 'representational and/or computational deficits' (e.g. Eubank & Grace, 1998; Hawkins, 2000; Lardiere, 2000; White, 2003), 'biased processing' (Carroll, 2005) and so on.

In sum, while the available explanations are plausible to a varying extent, it is clear that they are all broad-stroke attempts to account for a generic problem, and as such, their predictive power attenuates when it comes to intra-learner variability, a more microscopic though pervasive phenomenon. In particular, the existing explanations do not readily explain why variable use of grammatical morphemes may persist into the end-state grammar, even when environmental and psychological conditions have both been conducive to learning all along. Although a few of these explanations may seem able to account for acquisition variance at the individual level, for example, Carroll's (2005) attribution to L1-induced biased processing, none is as yet in a position to pinpoint the driving force behind the persistent variability.

Despite the apparent inadequacy, the existing accounts are not entirely unhelpful. For example, VanPatten's, and similarly, Wei's bifurcation of morphemes into features of '+/- meaning' or '+/- conceptually motivated', coupled with the general recognition that L1 may tamper with the acquisition process, could be substantiated to provide a foray into the complexity of the morphological problem, especially that of persistent variability. Such an endeavor would, however, presuppose conceptual restructuring on the researcher's part of constructs such as complexity and L1 influence, which have often been simplified dichotomously. Often, when applied, these constructs are construed as an either/or type of thing, that is, either complex or simple in the case of complexity and either present or absent in the case of L1 influence, only to camouflage their intricacy. Complexity and L1 influence, as research has amply shown, can each be underlain by a variety of factors interacting with one another (see, e.g. DeKeyser, 2005 on complexity; Andersen, 1983; Han, 2004, 2008; Kellerman, 1995; Odlin, 1989, 2005; Selinker, 1992 on L1 influence) and, most importantly, by virtue of their own mutual interaction, which is capable of forging greater complexity and lesser permeability to learning (Han, 2008).

A problem, therefore, with VanPatten's account as well as Wei's is that both have oversimplified complexity and ignored its interaction with L1 influence. Both accounts seem to suggest that the complexity of a grammatical morpheme is determined by its contribution to meaning expression in a sentence or utterance. Hence, forms that contribute less (i.e. having lower communicative value) are presumably more complex than forms contributing more (i.e. having higher communicative value). Take Wei's 4-M Model[2] as an example. As noted earlier, this model treats morphemes as unequal. Four types of morphemes are differentiated: content morphemes, which are directly elected by the speaker's semantic and pragmatic intentions; grammatical morphemes that are indirectly elected by the speaker's semantic and pragmatic intentions; and grammatical morphemes that are irrelevant to such intentions but are required by the grammatical frame of the target language, the latter further bifurcated into two other types: 'bridge' morphemes whose function is solely to satisfy the grammatical requirement within the maximal projection or the highest projection of a lexical head, for one type, and 'outsiders' whose realization depends on information outside the maximal projection morphemes, for the other. According to this view, the four types of morphemes are accessed at different stages of production (cf. Levelt, 1989) and hence are acquired at different points in time:

> content morphemes > early system morpheme >
> late system morphemes

As expressed in this 'implicational hierarchy' (Wei, 2000: 114), content morphemes are acquired before early system morphemes, which, in turn, are acquired before late system morphemes. Thus, in essence, such a hierarchy is predicated on the proximity of the different types of morphemes to the speaker's intended meaning.

For the purposes of the present study, it is relevant to note a specific prediction made by the 4-M model, namely that 'English plural is typically indirectly elected and therefore is an early system morpheme' (2000: 104). Indeed, by most of the extant accounts, English plural is considered non-complex and hence easy to acquire. R. Ellis (2003, 2005), for example, asserts that English plural is acquired early, by virtue of the fact that it is governed by a simple rule. On the other hand, such assertions seem at odds with observational findings suggesting that even advanced learners have trouble using English plural forms consistently in a native-like manner (Han, 2008). Han points out that extant accounts of the morphological problem have largely failed to cognize the fact that the hard-to-acquire grammatical morphemes are meaning-laden rather than meaningless,[3] although their meaning is abstract rather than concrete. They encode abstract concepts, such as 'definiteness' and 'number', rather than concrete referents, such as 'table' and 'desk', and are tied up with underlying conceptualizations. Drawing on linguistic relativism, Han argues that these grammatical forms are the most liable to L1 interference and hence the most susceptible to fossilization (cf. Selinker & Lakshmanan, 1992). A linguistic-relativism-based account, thus, makes predictions contrary to extant SLA accounts, as further discussed below.

Linguistic Relativism

Linguistic relativism, as most authors of the chapters in this volume have explicated, is a theory that predicts a relationship between language and cognition. Its central tenets are that language shapes cognition and/ or constrains its expression. In more concrete terms, speakers of a given language, be it his first or second, develop a particular world view, which bears both universality and uniqueness. In other words, on the one hand, the world view may have something in common with that of speakers of other languages, but it may be sufficiently distinct from it, on the other. An oft-used example in expositions of linguistic relativism is that of Eskimos speaking a language that has multiple lexical terms for *snow* and, at the same time, having a granular conception of snow.

The application of linguistic relativism to SLA is by no means a recent endeavor, even though recent SLA research has seen a distinct revival of interest in the linguistic theory (Odlin, 2005, 2008a). As early as in the 18th century, German philosopher von Humboldt (1836) remarked that

> To learn a foreign language should ... be to acquire a new standpoint in the world-view hitherto possessed, and in fact to a certain extent this is so, since every language contains the whole conceptual fabric and mode of presentation of a portion of mankind. But because we always carry over, more or less, our own world-view, and even our own language-view, this outcome is not purely and completely experienced. (von Humboldt, 1836/1960: 60)

In the above statement, von Humboldt made two important points: first, that language learning entails developing, correspondingly, a conceptual system for representing the world; and second, because first language learning experience has already provided for such a system, it will be impossible to fully develop a new conceptual system while learning a second language, and hence, second language learning cannot be completely successful. On this view, then, the lack of success in learning a second language is endemic. In a similar vein, Han and Odlin question 'whether the cognitive as well as the linguistic systems of second language learners can ever be identical' (Han & Odlin, 2006: 11).

Whereas von Humboldt was very general about the influence of the first language conceptual system on the learning of a second, Slobin (1996a) spoke to specific aspects of that system that are most likely to function to build resistance in the interlanguage to the influence of the target language and of its accompanying conceptual system. These aspects, according to Slobin, are independent of 'our perceptual, sensorimotor, and practical dealings with the world' (Slobin, 1996a: 91), which include, but are not limited to, aspect, number, definiteness and voice.

> Each native language has trained its speakers to pay different kinds of attention to events and experiences when talking about them. This training is carried out in childhood and is exceptionally resistant to restructuring in adult second-language acquisition. (Slobin, 1996a: 89)

Empirical research has shown that the L1-based cognitive, conceptual influence is particularly acute when second language learners are asked to spontaneously produce oral narratives evoking linguistic items that encode abstract notions. Studies investigating learners' expressions of motion, spatial and temporal relations (for reviews, see Cadierno, this volume; Odlin, 2005, 2008a) have revealed that learners' discourse is framed largely in the L1-based perspective. The manner in which learners verbalize events is consistent with how they would do so in their L1, a phenomenon characterized by Slobin as 'thinking for speaking'.

Thinking for speaking

Slobin (1987) proposed a modified form of linguistic relativism,[4] known as the thinking-for-speaking hypothesis. Utilizing two gerunds 'thinking' and 'speaking' and a purposive preposition 'for' in lieu of the traditional term 'thought and language', the hypothesis seeks to capture the online effects of language on thought processes. Slobin wrote:

> The activity of thinking takes on a particular quality when it is employed in the activity of speaking. In the evanescent timeframe of constructing utterances in discourse, one fits one's thought into available linguistic forms. A particular utterance is never a direct reflection of 'objective' or perceived reality or of an inevitable and universal mental representation of a situation. This is evident in any given language, because the same situation can be described in different ways; and it is evident across languages, because each language provides a limited set of options for the grammatical encoding of characteristics of objects and events. 'Thinking for speaking' involves picking those characteristics that (a) fit some conceptualization of the event, and (b) are readily encodable in the language. (Slobin, 1987: 435)

Thus, according to the thinking-for-speaking hypothesis, expression of experience in linguistic terms involves a special form of thought, mobilized for communication, which is filtered through and constrained by existing language.

In the case of L2 learning, L1 naturally functions as the filter, as has been documented in numerous studies on L2 sentence processing and narrative production. In terms of the latter, learners (advanced learners included) appear influenced by their L1-specific thinking for speaking, selecting items, accordingly, from their L2 mental grammar and lexicon to verbalize experience, as exemplified in several chapters in this volume.

Slobin (2003) identifies a number of avenues for research on thinking for speaking, and by extension, thinking for writing and thinking for translation, several of which have a direct bearing on L2 research. For example, he suggests examining 'ways in which one's native language shapes one's mastery of grammatical categories of a foreign language. That is, how well can one adapt one's thinking for speaking in a different system?' (Slobin, 2003: 436). He also recommends looking into 'the contents of grammatical categories' (2003: 436) that are especially resistant to change or that are deeply ingrained. Furthermore, he notes that thinking for speaking should be most evident in things that are 'easily and automatically said' in particular languages. Taken together, these insights suggest that unmarked structures, which are habitually used, in the L1 are most susceptible to transfer via thinking for speaking into L2 production, and that the effects tend to persevere. The present study was an attempt to substantiate this line of reasoning, through examining the use of English articles and plurals by an adult native speaker of Chinese who had been residing and working in an English-speaking country for 12 years.

English and Chinese

It is an indisputable fact that English and Chinese are typologically distant. Of numerous differences, they polarize, orthogonally, with respect to articles and plurals. English is an [+ART] and [+plural] language, whereas Chinese is [−ART] and [−plural]. More specifically, with respect to articles, English grammaticizes definiteness and indefiniteness into definite and/ or indefinite articles, but such grammaticization is largely absent in Chinese, where definiteness or indefiniteness is, instead, largely inferred from the discourse context.

With respect to plural marking, English typically uses the −s morpheme (and its variants) to overtly mark plurality on certain categories of nouns. According to Lucy (1992b), three classes of nouns can be distinguished, depending on how features of [+/− animate] and [+/− discrete] are combined, with different combinations having differential consequences for number marking. The first class of nouns are those that are [+animate] and [+discrete]. They, therefore, must take plural inflection when quantified. Examples thereof are *three boy(s)* and *four girl(s)*. A second category of nouns carries the settings of [−animate] and [+discrete], and these nouns must also take plural inflection, for example, *two book(s)* and *two pen(s)*. A third category of nouns are [−animate] and [−discrete]. They cannot take plural marking, and in order to be quantified, quantifiers and classifiers must be used. Examples are *two spoonfuls of sugar* and *three cups of tea*. These classes of nouns are, however, conflated in Chinese, where there is not a similar interaction between nouns and grammatical number marking. In Chinese, all nouns are inherently non-quantificational (i.e. [−discrete]), yet they all can be quantified (i.e. [+discrete]), by grammatical means of quantifiers and classifiers, for example, *liang3* (two) *ben3* (CL) *shu1* (book) for *two books* and *liang3* (two) *zhi1* (CL) *bi3* (pen) for *two pens*. Thus, the grammatical differences between English and Chinese are concomitant with cognitive, conceptual differences, as illustrated in Table 7.1.

Table 7.1 Conceptual and grammatical differences in number marking between English and Chinese

	English			*Chinese*
Conceptual categories	[+animate] [+discrete]	[−animate] [+discrete]	[−animate] [−discrete]	[±animate/ −discrete]
Grammatical means	plural morpheme	plural morpheme	quantifier + classifier	quantifier + classifier

Note that, according to Table 7.1, Chinese and English, in spite of many stark differences, have something in common: English has a subset of nouns overlapping with nouns in Chinese insofar as they both can be quantified using a numerical quantifier and a classifier. This similarity is, nevertheless, only superficial; underneath there is a fundamental difference between the two languages. In Chinese, all nouns can be *individuated* both conceptually and grammatically, whereas the subset of English nouns cannot. Take the concept of 'hair' as an example. The word in English encoding this concept belongs to the [−animate] and [−discrete] category of nouns and, as such, it cannot be individuated. Thus, in general, one cannot say 'two hairs',[5] but the concept can be quantified into, for example, 'a slew of hair', thus with the help of a classifier indicating massiveness. However, this word in Chinese behaves just like any other nouns in that conceptually, it *can* be individuated, and grammatically, it is done through using a quantifier and a classifier suggesting individuality, *liang3* (two) *gen1* (CL) *mao2* (hair). The cognitive and grammatical differences between the two languages, in light of linguistic relativism, transmit distinct world views, and in the present context, this translates into how objects (e.g. hair) are conceived by native speakers of English versus Chinese, and also into how the plural morpheme *–s* is interpreted and used.

For native speakers of Chinese learning English as the L2, it can be predicted, in light of Slobin's thinking-for-speaking hypothesis, that there will be interference from the L1, due to the fact that number is an unmarked concept (i.e. encoded with high frequency) in the L1 (and the L2). Moreover, following Tarone (1982, see also Tarone & Liu, 1996), it may be predicted that the transfer effects via thinking for speaking should be most evident in the interlanguage *vernacular*, namely spontaneous and informal production, where the learner pays the least attention to form.

The present longitudinal case study investigated two specific questions:

(1) Do number and definiteness marking in the L2 pattern after those in the L1?
(2) To what extent is the L2 user's mind still L1-relativized?

It was hoped that findings from the study would shed light on the two broader issues noted earlier, namely, intra-learner variability and persistence, and would thereby contribute to a more granular understanding than is currently available of the grammatical morpheme problem and of linguistic relativistic effects in SLA.

Method

Participant

The participant, pseudo-named Geng, was an adult male native speaker of Chinese, aged 50, who had been living and working in an English-speaking country for 12 years and who reportedly had high intrinsic and extrinsic motivation to improve his English. It is worth mentioning in passing that other aspects of the same participant's interlanguage have been reported elsewhere (Han, 2000, 2006).

Data

The data came from two sources. The first is two batches of Geng's spontaneous writings produced respectively in 2003 and 2007, and they were samples of email messages that Geng wrote to coworkers with whom he interacted on a daily basis. Each batch of samples contained approximately 9000 words. The second source of data is six tailor-made written tasks employed to elicit Geng's use of the target forms, namely articles and plurals. They include four translation tasks, a noun identification task and an error correction task, all of which were intended to verify findings from the analysis of the naturalistic data and to further probe Geng's use and mental representations of the target forms in order to pin down the constraints. A description of the tasks follows.

Elicitation tasks

The tasks are described in this section in the order they were administered: the translation tasks, the noun-identification task and the error correction task.

Four Chinese-to-English translation tasks were developed and employed in the study. Task 1 containing 10 sentences was purported to probe Geng's L2 marking of (a) plurality, (b) definiteness and (c) plurality and definiteness. To that end, three linguistic environments were provided: (a) an existential construction containing a quantified count noun; (b) a non-quantified count noun occupying the subject/topic position; and (c) a quantified non-count noun in a non-subject/non-topic position. Examples of each type are given below.

Example (1): Existential construction containing a quantified count noun

有	些	问题	仍	需要	解决。
you3	xie1	wen4ti2	reng2	xu1yao4	jie3jue2
have	some	problem	still	need	solve

Example (2): Non-quantified count noun occupying the subject/topic position

总统	作	了	一番	重要	讲话
zong2tong3	zuo4	le	yi4fan1	zhong4yao4	jiang3hua4
<u>President</u>	deliver	PFV	one CL	important	speech

Example (3): Quantified non-count noun in a non-subject/topic position

这	本	书	为	那	个	问题	提供	了	两 项	重 要	的	证据
zhe4	ben3	shu1	wei4	na4	ge4	wen4ti2	ti2gong4	le	liang3xiang4	zhong4yao4	de	zheng4ju4.
this	CL	book	for	that	CL	problem	provide	PFV	<u>two CL</u>	<u>important</u>	<u>NOM</u>	<u>evidence</u>

Task 2 involves translation into English of 20 Chinese sentences of four types: (a) an L1 topic–comment construction with the topic encoded by a count noun; (b) an L1 topic–comment construction with the topic encoded by a non-count noun; (c) an L1 non-topic–comment construction containing a count noun in a non-subject position; and (d) an L1 non-topic–comment construction containing a non-count noun in a non-subject position. An example of each type follows:

Example (4): Topic–comment construction with the topic encoded by a count noun

猫	很	可 爱
mao1	1hen2	ke3ai4
<u>Cat</u>	very	lovely

Example (5): Topic–comment construction with the topic encoded by a non-count noun

音乐	能	帮	我	放松
yin1yue4	neng2	bang1	wo3	fang4song1
<u>music</u>	can	help	me	relax

Example (6): Other construction containing a count noun in a non-subject position

中午	我们	吃	了	苹果
zhong1wu3	wo3men2	chi1	le	ping2guo3
noon	we	eat	PFV	<u>apple</u>

Example (7): Other construction containing a non-count noun in a non-subject position

他	从	小	到	大	受	了	很多	良好	的	教育
ta1	cong2	xiao3	dao4	da4	shou4	le	hen3duo1	liang2hao3	de	jiao4yu4
he	from	small	till	big	receive	PFV	much	good	NOM	<u>education</u>

The purpose of this task was to probe Geng's plural marking of count versus non-count nouns in his L2 rendering of Chinese topic–comment versus non-topic–comment constructions. The topic–comment sentences all express generic statements.

Task 3 involves 10 utterances[6] in Chinese to be translated into English, each beginning with a generic statement encoded in a topic–comment construction and thus having a noun occupy the initial position of the sentence/utterance. In this task, two topic–comment constructions were investigated: the *in situ* topic (i.e. base-generated NP) versus the derived topic (i.e. fronted/topicalized NP from the object position).

Example (8): Base-generated topic

<u>钢笔</u>	没有	铅笔	好用。
gang1bi3	mei2you3	qian1bi3	hao3yong4
pen	not have	pencil	good use

Example (9): Derived topic

<u>问题</u>	到处	可以	碰到。
wen4ti2	dao4chu4	ke2yi3	peng4dao4
<u>problem</u>	everywhere	may	encounter

The task was designed to probe Geng's L2 expression of the Chinese topic–comment construction and, in particular, to see how he would handle the definiteness of the sentence-initial nouns or topics, in expressing L1 generic statements in the L2.

Task 4 provides 15 Chinese sentences to be translated into English, involving quantified count versus quantified non-count nouns. These sentences were designed to tap Geng's L2 knowledge of plural marking vis-à-vis count versus non-count nouns.

Example (10): Quantified count noun

他	给	他 的	孙子	取	了	<u>两</u>	<u>个</u>	<u>名字</u>。
ta1	gei3	ta1 de	sun1zi3	qu3	le	liang3ge4		ming2zi4
he	to	he GEN	grandson	give	PFV	<u>two</u>	<u>CL</u>	<u>name</u>

Example (11): Quantified non-count noun

他 的	叔叔	患 有	<u>两</u>	<u>种</u>	<u>癌症</u>。
ta1 de	shu1shu1	huan4you3	liang2zhong3		ai2zheng4
he GEN	uncle	suffer-have	<u>two</u>	<u>CL</u>	<u>cancer</u>

In addition to the four translation tasks, the study employed a noun identification task, on which Geng was asked to indicate, out of 120 nouns (70 non-count nouns, 44 count nouns and 6 fillers), which of the nouns were countable (C), uncountable (NC) or neither (N/A). The purpose of this task was to probe Geng's metalinguistic knowledge vis-à-vis nouns, in particular, non-count nouns.

Finally, the study also employed an error correction task to mainly probe Geng's use of plurals. The task drew on texts written by Geng's English-speaking co-workers, with whom he had interacted on a daily basis. Specifically, 51 items were removed from the texts, 22 of which were target items and the rest of which were fillers. Constructed as such, the error correction task had an additional underlying purpose, namely, to indirectly gauge Geng's sensitivity to the type of input he had been exposed to from 2003 to 2007. This task required detection and suppliance of missing items.

Procedure

The naturalistic data collection has been an ongoing process, dating from 1995. On a regular basis, the case subject selectively downloaded bulks of his email writings and forwarded them to the researcher. For the purposes of the present study, data from 2003 and 2007 were sampled for analyses.

The six elicitation tasks were administered in the order presented above in the span of a week in March 2007, and all were timed, in order to maximize the possibility of getting at Geng's intuitions or default knowledge. Table 7.2 provides a summary of the tasks.

Analysis

Naturalistic data: The focus of analysis of naturalistic data was on articles and plurals. As mentioned, most existing research (see Chapter 6 for a review) has tended to examine a single grammatical morpheme, for example, articles. From that point of view, the present study was unique in that it targeted a 'cohort' of morphemes. The two chosen targets both concern nominal phrases and both can express the abstract notion of definiteness, in addition to the fact that plurals express the abstract concept of number.

Table 7.2 Elicitation tasks

Task	*Stimuli*	*Focus*	*Duration (minutes)*
Translation 1	10 sentences	(a) Plurality, (b) definiteness and (c) plurality and definiteness	5
Translation 2	20 sentences	Plural marking vis-à-vis count and non-count nouns	10
Translation 3	10 sentences	Definiteness marking in topic–comment constructions	5
Translation 4	15 sentences	Plural marking of quantified versus non-quantified nouns	8
Noun identification	120 nouns	Differentiating count and non-count nouns	10
Error correction	5 short chunks of text	Plural marking	10

It was believed that such an approach would yield a clearer and more reliable picture of the effects, if any, of L1-based thinking for speaking on L2 production than if either alone had been the focus of analysis. Furthermore, focusing on more than one morpheme was necessary to address the larger issue of intra-learner variability.

The analysis of the naturalistic data assumed both a target-oriented perspective, by examining instances of suppliance and non-suppliance of the morphemes in obligatory contexts, and an interlanguage-oriented perspective, from which both suppliance and over-suppliance (i.e. in so-called non-obligatory contexts) of the forms were examined. The latter perspective is often absent from most of the existing research (see, e.g. Lardiere, 2007; Robertson, 2000; White, 2003). The data were coded by the researcher iteratively until the intra-rater consistency reached 100%.

When data were examined for plural marking, two specific linguistic contexts were inspected: quantified nouns (e.g. _two books_) and non-quantified nouns (e.g. _books_). When data were examined for articles, both definite contexts and indefinite contexts were checked. In each case, tokens were tallied for each category. Pearson Chi-Square analyses were then conducted to see if there were any significant differences between 2003 and 2007.

Elicited data: The data elicited via the four translation tasks were analyzed qualitatively. Each response was carefully examined on its own and in relation to others to discern systematicity or lack thereof. The data from the noun identification task and error correction task, on the other hand, were analyzed quantitatively. Tokens of right and wrong answers were tallied to yield accuracy scores.

Results

Naturalistic data

Table 7.3 summarizes the results on Geng's plural marking for quantified and unquantified NPs. As shown, data from 2003 and 2007 converged on the pattern that quantified nouns are more accurately marked for plural than non-quantified nouns.

The Pearson Chi-Square tests reveal significant similarity between the 2003 and 2007 data ($\chi^2 = 47.917$, $p = 0.00$ for quantified NPs; $\chi^2 = 84.177$, $p = 0.00$ for unquantified NPs), suggesting stabilization of Geng's patterned use of the plural morpheme. These results also bear resemblance

Table 7.3 Percentage of accurate plural marking by Geng in obligatory contexts

Year	Quantified NPs (%)	Unquantified NPs (%)
2003	92	76
2007	96	79

Table 7.4 Percentage of accurate use of articles in obligatory contexts

Year	*'a'/'an' (%)*	*'the' (%)*
2003	82	64
2007	86	69

to those reported in Lardiere (2007) for Patty, an adult, female native speaker of Chinese who, as noted earlier, had resided in an English-speaking country for more than 20 years. Table 7.3 also appears to suggest that complete acquisition of plural marking of quantified nouns is possible for Geng, whereas the same outcome may not be possible for unquantified NPs. A Wilcoxon Signed Ranks Test indicates a significant, *stable* difference in Geng's plural marking of quantified nouns versus unquantified nouns ($Z = -4$, $p = 0.00$ for 2003; $Z = -4.123$, $p = 0.00$ for 2007).

Table 7.4 summarizes the results on Geng's use of articles in obligatory contexts. Again, data from 2003 and 2007 converged to the same pattern, namely that the indefinite article is used more accurately than the definite article.

Pearson Chi-Square analyses show significant similarity between 2003 and 2007 ($\chi^2 = 74.160$, $p = 0.00$ for the indefinite article; $\chi^2 = 79.871$, $p = 0.00$ for the definite article), which suggests long-term stabilization of Geng's idiosyncratic use of articles. Moreover, the Wilcoxon Signed Ranks Test indicates a significant, *stable* difference between Geng's definite and indefinite articles at both times ($Z = -4.243$, $p = 0.00$ for 2003; $Z = -4.123$, $p = 0.00$ for 2007).

Summing up, the quantitative results, based on obligatory usage, indicate that overall, Geng was more accurate in using plurals than articles. Furthermore, in terms of plural marking, he was more accurate in marking quantified nouns than unquantified nouns, and in terms of articles, more accurate in using the indefinite article than the definite article. The latter result, interestingly, differs from Lardiere's subject, Patty, a point to which I will return in Discussion.

Elicited data

To verify and further investigate the results from analyses of the naturalistic data, a number of elicitation tasks were administered to Geng, and these included four translation tasks, a noun identification task and an error correction task (see the section 'Elicitation tasks' above for a description). Results from each task are presented below.

Translation Task 1: Geng's performance on the first translation task, which targets (a) plural marking, (b) definiteness and (c) plural marking and definiteness, reveals a number of tendencies. With regard to (a), Geng's plural marking seems to always be accompanied by the presence of a quantifier, as shown by his turning, in one instance, '几项重大的研究'

into 'several research projects' and in another instance, '两项重要的证据' into 'two evidences'. These expressions also reveal that Geng was able, although not always, to differentiate count nouns from non-count nouns.

With regard to (b), Geng tended to mark a derived topic as definite, as illustrated in Examples (12) and (13).

Example (12)

(a)   具体   的   标准   我们 还不是 很清楚。(Prompt)
      Ju4ti3   de   biao1zhun3 wo2men2 hai2bu2shi4 hen3qing1chu3
      <u>concrete NOM criterion</u> we still not be very clear
(b)   <u>The specific standard</u> is not clear yet.   (Translation)

Example (13)

(a)   从   他 的   脸上   你可以   看出   他 经历   过   <u>很多磨难</u>。(Prompt)
      cong2 ta1 de   lian3shang4 ni3 ke2yi3 kan4chu1 ta1 jing1li4 guo4 hen3duo1muo2nan4
      from he GEN face   you can   see   he experience EXP <u>much hardship</u>
(b)   <u>The hardship</u> is apperently on his face. (Translation)

As Example (12) shows, '具体的标准' [see Example (12a)] is a derived topic, and Geng translated it into '*the* specific standard' [see Example (12b)]. In Example (13a), '磨难' is topicalized in Geng's translation, hence becoming a derived topic and was marked as definite, '*the* hardship'. Interestingly, however, when the prompt sentence contains a base-generated topic, Geng's marking of definiteness became random, as shown by Examples (14–16).

Example (14)

(a)   下午   三点,   <u>候选者</u>   到达   会场。   (Prompt)
      xia4wu3   san1dian3 hou4xuan2zhe3 dao4da2 hui4chang3
      afternoon 3 'clock   <u>candidate</u>   arrive   meeting site
(b)   <u>Candidates</u> arrives the site at 3:00 pm this afternoon. (Translation)

Example (15)

(a)   总统   做了   一番   重要   讲话。(Prompt)
      zong2tong3 zuo4le   yi1fan1 zhong4yao4 jiang3hua4
      <u>president</u> give PFV one CL important   speech
(b)   <u>The president</u> gives important speech. (Translation)

Example (16)

(a)   副总统   也讲了   一些   很重要   的   话。(Prompt)
      fu4zong2tong3 ye2jiang4le yi1xie1 hen3zhong4yao4 de   hua4
      <u>vice president</u> also speak PFV some   very important   NOM remark
(b)   <u>Vice president</u> gives an important speech as well. (Translation)

Examples (14a), (15a) and (16a) are strikingly similar in that they share the same topic–comment construction (i.e. having a base-generated topic), with the subject noun carrying the meaning of 'definite and specific'. Yet, as can be seen from Geng's translation, he plural-marked '候选者' as 'Candidates' (14b), defined '总统" as 'The president' (15b) and zero-marked '副总统' as 'vice president' (16b), thus utilizing three morphosyntactic means for expressing the same type of topic.

Finally, with regard to (c) plural and definiteness marking, Geng appeared to be able to dissociate plural marking from definiteness, as he consistently pluralized subject NPs in existential constructions, without marking them as definite or indefinite. An example is given below.

Example (17)

(a) 教室　　里　有　学生。(Prompt)
     jiao4shi4li3　you3xue2sheng1
     Classroom　inside have <u>student</u>

(b) <u>There are some students</u> in the classroom. (Translation)

Translation Task 2: Task 2 further investigates Geng's productive knowledge of count versus non-count nouns as well as his treatment of generic statements with a count or non-count noun functioning as the topic. Several findings are noteworthy. First, Geng continued to demonstrate a good working knowledge of count versus non-count nouns. For example, he rendered '一些很好的指点' into 'some very good advice', on the one hand, and '一些困难' into 'some difficulties', on the other. Second, Geng, consistently, rendered base-generated, generic topics into bare NPs, as illustrated in Examples (18) and (19).

Example (18)

(a) 猫　　很　　可爱。(Prompt)
     mao1　hen2　ke3ai4
     <u>cat</u>　very　lovely

(b) <u>Cat</u> is lovely. (Translation)

Example (19)

(a) <u>音乐</u>　能　帮我　放松。　(Prompt)
     yin1yue4 neng2 bang1wo3fang4song1
     <u>music</u>　can　help me　relax

(b) <u>Music</u> could help me relaxing.　(Translation)

Third, that Geng's plural marking favors quantified nouns over non-quantified nouns was again observed, as in Examples (20) and (21).

Example (20)

(a)   中午   我们   吃了   苹果。(Prompt)
      zhong1wu3 wo3men2 chi1le   ping2guo3
      noon   we   eat PFV   <u>apple</u>
(b)   We ate <u>apple</u> at noon. (Translation)

Example (21)

(a)   很多   人   喜欢   狗。(Prompt)
      hen3duo1ren2   xi3huan1gou3
      Many   person   like   <u>dog</u>
(b)   Many people like <u>dog</u>. (Translation)

Note that neither 'apple' in Example (20b) nor 'dog' in Example (21b) was plural marked, in the absence of a quantifier.

Translation Task 3: Task 3 further elicited Geng's L2 translation of L1-topic–comment constructions, importantly, differentiating (a) generic statements from non-generic interrogatives, and (b) based-generated topics from derived topics. The results largely confirmed two previously emerging findings. First is that Geng tended not to mark the definiteness of base-generated topics, using, therefore, bare NPs. Second is that Geng tended not to plural-mark unquantified nouns. These are illustrated in Example (22).

Example (22)

(a)   钢笔   没有   铅笔好用,   但 亚洲人   喜欢   用   钢笔。(Prompt)
      gang1bi3 mei2you3 qian1bi3hao3yong4 dan4 ya4zhou1ren2 xi3huan1yong4 gang1bi3
      <u>pen</u>   NEG   <u>pencil</u> good use   but <u>Asian</u>   like   use   <u>pen</u>
(b)   <u>Pen</u> is not as good as <u>pencil</u> but <u>Asian</u> like <u>pen</u> better. (Translation)

Geng, on the other hand, plural-marked the derived topics, as shown in Examples (23) and (24).

Example (23)

(a)   照片   不好   保管,   除非   放在   像本里。(Prompt)
      zhao4pian1bu4hao3 bao2guan3, chu2fei1 fang4zai4 xiang4ben2li3
      <u>photo</u>   NEG   preserve   unless   put PREP <u>album</u> inside
(b)   <u>Pictures</u> are difficult to reserve unless you put them in <u>album</u>. (Translation)

Example (24)

(a)   文章   写完   了   吗? 要 写 完   了 的   话   我们   就去   书店   看看。(Prompt)
      wen2zhang1xie3wan2 le   ma1 yao4xie3wan2 le   de   hua4 wo3men2 jiu4qu4 shu1dian4 kan4kan4
      <u>article</u>   write-finish PFV PRT if write-finish PFV COND   we   then go <u>bookstore</u> see see
(b)   Did you finish <u>the article</u>? If so, we should go to <u>bookstore</u>.   (Translation)

Example (23a) is a generic statement with a derived topic, '照片', which Geng plural-marked as 'pictures' [see Example (23b)], seemingly to express the meaning of non-specificity or indefiniteness. Example (24a) is a non-generic interrogative with a derived topic, '文章', which Geng marked as definite, 'the article'. Note also that Examples (23a) and (24a) each also contain an NP in a non-topic position, '像本' and '书店', and Geng marked it neither for definiteness nor for number, namely 'album' (23b) and 'bookstore' (24b).

Translation task 4: Task 4 zeroed in on Geng's plural marking of quantified count nouns versus quantified non-count nouns. The results were consistent with the emerging findings from the previous tasks. Specifically, Geng plural-marked quantified count nouns and, only occasionally, non-count nouns as well, as shown in Example (25).

Example (25)

(a)　他 的　　叔叔　　患 有　　<u>两种</u>　　<u>癌症</u>。(Prompt)
　　ta1 de　shu1shu　huan4you3 liang2zhong3ai2zheng4
　　he GEN　uncle　　suffer have <u>two CL</u>　<u>cancer</u>
(b)　His uncle gets <u>three kinds of cancers</u>. (Translation)

Noun identification task: This task sought to probe Geng's metalinguistic awareness of count versus non-count nouns. Table 7.5 displays the accuracy rate.

As seen in Table 7.5, the results from this task are consistent with what we have seen from the translation tasks. In other words, there was consistency between Geng's metalinguistic knowledge and his use of count and non-count nouns, as evident in his naturalistic production. It is also interesting to note that Geng's knowledge of non-count nouns somewhat surpassed his knowledge of count nouns. A Wilcoxon Signed Ranks Test indicates a significant difference between the two ($Z = -3.317$; $p < 0.05$). Overall, Geng's accuracy rate is high at the metalinguistic level, which may suggest two things: (a) that Geng's command of English was high and (b) that the relative lack of plural marking was due to performance factors, not the least of which was the influence of the L1-based thinking for speaking, a point to which I will return in Discussion.

Error correction task: It may be recalled that the error correction task drew on passages produced by Geng's native-speaking co-workers. Geng's performance on this task was rather minimal. The overall accuracy rate was 29% and merely 5% when it comes to the target items, namely plurals. He, in fact, did better on the filler items (e.g. pronouns) than the target items. Of the 21 missing plurals, Geng was only able to identify and supply

Table 7.5 Geng's accuracy vis-à-vis noun identification

Count nouns	*Non-count nouns*	*Overall accuracy*
75% (33/44)	86% (60/70)	87% (99/114)

one – not surprisingly, for a quantified count noun. These results indicate (a) that Geng was not able to detect the grammatical morpheme inadequacy of the passages, but more profoundly, (b) that he was insensitive to the input from interacting with his native-speaking co-workers. Clearly, where the grammatical morphemes are concerned, the input that had been available to him over the years had little impact on him. It is worth noting also that Geng was given 10 minutes for the task, but he 'finished' it in five minutes, commenting that he could not see much wrong in the texts.

In summary, the analytic results from the elicited data confirmed as well as expanded on those from the naturalistic data. On the converging side, Geng displayed, on the elicitation tasks just as he did in his natural production, a tendency to pluralize quantified nouns (including non-count nouns, from time to time) and ignore non-quantified count nouns. Moreover, he showed a tendency to underexpress definiteness of NPs. Where the latter is concerned, the elicited data shed critical light on the conditions under which NPs tended not to be marked for definiteness. Table 7.6 provides a summary of the patterns that emerged from the elicited data for number and definiteness marking.

Table 7.6 illustrates eight patterns, as follows: (i) when an NP functions as a base-generated topic in the L1 utterance, whose semantics is non-specific, it tends not to be marked at all (expressed by a bare NP) in the L2; (ii) when an NP functions as a base-generated topic that carries the meaning of 'specific' in the L1, it is variably marked in the L2; (iii) when an NP

Table 7.6 Patterns of Geng's L2 marking of definiteness and number

L1		L2	
Form	*Meaning*	*Form*	*Meaning*
Base-generated topic NP (a)	Non-specific	Bare NP	Non-specific
Base-generated topic NP (b)	Specific	NP variably marked for definiteness	Specific
Derived topic NP (a)	Non-specific	Bare NP	Non-specific
Derived topic NP (b)	Specific	NP marked as definite	Specific
Non-topic (a)	Non-specific	Bare NP	Non-specific
Non-topic (b)	Specific	NP marked as definite	Specific
Non-quantified NP	Singular non-specific	Bare NP	Non-specific
Quantified NP	Plural, specific	NP marked for plural	Specific

is a derived topic and carries the meaning of 'non-specific' in the L1, it tends to be expressed by a bare NP in the L2; (iv) when an NP is a derived topic and carries the meaning of 'specific' in the L1, it tends to be marked as definite in the L2; (v) when an NP appears in a non-topic position of an utterance and bears the semantics of 'non-specific' in the L1, it tends not to be marked for definiteness (expressed by a bare NP); (vi) when an NP appears in a non-topic position of an utterance and bears the meaning of 'specific' in the L1, it tends to be marked as definite in the L2; (vii) when an NP is non-quantified, it tends not to be marked for plural; and (viii) when an NP is quantified, it tends to be marked for plural.

Also worthy of note in Table 7.6 is that although the L2 exhibits some variation from the L1, in terms of form (see Columns 1 and 3), there is full correspondence between the L1 and the L2 in meaning (Columns 2 and 4). In other words, TL grammatical morphemes (i.e. articles and plurals) were *selectively* utilized in Geng's L2 to convey L1-based meanings, for instance, under conditions (iv), (vi) and (viii).

Finally, the elicited data collectively pointed up a discrepancy between Geng's metalinguistic knowledge and use of the L2. Data, in particular, from the noun identification task and the error correction task reveal that Geng, on the one hand, had a high metalinguistic awareness of the distinction between count and non-count nouns but, on the other, a limited, biased and selective ability to plural-mark nouns in his natural production.

Discussion

The present study set out to investigate two questions, repeated below for convenience:

(1) Do number and definiteness marking in the L2 pattern after those in the L1?
(2) To what extent is the L2 user's mind still L1-relativized?

Naturalistic data, sampled at two points in time, 2003 and 2007, and coupled with data elicited from six specially designed tasks, shed ample light on both questions. First of all, in terms of the first research question, the evidence is overwhelmingly suggestive that the number and definiteness marking in Geng's L2 English do pattern after those in his L1 Chinese. In respect of number marking, there was a clear tendency in Geng's naturalistic writing as well as elicited translation to plural-mark quantified nouns; less often did he plural-mark non-quantified nouns. Such a tendency coincides with a canonical fact in his L1, as described earlier in the 'English and Chinese' section. In addition to the results reported in the preceding section for the elicited data, Geng, in his natural writing, typically produced sentences such as Examples (26–28).

Example (26)
We have around <u>< 1500 boxes</u>.

Example (27)
I got some impression that they are hiring <u>C ++ developer</u>.

Example (28)
This is great!!! Especially after <u>so much frustrations</u>.

Example (28) illustrates overextension of an interlanguage rule, namely that *when a noun is quantified, it should be plural-marked*. Such overuse of plural marking[7] along with underuse [Example (27)], and seemingly target-like use [Example (26)], cannot be coherently explained unless one assumes that the underlying driving force was the L1-based thinking for speaking. It is how one would say it in one's L1, so to speak, or more precisely, it is how one would mean it in the L1 that drove the L2 production. The underlined NPs in Examples (26) and (28) both carried the L1 meaning of 'specific', while Example (27), as inferred from its discourse context, carried the L1 meaning of 'non-specific'. Thus, in Geng's L2, the concept of 'number' was associated more with a 'quantifier' than with a noun, form-wise, and meaning-wise with 'specific', resulting, therefore, in employing the plural morpheme predominantly for quantified nouns to encode the meaning of 'specificity'. From a target-oriented perspective, then, Geng's use of plurals was only partially accurate, for in the target language, English, plurals can also be applied to non-quantified nouns with the semantics being 'non-specific' (e.g. *Cats* are *cute*).

Similarly, in respect of definiteness marking, data gathered provide sufficient evidence indicating that Geng's L2 usage mirrors his L1 thinking for speaking. Specifically, as reported earlier, he demonstrated a tendency, on the translation tasks, to mark – or not mark – NPs as definite under conditions corresponding with the L1-intended meaning (see Table 7.6). Examples (29–31), pulled from Geng's naturalistic data, further illustrate the function of the L1 thinking for speaking in L2 production.

Example (29)
I'm looking for <u>the file</u> you send me.

Example (30)
They couldn't solve <u>the problem</u> at this moment.

Example (31)
I'll <u>park car</u> to some convenient place and <u>take train</u> home.

In all three instances, the use (or non-use) of the definite article 'the' fully corresponds to the L1 way of speaking. In Examples (29) and (30), 'the' transmits the L1 meaning of '这个' ('this'). Indeed, that Geng's use of the definite article 'the' patterns after the Chinese demonstrative

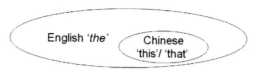

Figure 7.1 English 'the' versus Chinese 'this/that'

determiner is a contributing factor to his underuse of 'the' in his L2. In Geng's L1, Chinese, as noted earlier, definiteness or indefiniteness is generally not marked grammatically, but in a subset of cases, demonstrative determiners may be used to convey definiteness, especially when specificity is emphasized. This form–meaning–function mapping, however, appears far less frequently when compared with the definite article 'the' in English (Lardiere, 2007; Robertson, 2000). This is illustrated in Figure 7.1.

Likewise, Geng's use of the English indefinite article 'a/an' also appears to be driven by his L1 thinking for speaking. In Geng's L2, 'a/an' encodes the meaning of 'one', a numerical quantifier, rather than indefiniteness or lack of specificity, as shown in Examples (32–34) taken from Geng's naturalistic data.

Example (32)
If that's the case, then we need to <u>have a quick way</u> to reach them.

Example (33)
... you should <u>take rest</u> for another day.

Example (34)
I will then configure it <u>in a right way</u>.

Had Examples (32) and (34) been said in Chinese, '一个' or '一种' ('one') would have been used but would not have been used in Example (33).

According to Table 7.4, Geng's naturalistic use of the indefinite article 'a/an' was more accurate than that of the definite article 'the'. This finding, I contend, is accidental, for two reasons. First, in natural production the speaker or writer is guided largely by the discourse topic as well as by his/her choice of what to express and how to express it. Thus, it may have been that the topics and choices Geng had may have provided more opportunities to use 'a/an' for his intended meaning of 'one', which appeared target-like in some cases. Second, results from the elicited data have indicated that Geng had greater trouble with marking indefiniteness or non-specificity than definiteness or specificity, in line with the characteristics of his L1.

Judging from the above findings, little doubt remains that Geng's mind was still largely L1-relativized (Question 2). The persistent intra-learner variability, manifested as overuse, underuse and target-like use vis-à-vis the same grammatical form, suggests that conceptual restructuring had

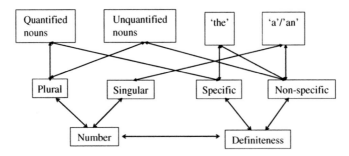

Figure 7.2 Form-meaning-concept mapping of plurals and articles in English

barely occurred for Geng. Figure 7.2 provides a glimpse of the complexity involved in fully acquiring English plurals and articles.

Figure 7.1 shows that the abstract concepts of 'number' and 'definiteness' (bottom tier) are separate as well as related (cf. Lardiere, 2007). Semantically they each are expressed as 'plural' and 'singular', on the one hand, and 'specific' and 'non-specific', on the other (middle tier). These meanings can then be encoded in a variety of forms between plurals and articles. For example, the meaning of plural can be expressed by both quantified and unquantified nouns. What is complicated is that multiple forms can encode the same meaning and, vice versa, multiple meanings can be expressed via one and the same form. Accordingly, full acquisition of articles and plurals entails not just mapping individual forms onto individual meanings, but rather, integrated mapping of a cohort of forms onto the same or different meanings and onto the same or different concepts. In a nutshell, full acquisition would not be possible without conceptual learning, or rather, conceptual *restructuring* in the case of L2 acquisition.

Findings from the present study indicate, however, that such a conceptual restructuring may not be possible, at least in Geng's case. The attested persistence of variable use of grammatical morphemes in Geng's naturalistic production, coupled with evidence from his performance on the error correction task suggesting that further exposure to TL input would be of little use, backs up a linguistic relativist thesis, which underlies the thinking-for-speaking hypothesis:

> The grammaticized categories that are most susceptible to [L1] influence have something important in common: they cannot be experienced directly in our perceptual, sensorimotor, and practical dealings with the world.
>
> ...
>
> Distinctions of aspect, **definiteness**, voice, and the like, are, *par excellence*, distinctions that can only be learned through language, and

have no other use except to be expressed in language ... Once our minds have been trained in talking particular points of view for the purpose of speaking, it is exceptionally difficult for us to be retrained. (Slobin, 1996a: 91; emphasis added)

Where did Geng fossilize, precisely?

To answer this question, let us look more closely at how English and Chinese differ in the linguistic category of definiteness. Table 7.7 illustrates the difference.

Jacobson (1959: 142) argues that 'the true difference between languages is not in what may or may not be expressed but in what must or must not be conveyed by the speakers'. Following this argument, the concepts of definiteness and indefiniteness may be expressed in both English and Chinese, but as Table 7.7 shows, the two languages differ in whether definiteness and indefiniteness must or must not be conveyed by their speakers: Whereas in English they must, in Chinese they are non-obligatory. Importantly, the obligatory (or non-obligatory) grammatical morphemes, as Slobin (1996a: 84) points out, 'may do more than simply direct attention-while-speaking to their semantic content. This direct attention may have consequences for what is said and unsaid in any particular language'. Relating this insight to the case subject in question, Geng's L2 grammaticization of definiteness and indefiniteness resembles more the L1 thinking-for-speaking pattern than that of the TL, and consequently, it is likely that his L2 production occasion misinterpretations from his native-speaking interlocutors in relation to what is said and what is unsaid. This, however, is an empirical question yet to be investigated.

From a target-oriented perspective, Geng appears to have learned how to mark definiteness, indefiniteness and number (form-wise), but, as a function of his deeply ingrained L1 thinking for speaking, has only partially acquired what to mark and, marginally, when to mark it. Figure 7.3 illustrates the areas of fossilization.

The present study has demonstrated that the *what* and *when* are the hardest to acquire, as it requires conceptual restructuring. The fact that the set of grammaticized distinctions (or lack thereof) of the abstract concepts

Table 7.7 Concept and grammaticization in English and Chinese

	Grammaticization	
Concept	*English*	*Chinese*
Indefiniteness	a/the/pl./zero	zero
Definiteness	the	zero (or occasionally, this/that or word order)

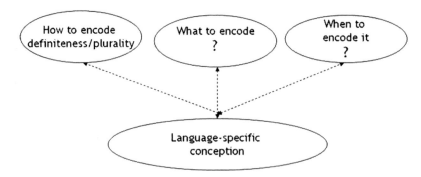

Figure 7.3 Geng's areas of fossilization in respect of number and definiteness marking

in the L1 has trained its speakers to attend to certain particular features of events while speaking (Slobin, 1996a) leaves little hope that such conceptual restructuring can ever be complete in L2 acquisition.

The thinking-for-speaking hypothesis appears to provide an adequate explanation not only for the persistence of the grammatical morpheme problem but also that of other seemingly unrelated problems in Geng's L2. In the longitudinal set of naturalistic data spanning 12 years (1995–2007), Geng was frequently found to produce utterances such as Examples (35–39).

Example (35)
I'm not sure if we could shut down <u>all machines</u> for <u>long time</u> as you suggested, it's our machine. Do you have <u>other way</u> to test it?

Example (36)
I wish you <u>a good luck</u> in job hunting!

Example (37)
This <u>will take care of</u> this week.

Example (38)
There <u>is some preparation need to</u> be done ...

Example (39)
We find a number of lists, <u>could show</u> us this weekend.

Examples (35–39) appear to speak to a disparate set of grammatical problems that are, nonetheless, related in the current perspective: They were driven by a common underlying force, namely, L1 thinking for speaking. Again, it is the way one would say it in Chinese, so to speak, that gave rise to these expressions.[8]

Conclusion

The study reported in this chapter tackles a persistent and pervasive learnability problem in L2 acquisition, namely, grammatical morpheme inadequacy. From a linguistic relativism perspective, the study zeroed in on definiteness and plural marking in the longitudinal samples of naturalistic L2 English writing by one adult, male native speaker of Chinese, who had had ample exposure to the target language, adequate motivation to learn and sufficient opportunity to practice. The analysis was augmented by data elicited from the case subject via six specially designed tasks. Results converged in showing that the subject's use of articles (definite and indefinite) and plurals patterned largely after his L1 thinking for speaking and that in spite of his long-term experience with the target language, the subject's mind largely remained L1-relativized. The data manifest, *par excellence*, fossilized intra-learner variability, and the understanding of this phenomenon has generally been shallow and fragmentary. Among other things, overuse, target-like use and underuse *concurrently* transpired and persisted in the subject's use of the grammatical forms in question. Lack of conceptual restructuring is ascribed to as a leading cause of the fossilized variability. To invoke Levelt's (1989) speech production model, *the problem is rooted in the Conceptualizer and its interface with the Formulator*.

Findings from the study, by virtue of their source being confined to one case subject, are necessarily of limited generalizability, from a research standpoint. They, nevertheless, derive from an in-depth qualitative analysis, and hence are trustworthy, with 'analytic generalization' (Dörnyei, 2007; Duff, 2008). In view of the well-established, dual fact that learners differ from one another and that fossilization is fundamentally an idiosyncratic process (Han, 2004; Selinker, 1992), I would call for more longitudinal case studies, not so much to validate the specific findings reported here but the theory and methodology employed in the current study. As shown, the thinking-for-speaking hypothesis provides a coherent account of what appears, from a target-oriented perspective, to be random variations and differential command of the target language forms. Also shown in the present study is that naturalistic data alone, albeit longitudinal, are insufficient to motivate a robust understanding of the learnability problem unless supplemented by focused data elicited via contrived tasks. Additionally, adopting an analytic approach focusing on a cohort of forms, as opposed to a synthetic approach that isolates forms, is critical to unveiling the nature of the grammatical morpheme problem.

Finally, for the present line of inquiry, a future direction[9] would be to probe into effects of the L1 thinking for speaking for L2 perception and comprehension (cf. Cadierno, this volume). Until we have sufficient evidence for both production and comprehension, our understanding will remain incomplete of the impact of an L1-relativized mind on the L2 process and outcome.

Acknowledgements

This study was reported at the linguistic relativity colloquium at the AAAL 2007 conference. I am grateful for the feedback from Scott Jarvis and Diane Larsen-Freeman. Terence Odlin and Teresa Cadierno have read earlier versions of this chapter and provided perceptive and constructive comments. None of these individuals are responsible for any errors that remain.

Notes

1. Communicative value refers to the relative weight of a linguistic form to the meaning of a sentence in which the form appears.
2. The 4-M model was originally proposed by Myers-Scotton and Jake (2001), which in turn was premised on Levelt's (1989) speech production model. Levelt distinguishes three levels of speech production, the conceptualizer, the formulator and the articulator.
3. On cognitive linguistic accounts, all forms or constructions are meaningful.
4. Traditional research on linguistic relativity focuses on the influence of language on non-linguistic cognition, the goal being to establish 'an independent cognitive interpretation of reality' (Lucy, 2000: xii). Slobin argues that 'research on linguistic relativity is incomplete without attention to the cognitive processes that are brought to bear, *online*, in the course of using language' (2003: 158).
5. Exceptions do exist for pragmatic reasons (see note 6 in Han, 2008).
6. In Chinese, one utterance may contain several sentences, for example:
   纽约的房子很贵，只有中产阶级的人买得起，我想等我 攒够了钱后再开始买房子。
   (Houses in New York are expensive. Only middle-class people can afford them. I'd like to wait until I have saved enough money before I begin to shop for one.)
7. The use of plurals in non-obligatory contexts.
8. Note that this claim is made in reference to resilient or long-stabilized interlanguage features only, hence with no presumption that all grammatical transfer is conceptual transfer.
9. Odlin (personal communication, November 2008) suggested that it would also be interesting to explore if grammatical marking of number and definiteness have any non-linguistic cognitive effects. Based on Lucy's (1992b) study of speakers of Yucatec and given the similarity between Chinese and Yucatec at least in terms of number marking, it is reasonable to hypothesize, I think, that the grammatical marking of number in Chinese *can* have non-linguistic cognitive effects and that such effects will persist, just like the linguistic cognitive effects shown in the present study, perhaps with the two sets of effects being correlated.

Chapter 8

Conclusion: On the Interdependence of Conceptual Transfer and Relativity Studies

TERENCE ODLIN

Definitions

Although notions such as linguistic relativity, conceptual transfer and language transfer have prompted many discussions, these notions are at one level easy to define. Linguistic relativity concerns the putative influence of language on cognition, especially the influence of linguistic structures not common to all languages. Language transfer is the influence of one language on another and, in cases of second language acquisition (SLA), is most typically the influence of a native language on a new language to be acquired. Conceptual transfer is a more specific type of crosslinguistic influence where linguistic relativity is also involved. These thumbnail definitions do not, of course, take into account the complexity of the issues entailed, but they indicate demarcations between transfer and relativity, on the one hand, and between language transfer and conceptual transfer.

The demarcation between relativity and transfer might seem surprising to anyone who takes it as self-evident that the two notions are indeed distinct. However, any inquiry into relativity or conceptual transfer needs to avoid the circularity of claiming that all relativity is transfer (or vice versa). The reasoning of such claims might have it that any relativity effect involves linguistic influence or that any linguistic influence is also cognitive. While it is true that any relativity must involve language and while it is also true that language is one manifestation of cognition, careful analyses of conceptual transfer (e.g. Jarvis & Pavlenko, 2008) inevitably assume some distinction between language and cognition. In other words, it proves necessary to conceive of relativity as a phenomenon that involves influence on something *beyond* language. One leading investigator (Lucy, 1992a) has emphasized the danger of ignoring the nonlinguistic dimension and has criticized much of the earlier anthropological work on relativity since 'it did not provide clear evidence for a nonlinguistic [i.e. cognitive] correlate with grammatical patterns' (Lucy, 1992a: 259). For SLA researchers, the most important implication of the tripartite division between relativity, transfer and conceptual transfer is that not everything counting as language transfer necessarily counts as evidence of relativity or conceptual transfer. The relation between transfer and conceptual transfer will be discussed further on in this chapter, but some implications of the cognition/language distinction need attention first.

There are good reasons to view cognition as prior to language. Most significant is the somewhat delayed emergence of language in child development: infants in their first few months of life have virtually no abilities to use or understand language, yet various cognitive capacities have been identified in decades of work on developmental psychology from Jean Piaget to Dan Slobin. Although most of the references to Slobin in the current volume cite his recent work on what he has termed 'thinking for speaking', one of his best-known earlier analyses is titled 'Cognitive Prerequisites for the Development of Grammar' (1973). In one sense his position on relativity is a natural extension of such cognitivist research although with increasing emphasis on the importance of language-specific structures that can affect cognitive development in the course of child language acquisition. Some of the assumptions of another relativistic researcher, Bowerman (1996b), likewise suggest that certain aspects of cognitive development unfold somewhat independently of language, where she thus views as credible, for instance, the results obtained by Johnston and Slobin (1979) on a common developmental order in locative expressions in four typologically different languages, an order that Johnston and Slobin deem a reflection of successive stages of cognitive development. In her work and in Slobin's there is no contradiction between taking relativity seriously and positing cognitive characteristics that may be prior to language or independent of it; as Lucy (1992a: 95) observes, researchers can look at typological variation in language in different yet complementary ways. They can emphasize common elements underlying structures that are different, or they can emphasize crosslinguistic diversity and investigate possible cognitive effects.

Universals, Typology and Contrastive Analysis

SLA researchers will benefit from adopting the view that typology can help reconcile the seeming opposition between relativity and universals. In fact, there is nothing new in seeing the two as reconcilable; for instance, one relativist from a century ago wrote, 'the occurrence of the most fundamental grammatical concepts in all languages must be considered proof of the unity of fundamental psychological processes' (Boas, 1911/1966: 67).

This universalist stance does not deny the significance of typological variation (which Boas himself stressed) or the possible effects of such variation on language processing. Indeed, no crosslinguistic grammatical comparison seems feasible without assuming some semantic or conceptual similarity. This necessity is evident in a comparative grid of noun phrase (NP) structures given by Lucy (1992b: 78) in an empirical study of relativity. Although his study focuses on the differences between English and Yucatec Maya, the grid also provides information on three other languages: Chinese, Tarascan and Hopi. Interestingly, Lucy uses the term *contrastive analysis* (1992b: 18) to refer to such comparisons. Although his study does not involve SLA, the implications of his position are also important for work on language transfer and conceptual transfer.

In the grid that Lucy provides, Yucatec and Chinese are viewed as using the same grammatical means to code pluralization. In effect, where English obligatorily uses the contrast between singular and plural marking in denoting nouns that are either [+animate] (e.g. *cats* and *humans*) or [−animate, +discrete] (e.g. *sticks* and *stones*), but not nouns that are [−animate, −discrete] (thus, the ungrammaticality of **informations*), Chinese and Yucatec do not make any obligatory coding distinctions (elsewhere in his study, Lucy does note that Yucatec allows for some non-obligatory pluralization patterns). Such structural contrasts have naturally invited the question of whether there are any cognitive differences in how speakers of different languages process information such as animacy. Lucy's empirical study found strong support for a relativistic interpretation. In various tasks such as picture description, Yucatec and English speakers differed significantly in how they described and what they remembered about the pictures. Given the similarity of the Yucatec and Chinese systems in terms of the features in Lucy's grid, it seems likely that an empirical study would yield similar results.

The contrasts between NPs in Chinese and English do not end with singular/plural distinctions, of course, nor do the possibilities for conceptual transfer involving other contrasts. In Chapter 7, Han looks at the use of both plurals and articles in the writing of a Chinese speaker called Geng. She identifies a very clear difference in Geng's plural marking, where he more frequently uses plural endings in quantified NPs (versus unquantified), and this pattern persisted over a four-year period (the term *quantified* as used by Han refers solely to explicit numerical determiners). Han attributes this greater success with quantified NPs to the influence of the classifier system of Geng's native language. In Chinese it is not sufficient to use a numeral and a noun such as in English *two books* or *two tickets*; also needed are classifiers that subcategorize NPs according to the semantic type of the head noun where, for instance, the classifier *ben3* is needed for *liang3 ben3 shu1*, in which the final word is the head noun (books) and the first is the numeral (with the Arabic numerals specifying tones).

A different classifier, *zhang1*, is required, however, for another semantic category as seen in *liang3 zhang1 piao4* (two tickets).

One fact that Han calls 'canonical' is the restriction of classifiers where they do not occur in all Chinese NPs. Han focuses on quantified NPs, which require such classifiers, but there is also a relevant generalization of Li and Thompson (1987: 823) that referential NPs take classifiers while non-referential NPs do not, so that generic and other non-specific NPs regularly appear without classifiers. In the results of Han's translation tests, the contrast between referential and non-referential NPs in Chinese appears relevant to the use of articles as well as plurals in English where, for instance, Geng translated one Chinese sentence as *We ate apple at noon* instead of as either *We ate apples at noon* or *We ate an apple at noon*. The context that Geng apparently assumed during his translation is non-specific, given the absence of a classifier in the Chinese original. However, such cases point to the difficulties of teasing apart the possible effects of not only categories in the L1 but also those in the L2, and in English these involve, of course, categories such as definiteness/indefiniteness and noun countability, among others. The fact that more often than not Geng did manage to successfully use both definite and indefinite articles suggests that he has come to terms with some – though not all – of the challenges of the new system of English, as does his modest improvement in overall article use in the four-year interval. If relativistic effects of the Chinese classifier system impede Geng's progress, as Han plausibly argues, they at least do not keep him at the very early stages of mastery of English articles evident in a study of article use by Finnish speakers (Jarvis, 2002), many of whom had taken English for over five years.

Fossilization and Dynamic Language Systems

The change that Geng shows in his use of articles and plurals is, as noted, only a modest improvement. The fact that he still has a long way to go for complete control of these structures supports Han's argument that his English has fossilized in these areas (cf. Han & Odlin, 2006: 11–12). On the other hand, the fact that he does show some improvement makes another interpretation possible, namely, that the grammar of Chinese may never be an absolute bar to mastery of English but rather a strong influence that can eventually be overcome. The longitudinal approach that Han uses to investigate fossilization can help immensely to understand what does or does not change (cf. Han, 2004; Long, 2003). Especially significant would be evidence in future data collection of either further progress in Geng's use of articles and plurals or a lack thereof, and obviously, comparable longitudinal studies of other individuals are likewise desirable.

In Chapter 3, Stam explores in yet other ways the problem of change or lack thereof not only in an individual's L2 but also in the L1. One conclusion she reaches is that 'L2 thinking for speaking is not static'. However, she also finds that 'not all aspects of thinking for speaking change equally', and this conclusion opens up the difficult but fascinating question of what does and does not change. In her study of an L1 speaker of Spanish using L2 English, Stam found complex variation where, for instance, the expression of path in English differed in data collected in 2006 from data collected in 1997, while the expression of manner did not. In contrast, the individual's L1 Spanish showed no change in either path or manner. Even so, the L1 as well as the L2 did show changes in gestural patterns indicating path even when there was no change in manner gestures in either language.

Stam's findings about L1 influence on L2 spatial expressions are buttressed by Cadierno's investigation (Chapter 1), in which she found different expressions of motion in L2 Danish that varied largely in the motion patterns seen in different L1 data sets for Russian, German and Spanish. Both in comparing diverse L1 groups and in investigating the performance of many individuals, Cadierno provides further support for the thinking-for-speaking interpretation of conceptual transfer in earlier work (e.g. Cadierno, 2008). Although the studies of Stam and Cadierno share certain theoretical perspectives, some differences are also notable, as where Stam's research also considers the issue of bidirectional transfer (cf. Pavlenko & Jarvis, 2002) and also the coordination of spoken language with gestures (cf. Gullberg, 2008). How much the L2 can change toward target norms lies at the heart of the problem of fossilization, but no less interesting is the question of how much the L1 can change as a result of L2 influence (e.g. Cook, 2002). Pavlenko and Jarvis have emphasized the problematic character of the notion of an L1 or L2 'endstate', a common assumption of much research on putative Universal Grammar (e.g. White, 2003: 35). If, contrary to UG assumptions, the L1 can change as a result of L2 influence, even the native language has some of the unstable – or dynamic – character sometimes viewed as unique to interlanguage competence. Stam's conclusion that not all changes are equal certainly invites further work on the relative stability of the L1 in comparison with L2, but the dynamic nature of both should be assumed as a starting point for research.

Along with reality of the L1 and L2 both being dynamic systems, the question of fossilization shows further complications because it is not clear how much of a difference improved second language instruction can make for ultimate attainment. Slobin (1993, 1996) and Ellis (2008) have viewed the L1 as a source of too much 'entrenchment' (to use Ellis' term) to allow for full attainment of the new language. This pessimism has a long intellectual history where, for instance, the 19th century philosopher Humboldt (1836/1988) likewise took a skeptical stance. Nevertheless, another well-known relativist, Whorf (1956), had a more positive outlook, especially with regard to what linguistics could do to enhance language teaching (Odlin, 2005, 2008a). Two recent studies of difficult areas of L2 grammar indicate that with a better theoretical approach, structures such as the French partitive and English modals are not so intractable as they have often seemed to learners and teachers (Achard, 2008; Tyler, 2008). To the extent that further work achieves similar results, such research chips away at the notion of any insurmountable entrenchment. Yet, whether the pessimists or optimists ultimately win the debate, a very long research program seems unavoidable.

Meanings and Concepts

Most of the chapters in this volume investigate acquisition patterns involving grammatical structures whose meaning changes according to certain formal or functional conditions. In Hasko's study (Chapter 2), for instance, the subtle semantic contrast between unidirectional and bidirectional verbs in Russian is shown to be quite difficult for native speakers of English. Hasko characterizes unidirectional verbs as those denoting motion events that continuously 'flow' in one direction at a particular moment, whereas bidirectional verbs lack at least some of that information. Using a story narration task, Hasko found that native speakers of Russian were especially likely to employ unidirectional verbs in parts of the story that involved a chase, where either the pursuers or the pursued moved in ways denoted by such verbs. The English speakers, in contrast, proved inconsistent at best in making the unidirectional/bidirectional distinction. For example, while some learners correctly used the unidirectional form underlined in *Bednaia soboka bezhit* ((The) poor dog is running), some erroneously used a bidirectional form as in *Olen' begnet* ((The) deer is running). It might seem to some readers that verb aspect is involved in such directionality contrasts, but Hasko indicates that both Russian forms are imperfective (and hence the translation of both into English as present progressives). Directionality is, rather, an additional semantic contrast found in the Russian verb system, with no grammatical pattern in English that can facilitate positive transfer. Such a facilitating influence might be evident in some future study of learners of Russian with a different L1 such as Polish, another Slavic language and one that has so-called determinative verbs that seem similar to the unidirectional ones of Russian. In any case, the lack of a close grammatical correspondence between English and Russian seems to be the source of the difficulty studied by Hasko.

The directionality contrast is only one of many examples that could be cited as areas of potential difficulty for learners. Another example is the distinction between the so-called subject and topic particles of Japanese, which prove to be quite difficult for speakers of English, yet are not so hard for speakers of Korean, which has a similar system (Nakahama, 2003). Still another example is the distinction between two verbs in Spanish, *ser* and *estar*, which are both translatable as *be* (and its conjugated forms) and which are quite problematic for speakers of English (Whitley, 2002). In such cases, learners must come to terms with contrasts involving both form and meaning. Teachers of English can likewise point to similar problems such as the well-known difficulty of the *in/on* prepositional distinction (e.g. Arabski, 1979, Coventry *et al.*, this volume). In this case as well as in the *ser/estar* distinction – and in many others as well – the boundary between lexis and grammar is fuzzy (cf. Heine *et al.*, 1991); indeed, the lexical split between English *know* and Spanish *saber/conocer* shows a difficulty similar to the *ser/estar* split even though the latter is sometimes considered a grammatical problem and the former a lexical problem.

In such cases of semantic disparity between structures in two languages, what Stringer calls 'lexical relativity' (Chapter 5), the consequences of the disparity for acquisition are often significant, and learners must attend to new distinctions, which in many cases play a major systemic role in the new language. Not so clear, however, is whether those difficulties always qualify as cases of negative conceptual transfer. In fact, the findings of the study by Coventry *et al.* (Chapter 4) indicate that the *in/on* contrast in English does not lead to any significantly different results in picture recognition when the performance of English speakers is compared with that of speakers of Spanish, a language with one word (*en*) denoting most of the meanings coded by the two distinct prepositions in English. Coventry *et al.*, do not see their results as falsifying the large body of research indicating effects of thinking for speaking, but they plausibly argue that those effects are task-dependent, with factors such as time and type of picture being potential influences on the experimental results. Their findings are also consistent with earlier work that has not yielded evidence of linguistic relativity (e.g. Au, 1983; Maratsos *et al.*, 2000). As the body of empirical research grows, the findings that support or do not support relativity interpretations will probably lead to an ever more complex mosaic of results raising questions about the exact circumstances under which language may have significant effects on cognition. If so, the findings will help clarify where conceptual transfer begins and ends.

Along with the problem of task dependence, another challenge for researchers will be to understand better just what *conceptual* may or may not mean. While the definition of relativity as the influence of language on cognition is straightforward, as is the definition of conceptual transfer, no one should assume that cognition itself is thoroughly understood. In psychology there have been several competing approaches on how to characterize concepts (Hampton, 1997). Moreover, what now often goes by the name *cognitive science* raises still more questions and many of the questions have engaged thinkers over a long span of centuries. This observation does not deny the importance of recent work, and indeed much of it often seeks empirical support to narrow the range of controversies that have exercised countless philosophers from antiquity to the present. Lakoff and Johnson (1999: 22), for instance, have argued that 'human concepts are not just reflections of an external reality, but that they are crucially shaped by our bodies and brains, especially by our sensorimotor system'. In their detailed discussion, they seek to synthesize work on neuroscience, linguistics, psychology, philosophy and other fields, and among the phenomena they discuss are color and spatial concepts. In fact, their treatment of the latter is consistent with thinking-for-speaking approaches. Lakoff and Johnson stress the importance of looking, where possible, for empirical verification of cognitive science theories, and a recent study by Dodge and Lakoff (2005) presents evidence consistent with the typological distinctions that Cadierno and others have used in investigating conceptual transfer in spatial cognition. The evidence that Dodge and Lakoff review comes from neurolinguistics and computer science as well as from studies in typology and cognitive linguistics, and while they see many unresolved issues in the findings, they suggest that 'these path- and manner-related schemas may each be computed by the neural circuitry of different functional brain networks' (Dodge & Lakoff, 2005: 83).

Even while many challenges arise for investigations of conceptual domains such as space and color, these domains seem uncontroversial as sites for the study of the relation between language and cognition in SLA. Nevertheless, there remain other domains that may involve conceptual transfer but which are problematic as to their exact place in a fully verified account of cognition. One such domain is discourse processing. In Chapter 6, Ekiert sees conceptual transfer at work in how articles are supplied or omitted in the English of L1 Polish speakers. In her analysis of the interlanguage of three individuals, articles proved to be more frequent in NPs having an especially important role in the overall narrative in the discourse tasks used in the investigation. In Polish there are no articles, whereas in English articles prove to be quite important, primarily serving as a way to mark definiteness. While a very superficial contrastive analysis might claim definiteness to be a semantic category absent in Polish, Ekiert makes clear that articles are not the only structures realizing definiteness, and Polish has, like English, other structures functioning thus (for example, demonstratives and possessives), which play a major systemic role in structuring narratives. When learners attempt to construct discourse in English, Ekiert appears to suggest that they must make decisions at the conceptual level about the identifiability of referents, and she sees Polish grammar as an important influence on that decision-making. Two questions that inevitably arise for this interesting analysis are, first, exactly how the decision-making process in such cases interacts with Polish and, second, whether the process itself should be considered as the 'concept' in conceptual transfer. Full answers to both of these questions are naturally beyond the scope of Ekiert's study, and indeed they would require much more work both within and outside of SLA.

Discourse processing is just one of the cognitive domains requiring further study; another is emotion, which gets intermittent attention in cognitive linguistics. Even while speakers and listeners process discourse in terms of spatial constructions, personal reference, times of events and so on, they often have feelings intertwined with such information, and the affective stances they take can be manifest in language in myriad ways (Ochs & Schieffelin, 1989). Affective expression might seem to be a concern only for those who study interjections such as *Gosh!* or *Wow!*, or vocabulary such as *hope* and *fear*, or metaphoric uses such as *pain* or *heat*, but affect permeates the structure of language including many areas of syntax. For example, focus constructions in many languages play important roles in expressing certain affective stances that lead to strengthening an assertion, and so syntactic patterns themselves can serve as intensifiers (Irvine, 1990; Odlin, 2008b). One characteristic of focus constructions that makes them especially interesting is that they are, to some extent, language-specific. Even languages as historically related as German and English vary considerably in how focus is used as seen in studies of translation as well as SLA (cf. Caillies, 2006; Doherty, 2001). It thus may be wondered if language-specific affective constructions are linked to other language-specific cognitive domains. Some SLA analysis do take that position in general terms (e.g. Jarvis & Pavlenko, 2008), but empirically detailing how areas like focus constructions fit the theory remains to be done.

The first part of this chapter argued for the need to distinguish language from cognition. By the logic of that distinction, it is also necessary to differentiate meanings from concepts. Not all linguists, psychologists or philosophers are willing to make that distinction, however, and in many studies concepts do not differ from meanings. Levinson (1997) cites thinkers taking different sides on the question: 'lumpers', to use his term, conflate meanings and concepts, whereas 'splitters' do not. Levinson himself is a splitter, and while space does not permit a thorough summary of all the reasons he gives to prefer splitting, one should be considered. As he points out, sentences such as *Tomorrow I leave here* pose a serious problem for anyone who simply equates the meaning of a sentence with the thought it expresses. Every word in the sentence can change the 'thought' according to when it is uttered (Is *tomorrow* January 22nd or March 19th?), who utters it (Is *I* Emily Dickinson or Albert Einstein?), and so on. So-called indexical words such as *tomorrow* and *I* have conventional meanings relatively independent of particular concepts (e.g. January 22nd or March 19th). Levinson does acknowledge that meanings and concepts must be related in some fashion, but if his view is essentially correct, a major challenge for cognitive science will be to detail all the ways in which meanings and concepts interact. One key part of this challenge is to understand what has often been called the meaning of meaning (e.g. Lyons, 1977; Ogden & Richards, 1923). While the study of meaning is often equated with semantics both in everyday speech and in many linguistic analyses, a satisfactory account must also include pragmatics. Indeed cognitive linguists in SLA as well as in other fields are increasingly aware of the interconnections between pragmatics and syntax and the implications for acquisition (cf. Tomasello, 1998; Tyler, 2008). As with the multiple areas of cognition such as affect and discourse processing, there exist many domains in semantics and pragmatics that require close study if the relation between meanings and concepts is to be well understood.

From the likelihood that meanings and concepts are distinct (although related), it follows that investigations of transfer have not necessarily identified conceptual transfer simply from marshalling evidence of semantic or pragmatic influences. Not all of what counts as meaning transfer (semantic or pragmatic) will inevitably count also as conceptual transfer. In Poland an error said to arise frequently among Poles fluent in English appears in the faulty semantics of *We were at the theater last night with my brother* when the *we* has a singular, not a plural, first-person reference (Gotteri & Michalak-Gray, 1997: 180–181). Semantic errors such as this one arise from the influence of a syntactic pattern in Polish (and other Slavic languages) known as the comitative, an example of which can be found in other discussions (Odlin, 2005, 2008a). Sentences such as *We were at the theater last night with my brother* do illustrate syntactic, semantic and pragmatic transfer, but an argument for conceptual transfer is highly dubious. If the transfer of meanings were to be equated with the transfer of concepts, one would have to argue that the use of the comitative in English reflects some conceptual difficulty involving singular and plural number among speakers of Polish and other Slavic languages (who, from what Slavic linguists have told me, sometimes make similar errors). If such a broad interpretation of conceptual transfer will not suffice, it seems best to posit an inclusion relation where all conceptual transfer is also meaning transfer but where not all meaning transfer is conceptual transfer. Thus conceptual transfer should be seen as a subset of meaning transfer.

The Diversity of Approaches to Relativity

Although the subset relation posited here seems necessary, it does not specify exactly what might be evidence for conceptual transfer. The studies of thinking for speaking in this volume follow the very productive approach to relativity advanced by Slobin and others, but other topics such as thinking for listening likewise merit further research (Ellis, 2008). Moreover, the approach taken by Lucy discussed earlier in this chapter represents another promising path, as does the research program of Levinson and colleagues on spatial orientation (Levinson, 2003). While all are 'relativist' in some sense, these diverse approaches show somewhat different theoretical assumptions, different structures focused on and different research methods. Lucy, for example, has stressed the special status of grammar, since many grammatical structures are frequent and may instantiate what Whorf called 'habitual thought' or what Ellis has termed 'entrenchment'. Lucy's emphasis on grammar as well as any similar approach must assume the truth of at least the general view of cognitive linguists such as Langacker (2008: 67) 'that grammar subserves meaning rather than being an end in itself'. That view runs counter to the formalist assumptions seen in some of the polemics on Universal Grammar (e.g. Gregg, 1989), but empirical support for the cognitivist view is steadily growing.

Not only morphology or syntax may prove important domains to study. The investigations by Levinson and others have focused on lexical patterning in the construal of space among speakers of several typologically different languages. Many of those languages have small numbers of speakers, however, and other problems might also make conceptual transfer research difficult to undertake. Even so, studies of pidgins and other varieties that often arise in contact even among small populations suggest that such SLA research on grammar and lexis is by no means impossible (e.g. Koch, 2000). The lexicon is sometimes viewed as the site *par excellence* for the study of relativity, although folk beliefs about the alleged dozens of words for snow in Eskimo have contributed to the abiding skepticism of many linguists about relativity – indeed, Eskimo does *not* abound in snow terms (Pullum, 1991). Nevertheless, some research on the cognitive effects of lexis is not easily dismissed, as seen in work by Loftus and Palmer (1974), which indicated that different verbs such as *hit* or *crash* could induce different memories of a scene in a film showing a car striking a wall, in terms of participants' judgments about the speed of the car. Some skeptics such as Pinker (1994) have tried to discount such evidence, but it does seem consistent with the findings about memory that Lucy obtained in his study of grammatical patterns. The fact that the border between lexis and grammar is often hazy or even nonexistent (as several of the chapters in this volume suggest) makes it all the more desirable to look at the interaction of the two domains as various chapters in this volume do (e.g. Cadierno; Hasko), and future study seems likely to provide further evidence of thinking for speaking and other effects.

Work on relativity and work on conceptual transfer are interdependent, and the symbiosis of the two fields will probably increase in the coming years. Along with the experimental refinements, there is likewise a growing awareness of the complexity of the issues, including the questions of how to determine where conceptual transfer begins and ends and just what cognition itself is. Consistent findings from current studies to ones in the future will be one measure of progress, and it seems reasonable to expect that further work in cognitive linguistics can contribute more not only to the study of transfer and relativity but also to helping promote instruction that can minimize whatever entrenchment in SLA arises from crosslinguistic differences in semantics and pragmatics and from differences in patterns of mapping from form to meaning. The success (or lack thereof) of such improved instruction will be theoretically as well as practically significant since it can tell us much about how adaptable to change language and cognition can be.

References

Abbott, B. (2005) Definiteness and indefiniteness. In L. Horn and G. Ward (eds) *The Handbook of Pragmatics* (pp. 122–149). Oxford: Blackwell.

Achard, M. (2008) Teaching construal: Cognitive pedagogical grammar. In P. Robinson and N. Ellis (eds) *Handbook of Cognitive Linguistics and Second Language Acquisition* (pp. 432–455). New York: Routledge.

Adjemian, C. (1983) The transferability of lexical properties. In S. Gass and L. Selinker (eds) *Language Transfer in Language Learning* (pp. 250–268). Rowley, MA: Newbury House.

Aitchison, J. (1994) *Words in the Mind. An Introduction to the Mental Lexicon* (2nd edn). Oxford: Blackwell.

Andersen, R. (1983) Transfer to somewhere. In S. Gass and L. Selinker (eds) *Language Transfer in Language Learning* (pp. 177–201). Rowley, MA: Newbury House.

Apreszjan, J.D. and Pàll, E. (1982) *Orosz ige–magyar ige* [*Russian Verb–Hungarian Verb*]. Budapest: Tankönyvkiadó.

Arabski, J. (1979) *Errors as Indications of the Development of Interlanguage*. Katowice: University of Silesia.

Aske, J. (1989) Path predicates in English and Spanish: A closer look. *Proceedings of the 15th Annual Meeting of the Berkeley Linguistics Society* (pp. 1–14). Berkeley, CA: Berkeley Linguistics Society.

Athanasopoulos, P. (2006) Effects of the grammatical representation of number on cognition in bilinguals. *Bilingualism: Language and Cognition* 9, 89–96.

Athanasopoulos, P. (2007, April) The role of proficiency, age of acquisition, and cultural immersion on the changing cognitive state of the L2 learner. Paper presented at the American Association of Applied Linguistics Conference, Costa Mesa, CA.

Au, T. (1983) Chinese and English counterfactuals: The Sapir–Whorf hypothesis revisited. *Cognition* 15, 155–187.

Baker, M.C. (1988) *Incorporation: A Theory of Grammatical Function Changing*. Chicago, IL: University of Chicago Press.

Bardovi-Harlig, K. (1987) Markedness and salience in second-language acquisition. *Language Learning* 37 (3), 385–407.

Bardovi-Harlig, K. (2000) *Tense and Aspect in Second Language Acquisition: Form, Meaning and Use*. Oxford: Blackwell.

Berman, R.A. and Slobin, D.I. (1994) *Relating Events in Narrative: A Crosslinguistic Developmental Study*. Hillsdale, NJ: Lawrence Erlbaum Associates.

Bialystok, E. and Sharwood Smith, M. (1985) Interlanguage is not a state of mind: An evaluation of the construct for second-language acquisition. *Applied Linguistics* 6, 101–117.

Bickerton, D. (1981) *Roots of Language*. Ann Arbor, MI: Karoma Publishers.

Bley-Vroman, R. (1983) The comparative fallacy in interlanguage studies: The case of systematicity. *Language Learning* 33, 1–17.

Bley-Vroman, R. and Joo, H-R. (2001) The acquisition and interpretation of English locative constructions by native speakers of Korean. *Studies in Second Language Acquisition* 23, 207–219.

Bloom, P. (2000) *How Children Learn the Meanings of Words*. Cambridge, MA: MIT Press.

Boas, F. (1911/1966) *Introduction to Handbook of American Indian Languages*. Lincoln: University of Nebraska Press.

Boroditsky, L. (2001) Does language shape thought? Mandarin and English speakers' conceptions of time. *Cognitive Psychology* 3 (1), 1–22.

Bosque, I. and Demonte, V. (1999) *Gramática Descriptiva de la Lengua Española*. Madrid: Espasa.

Bowerman, M. (1981) The child's expression of meaning: Expanding relationships among lexicon, syntax and morphology. In H. Winitz (ed.) *Native Language and Foreign Language Acquisition* (pp. 172–189). New York: New York Academy of Science.

Bowerman, M. (1982) Reorganizational processes in lexical and syntactic development. In E. Wanner and L.R. Gleitman (eds) *Language Acquisition: The State of the Art* (pp. 319–345). Cambridge: Cambridge University Press.

Bowerman, M. (1996a) Learning how to structure space for language: A crosslinguistic perspective. In P. Bloom, M.A. Peterson, L. Nadel, and M.F. Garrett (eds) *Language and Space* (pp. 385–436). Cambridge, MA: MIT Press.

Bowerman, M. (1996b) The origins of children's spatial semantic categories: Cognitive vs linguistic determinants. In J.J. Gumperz and S.C. Levinson (eds) *Rethinking Linguistic Relativity* (pp. 145–176). Cambridge: Cambridge University Press.

Bowerman, M. and Choi, S. (2001) Shaping meanings for language: Universal and language-specific in the acquisition of spatial semantic categories. In M. Bowerman and S.C. Levinson (eds) *Language Acquisition and Conceptual Development* (pp. 475–511). Cambridge: Cambridge University Press.

Bowerman, M. and Levinson, S. (eds) (2001) *Language Acquisition and Conceptual Development*. Cambridge: Cambridge University Press.

Brown, A. (2007) Crosslinguistic influence in first and second languages convergence in speech and gesture. Unpublished PhD dissertation, Graduate School of Arts and Sciences, Boston University.

Brown, A. and Gullberg, M. (2008) Bidirectional crosslinguistic influence in L1-L2 encoding of manner in speech and gesture: A study of Japanese speakers of English. *Studies in Second Language Acquisition* 30 (2), 225–251.

Brown, R. (1973) *A First Language*. Cambridge, MA: Harvard University Press.

Butler, Y. (2002) Second language learners' theories on the use of English article: An analysis of the metalinguistic knowledge used by Japanese students in acquiring the English article system. *Studies in Second Language Acquisition* 24, 451–480.

Butt, J. and Benjamin, C. (2000) *A New Reference Grammar of Modern Spanish*. London: Edward Arnold.

Cadierno, T. (2004) Expressing motion events in a second language: A cognitive typological perspective. In M. Achard and S. Niemeier (eds) *Cognitive Linguistics, Second Language Acquisition, and Foreign Language Teaching* (pp. 13–49). Berlin: Mouton de Gruyter.

Cadierno, T. (2007, April) Thinking-for-speaking in a foreign language: On the expression of motion events. Paper presented at the American Association of Applied Linguistics Conference, Costa Mesa, CA.

Cadierno, T. (2008) Learning to talk about motion in a foreign language. In P. Robinson and N.C. Ellis (eds) *Handbook of Cognitive Linguistics and Second Language Acquisition* (pp. 239–275). New York/London: Routledge.

Cadierno, T. and Lund, K. (2004) Cognitive linguistics and second language acquisition: Motion events in a typological framework. In B. VanPatten, J. Williams, S. Rott and M. Overstreet (eds) *Form-Meaning Connections in Second Language Acquisition* (pp. 139–154). Mahwah, NJ: Lawrence Erlbaum Associates, Publishers.

Cadierno, T. and Ruiz, L. (2006) Motion events in Spanish L2 acquisition. *Annual Review of Cognitive Linguistics* 4, 183–216.

Caillies, M. (2006) Information highlighting and the use of focusing devices in advanced German learner English. Unpublished PhD dissertation, University of Marburg.

Carroll, M. (1997) The acquisition of English. In A. Becker and M. Carroll (eds) *The Acquisition of Spatial Relations in a Second Language* (pp. 35–78). Amsterdam: Benjamins.

Carroll, S. (2005) Input and SLA: Adults' sensitivity to different sorts of cues to French gender. *Language Learning* 55 (1) 79–138.

Celce-Murcia, M. and Larsen-Freeman, D. (1999) *The Grammar Book: An ESL Teacher's Course*. Boston: Heinle & Heinle.

Cenoz, J., Hufeisen, B. and Jessner, U. (eds) (2001) *Cross-Linguistic Influence in Third Language Acquisition: Pyscholinguistic Perspectives*. Clevedon: Multilingual Matters.

Chafe, W.L. (1976) Givenness, contrastiveness, definiteness, subjects, topics and point of view. In C. Li (ed.) *Subject and Topic* (pp. 25–56). New York: Academic Press.

Chaudron, C. and Parker, K. (1990) Discourse markedness and structural markedness: The acquisition of English noun phrases. *Studies in Second Language Acquisition* 12, 43–63.

Chesterman, A. (1991) *On Definiteness: A Study with Special References to English and Finnish*. New York: Cambridge University Press.

Choi, S. and Bowerman, M. (1991) Learning to express motion events in English and Korean: The influence of language-specific lexicalization patterns. *Cognition* 41, 83–121.

Choi, S. and Lantolf, J.P. (2008) Representation and embodiment of meaning in L2 communication: Motion events in the speech and gesture of advanced L2 Korean and L2 English speakers. *Studies in Second Language Acquisition* 30 (2), 191–224.

Choi, S., McDonough, L., Bowerman, M. and Mandler, J.M. (1999) Early sensitivity to language-specific spatial categories in English and Korean. *Cognitive Development* 14, 241–268.

Chomsky, N. (1995) *The Minimalist Program*. Cambridge, MA: MIT Press.

Cienki, A. (1989) *Spatial Cognition and the Semantics of Prepositions in English, Polish, and Russian*. München: Verlag Otto Sagner.

Clahsen, H. and Felser, C. (2006) Continuity and shallow structures in language processing. *Applied Psycholinguistics* 27 (1), 107–126.

Clark, R.J. (1995) *Story Cards: Aesop's Fables*. Brattleboro, VT: Pro Lingua.

Cook, V. (ed.) (2002) *Effects of the Second Language on the First*. Clevedon: Multilingual Matters.

Coventry, K.R. and Garrod, S.C. (2004) *Saying, Seeing and Acting. The Psychological Semantics of Spatial Prepositions*. Essays in Cognitive Psychology Series. Hove and New York: Psychology Press.

Coventry, K.R. and Prat-Sala, M. (2001) Object-specific function, geometry and the comprehension of "in" and "on". *European Journal of Cognitive Psychology* 13, 509–528.

Dasinger, L. (1995) The development of discourse competence in Finnish children: The expression of definiteness. Unpublished doctoral dissertation, University of California at Berkley.

DeKeyser, R. (2000) The robustness of critical period effects in second language acquisition. *Studies in Second Language Acquisition* 22, 499–533.

DeKeyser, R. (2005) What makes learning second language grammar difficult? A review of issues. *Language Learning* 55 (1), 1–25.

De Knop, S. and Dirven, R. (2008) Motion and location in German, French and English: A typological, contrastive and pedagogical approach. In S. De Knop and T. De Rycker (eds) *Cognitive Approaches to Pedagogical Grammar* (pp. 295–324). Berlin/New York: Mouton de Gruyter.

Dekydtspotter, L., Schwartz, B.D., Sprouse, R.A. and Bullock, G. (2008) Locative Verbs in Korean-English and the Universal Grammar Question Revisited: Disentangling Lexical Semantics, Syntax and Pragmatics. Ms., Indiana University.

Dodge, E. and Lakoff, G. (2005) Image schemas: From linguistic analysis to neural grounding. In B. Hampe (ed.) *From Perception to Meaning: Image Schemas in Cognitive Linguistics* (pp. 57–91). Berlin: Mouton de Gruyter.

Doherty, M. (2001) Discourse theory and translation of clefts between English and German. In I. Kenesei and R. Harnish (eds) *Perspectives on Semantics, Pragmatics, and Discourse* (pp. 273–292). Amsterdam: Benjamins.

Dörnyei, Z. (2007) *Research Methods in Applied Linguistics.* Oxford: Oxford University Press.

Driagina, V. (2007) Crossing and bridging spaces in a second language: Acquisition of motion talk by American learners of Russian. Unpublished Doctoral dissertation, Pennsylvania State University, University Park.

Duff, P. (2008) *Case Study Research in Applied Linguistics.* Mahwah, NJ: Lawrence Erlbaum.

Dulay, H.C. and Burt, M.K. (1974) Natural sequences and child second language acquisition. *Language Learning* 24 (1), 37–53.

Duncan, S.D. (1996) Grammatical form and 'thinking-for-speaking' in Mandarin Chinese and English: An analysis based on speech-accompanying gesture. Unpublished PhD dissertation, Department of Psychology, The University of Chicago.

Duncan, S.D. (2001) Co-expressivity of speech and gesture: Manner of motion in Spanish, English, and Chinese. In *Proceedings of the 27th Berkeley Linguistic Society Annual Meeting* (pp. 353–370). Berkeley, CA: Berkeley Linguistics Society.

Duncan, S.D. (2002) Gesture, verbal aspect, and the nature of iconic imagery in natural discourse. *Gesture* 2 (2), 183–206.

Ellis, N.C. (1995) The psychology of foreign language vocabulary acquisition: Implications for CALL. *Computer Assisted Language Learning* 8, 103–128.

Ellis, N.C. (2006) Selective attention and transfer phenomena in L2 acquisition: Contingency, cue competition, salience, interference, overshadowing, blocking, and perceptual learning. *Applied Linguistics* 27 (2), 164–194.

Ellis, N.C. (2008) Usage-based and form-focused language acquisition: The associative learning of constructions, learned attention, and the limited L2 state. In P. Robinson and N.C. Ellis (eds) *Handbook of Cognitive Linguistics and Second Language Acquisition* (pp. 372–405). New York/London: Routledge.

Ellis, R. (1994) *The Study of Second Language Acquisition.* Oxford: Oxford University Press.

Ellis, R. (2003) *Task-based Language Learning and Teaching.* Oxford: Oxford University Press.

Ellis, R. (2005) Measuring implicit and explicit knowledge of a second language: A psychometric study. *Studies in Second Language Acquisition* 27 (2), 141–172.

Emonds, J.E. (1985) *A Unified Theory of Syntactic Categories*. Dordrecht: Foris.

Emonds, J.E. (2000) *Lexicon and Grammar: The English Syntacticon*. Berlin: Mouton de Gruyter.

Engberg-Pedersen, E. and Trondhjem, F.B. (2004) Focus on action in motion descriptions: The case of West-Greenlandic. In S. Strömqvist and L. Verhoeven (eds) *Relating Events in Narrative. Typological and Contextual Perspectives* (pp. 59–88). Mahwah, NJ: Lawrence Erlbaum.

Eubank, L. and Grace, S. (1998) V-to-I and inflection in nonnative grammars. In M. Beck (ed.) *Morphology and Its Interfaces in L2 Knowledge* (pp. 69–88). Amsterdam: John Benjamins.

Feist, M.I. and Gentner, D. (1998) On plates, bowls and dishes: Factors in the use of English "in" and "on". In M.A. Gernsbacher and S.J. Derry (eds) *Proceedings of the Twentieth Annual Conference of the Cognitive Science Society* (pp. 345–349). Mahwah, NJ: Lawrence Erlbaum Associates.

Feist, M.I. and Gentner, D. (2007) Spatial language influences memory for spatial scenes. *Memory & Cognition* 35 (2), 283–296.

Filipović, L. (2007) *Talking about Motion: A Crosslinguistic Investigation of Lexicalization Patterns*. Amsterdam/Philadelphia: John Benjamins.

Fodor, J.A. (1975) *The Language of Thought*. New York: Crowell.

Fodor, J.A. (1998) *Concepts: Where Cognitive Science Went Wrong*. Oxford: Clarendon Press.

Fodor, J.A. and Sag, I. (1982) Referential and quantificational indefinites. *Linguistics and Philosophy* 5, 355–398.

Foote, I. (1967) *Verbs of Motion*. Cambridge: Cambridge University Press.

Forsyth, J. (1970) *A Grammar of Aspect. Usage and Meaning in the Russian Verb*. Cambridge: Cambridge University Press.

Franceschina, F. (2005) *Fossilized Second Language Grammars: The Acquisition of Grammatical Gender* (Vol. 38). Amsterdam: John Benjamins.

Freleng, I. (Director). (1950) *Canary Row [Animated Film]*. New York: Time Warner.

Fukui, N. (1993) Parameters and optionality. *Linguistic Inquiry* 24 (3), 399–420.

Fukui, N. (1995) The principles and parameters approach: A comparative syntax of English and Japanese. In M. Shibatani and T. Bynon (eds) *Approaches to Language Typology* (pp. 327–373). Oxford: Oxford University Press.

Gagarina, N. (2009) Verbs of motion in Russian: An acquisitional perspective. In V. Hasko (ed.) *Special Forum on Teaching and Learning Russian Verbs of Motion in the Slavic and East European Journal* 53 (3), 451–470.

Gallistel, C.R. (2002) Language and spatial frames of reference in mind and brain. *Trends in Cognitive Science* 6, 321–322.

Gelman, R. and Butterworth, B. (2005) Number and language: How are they related. *Trends in Cognitive Science* 9 (1), 6–10.

Gennari, S., Sloman, S., Malt, B. and Fitch, T. (2002) Motion events in language and cognition. *Cognition* 83, 49–79.

Gentner, D. and Goldin-Meadow, S. (eds) (2003) *Language in Mind: Advances in the Study of Language and Thought*. Cambridge, MA: MIT Press.

Goldin-Meadow, S. (2000) Beyond words: The importance of gesture to researchers and learners. *Child Development* 71 (1), 231–239.

Goldin-Meadow, S. (2003) *Hearing Gesture: How Our Hands Help Us Think*. Cambridge, MA: The Belknap Press of Harvard University Press.

Goldschneider, J.M. and DeKeyser, R.M. (2001) Explaining the "natural order of L2 morpheme acquisition" in English: A meta-analysis of multiple determinants. *Language Learning* 51 (1), 27–77.

Golinkoff, R.M., Hirsh-Pasek, K., Cauley, K.M. and Gordon, L. (1987) The eyes have it: Lexical and syntactic comprehension in a new paradigm. *Journal of Child Language* 14, 23–45.

Gordon, P. (2004) Numerical cognition without words: Evidence from Amazonia. *Science* 306, 496–499.

Gotteri, N. and Michalak-Gray, J. (1997) *Polish*. London: Teach Yourself Books.

Granger, S. (2002) Bird's-eye view of computer learner corpus research. In S. Granger, J. Hung and S. Petch-Tyson (eds) *Computer Learner Corpora, Second Language Acquisition and Foreign Language Teaching* (pp. 3–33). Amsterdam/Philadelphia: John Benjamins.

Gregg, K. (1989) Second language acquisition theory: A generativist perspective. In S. Gass and J. Schachter (eds) *Linguistic Perspectives on Second Language Acquisition* (pp. 15–40). Cambridge: Cambridge University Press.

Gropen, J., Pinker, S., Hollander, M. and Goldberg, R. (1991) Affectedness and direct objects: The role of lexical semantics in the acquisition of verb argument structure. *Cognition* 41, 153–195.

Gullberg, M. (2006) Some reasons for studying gesture and second language acquisition (Hommage à Adam Kendon). *IRAL* 44 (2), 103–124.

Gullberg, M. (2008) Gestures and second language acquisition. In P. Robinson and N. Ellis (eds) *Handbook of Cognitive Linguistics and Second Language Acquisition* (pp. 276–305). New York/London: Routledge.

Gullberg, M. and McCafferty, S.G. (2008) Introduction to gesture and SLA: Toward an integrated approach. *Studies in Second Language Acquisition* 30 (2), 133–146.

Gumperz, J.J. and Levinson, S.C. (eds) (1996) *Rethinking Linguistic Relativity*. Cambridge: Cambridge University Press.

Haastrup, K. and Henriksen, B. (2000) Vocabulary acquisition: Acquiring depth of knowledge through network building. *International Journal of Applied Linguistics* 10, 221–240.

Hampton, J.A. (1997) Psychological representation of concepts. In M. Conway (ed.) *Cognitive Models of Memory* (pp. 81–110). Cambridge, MA: MIT Press.

Han, Z-H. (1998) Fossilization: An investigation into advanced L2 learning of a typologically distant language. Unpublished PhD dissertation, University of London, London.

Han, Z-H. (2000) Persistence of the implicit influence of NL: The case of the pseudo-passive. *Applied Linguistics* 21 (1), 78–105.

Han, Z-H. (2004) *Fossilization in Adult Second Language Acquisition*. Clevedon: Multilingual Matters.

Han, Z-H. (2006) Can grammaticality judgment be a reliable source of evidence on fossilization? In Z-H. Han and T. Odlin (eds) *Studies of Fossilization in Second Language Acquisition* (pp. 56–82). Clevedon: Multilingual Matters.

Han, Z-H. (2008) On the role of meaning in focus on form. In Z-H. Han (ed.) *Understanding Second Language Process* (pp. 45–79). Clevedon: Multilingual Matters.

Han, Z-H. and Larsen-Freeman, D. (2005) On the role of "meaning" in focus on form. Paper presented at the Second Language Research Forum, New York City, NY.

Han, Z-H. and Odlin, T. (2006) Introduction. In Z-H. Han and T. Odlin (eds) *Studies of Fossilization in Second Language Acquisition* (pp. 1–20). Clevedon: Multilingual Matters.

Harley, B. (1989) Transfer in the written compositions of French immersion students. In H.W. Dechert and M. Raupach (eds) *Transfer in Language Production* (pp. 3–19). Norwood, NJ: Ablex.

Harley, B. (1995) The lexicon in language research. In B. Harley (ed.) *Lexical Issues in Language Learning* (pp. 1–28). Amsterdam: Benjamins.

Harley, B. and King, M.L. (1989) Verb lexis in the written compositions of young L2 learners. *Studies in Second Language Acquisition* 11, 415–439.

Hasko, V. (2009) The locus of difficulties in the acquisition of Russian verbs of motion by highly proficient learners. In V. Hasko (ed.) *Special Forum on Teaching and Learning Russian Verbs of Motion in the Slavic and East European Journal* 53 (3), 451–470.

Hasko, V. (2010) Motion domains of motion in Russian and English: Corpus-based analysis. In V. Hasko and R. Perelmutter (eds) *New Approaches to Slavic Verbs of Motion* (pp. 197–224). Amsterdam/Philadelphia: John Benjamins.

Hasko, V. and Perelmutter, R. (eds) (2010) *Multiple Approaches to Slavic Verbs of Motion*. Amsterdam/Philadelphia: John Benjamins.

Hawkins, J.A. (1978) *Definiteness and Indefiniteness*. London: Croom Helm.

Hawkins, R. (2000) Persistent selective fossilization in second language acquisition and the optimal design of the language faculty. *Essex Research Reports in Linguistics* 34, 75–90.

Heine, B., Claudi, U. and Hünnemeyer, F. (1991) *Grammaticalization: A Conceptual Framework*. Chicago: University of Chicago Press.

Henriksen, B. (1999) Three dimensions of vocabulary development. *Studies in Second Language Acquisition* 21, 303–317.

Hespos, S.J. and Spelke, E.S. (2004) Conceptual precursors to language. *Nature* 430, 453–456.

Hickmann, M. and Robert, S. (eds) (2006) *Space in Languages: Linguistic Systems and Cognitive Categories*. Amsterdam/Philadelphia: John Benjamins.

Hirschbuhler, P. (2004) Alternating vs. non-alternating 'fill'-verbs: where does the difference come from? Paper presented at the Workshop on Event Structures in Linguistic Form and Interpretation, University of Leipzig.

Hirsh-Pasek, K. and Golinkoff, R.M. (1996) The preferential looking paradigm reveals emerging language comprehension. In D. McDaniel, C. McKee and H. Cairns (eds) *Methods for Assessing Children's Syntax* (pp. 105–124). Cambridge, MA: MIT Press.

Hohenstein, J.M., Eisenberg, A.R. and Naigles, L.R. (2006) Is he floating across or crossing afloat. Cross-influence of L1 and L2 Spanish-English bilingual adults. *Bilingualism: Language and Cognition* 9 (3), 249–261.

Hohenstein, J.M., Naigles, L.R. and Eisenberg, A.R. (2004) Keeping verb acquisition in motion: A comparison of English and Spanish. In D.G. Hall and S.R. Waxman (eds) *Weaving a Lexicon* (pp. 569–602). Cambridge, MA: MIT Press.

Huang, S. (1999) The evidence for a grammatical category *definite article* in spoken Chinese. *Journal of Pragmatics* 34, 77–94.

Huebner, T. (1983) *A Longitudinal Analysis of the Acquisition of English*. Ann Arbor, MI: Karoma Press.

Ibarretxe-Antuñano, I. (2004) Motion events in Basque narratives. In S. Strömqvist and L. Verhoeven (eds) *Relating Events in Narrative. Typological and Contextual Perspectives* (pp. 89–111). Mahwah, NJ: Lawrence Erlbaum.

Ijaz, H. (1986) Linguistic and cognitive determinants of lexical acquisition in a second language. *Language Learning* 36, 401–451.

Inagaki, S. (2001) Motion verbs with goal PPs in the L2 acquisition of English and Japanese. *Studies in Second Language Acquisition* 23, 153–170.

Inagaki, S. (2002) Motion verbs with locational/directional PPs in English and Japanese. *Canadian Journal of Linguistics/Revue canadienne de linguistique* 47, 187–234.

Ionin, T., Ko, H. and Wexler, K. (2008) The role of semantic features in the acquisition of English articles by Russian and Korean speakers. In J. Liceras, H. Zobl and H. Goodluck (eds) *The Role of Formal Features in Second Language Acquisition* (pp. 226–268). New York: Lawrence Erlbaum.

Irvine, J. (1990) Registering affect: Heteroglossia in the linguistic expression of emotion. In C. Lutz and L. Abu-Lughod (eds) *Language and the Politics of Emotion* (pp. 126–161). Cambridge: Cambridge University Press.

Isachenko, A. (1960) *The Grammatical System of Russian Compared with Slovak: Morphology.* Bratislava: The Slovak Academy of Sciences Press.

Jackendoff, R. (1990) *Semantic Structures.* Cambridge, MA: MIT Press.

Jacobson, R. (1959) Boas' view of grammatical meaning. *American Anthropologist* 61, 139–145.

Janda, L. (1988) The mapping of elements of cognitive space onto grammatical relations: An example from Russian verbal prefixation. In B. Rudzka-Ostyn (ed.) *Topics in Cognitive Linguistics* (pp. 327–343). Amsterdam: John Benjamins.

Jarvis, S. (1998) *Conceptual Transfer in the Interlingual Lexicon.* Bloomington, IN: Indiana University Linguistics Club Association.

Jarvis, S. (2002) Topic continuity in L2 English article use. *Studies in Second Language Acquisition* 24, 387–418.

Jarvis, S. (2007) Theoretical and methodological issues in the investigation of conceptual transfer. *Vigo International Journal of Applied Linguistics* 4, 43–71.

Jarvis, S. and Odlin, T. (2000) Morphological type, spatial reference, and language transfer. *Studies in Second Language Acquisition* 22, 535–556.

Jarvis, S. and Pavlenko, A. (2008) *Crosslinguistic Influence in Language and Cognition.* New York: Routledge.

Jiang, N. (2004) Morphological insensitivity in second language processing. *Applied Psycholinguistics* 25, 603–634.

Johnson, J. and Newport, E. (1989) Critical period effects in second language learning: The influence of maturational state on the acquisition of English as a second language. *Cognitive Psychology* 21, 60–99.

Johnston, J.R. and Slobin, D.I. (1979) The development of locative expressions in English, Italian, Serbo-Croatian and Turkish. *Journal of Child Language* 6, 531–547.

Joo, H-R. (2003) Second language learnability and the acquisition of the argument structure of English locative verbs by Korean speakers. *Second Language Research* 19, 305–328.

Juffs, A. (1996) *Learnability and the Lexicon: Theories and Second Language Acquisition Research.* Amsterdam: John Benjamins.

Kagan, O. (2010) Aspects of motion: On the semantics and pragmatics of indeterminate aspect. In V. Hasko and R. Perelmutter (eds) *New Approaches to Slavic Verbs of Motion* (pp. 141–162). Amsterdam/Philadelphia: John Benjamins.

Kaplan, R. (1966) Cultural thought patterns in inter-cultural education. *Language Learning* 16, 1–20.

Kellerman, E. (1995) Crosslinguistic influence: Transfer to nowhere? *Annual Review of Applied Linguistics* 15, 125–150.

Kellerman, E. and Van Hoof, A. (2003) Manual accents. *International Review of Applied Linguistics* 41, 251–269.

Kim, J.H. and Han, Z-H. (2007) Recasts in communicative EFL classes: Do teacher intent and learner interpretation overlap? In A. Mackey (ed.) *Conversational Interaction in Second Language Acquisition: A Series of Empirical Studies* (pp. 269–300). Oxford: Oxford University Press.

Kim, M. (1999) A cross-linguistic perspective on the acquisition of locative verbs. Doctoral dissertation, University of Delaware.

Kita, S. (1993) Language and thought interface: A study of spontaneous gestures and Japanese mimetics. Unpublished PhD dissertation, Department of Psychology and Linguistics, The University of Chicago.

Kita, S. and Özyürek, A. (2003) What does cross-linguistic variation in semantic coordination of speech and gesture reveal?: Evidence for an interface representation of spatial thinking and speaking. *Journal of Memory and Language* 48, 16–32.

Klein, W. (1986) *Second Language Acquisition*. Cambridge: Cambridge University Press.

Klein, W. and Dittmar, N. (1979) *Developing Grammars: The Acquisition of German Syntax by Foreign Workers*. Berlin: Springer.

Koch, H. (2000) Central Australian aboriginal English: In comparison with the morphosyntactic categories of Kaytetye. *Asian Englishes* 23, 32–58.

Kopecka, A. (2010) Motion events in Polish: Lexicalization patterns and the description of manner. In V. Hasko and R. Perelmutter (eds) *New Approaches to Slavic Verbs of Motion* (pp. 225–246). Amsterdam/Philadelphia: John Benjamins.

Korchmaros, V. (1983) Definiteness as semantic content and its realization in grammatical form. *Studia Uralo-Altaica* 19, 1–125.

Kramsky, J. (1972) *The Article and the Concept of Definiteness in Language*. The Hague, The Netherlands: Mouton.

Kryk, B. (1987) *On Deixis in English and Polish*. Frankfurt am Main, Germany: Peter Lang.

Kwon, E.Y. and Han, Z-H. (2008) Language transfer in child SLA: A longitudinal case study of a sequential bilingual. In J. Philp, R. Oliver and A. Mackey (eds) *Second Language Acquisition and the Younger Learner: Child's Play?* (pp. 303–332). Amsterdam: John Benjamins.

Lado, R. (1956) *Linguistics across Cultures*. Ann Arbor, MI: University of Michigan Press.

Lakoff, G. and Johnson, M. (1999) *Philosophy in the Flesh: The Embodied Mind and its Challenge to Western Thought*. New York: Basic Books.

Landau, B. and Jackendoff, R. (1993) "What" and "where" in spatial language and spatial cognition. *Behavioral and Brain Sciences* 16, 217–265.

Langacker, R. (1998) Conceptualization, symbolization, and grammar. In M. Tomasello (ed.) *The New Psychology of Language: Cognitive and Functional Approaches to Language Structure* (pp. 1–40). Mahwah, NJ: Lawrence Erlbaum.

Langacker, R. (2008) Cognitive grammar as a basis for language acquisition. In P. Robinson and N. Ellis (eds) *Handbook of Cognitive Linguistics and Second Language Acquisition* (pp. 66–88). New York: Routledge.

Lardiere, D. (1998) Dissociating syntax from morphology in a divergent L2 end-state grammar. *Second Language Research* 14 (4), 359–375.

Lardiere, D. (2000) Mapping features to forms in second language acquisition. In J. Archibald (ed.) *Second Language Acquisition and Linguistic Theory* (pp. 102–129). Oxford: Blackwell.

Lardiere, D. (2004) Knowledge of definiteness despite variable article omission in second language acquisition. In A. Brugos, L. Micciulla and C.E. Smith (eds) *Proceedings of the 28th Annual Boston University Conference on Language Development* (pp. 328–339). Somerville, MA: Cascadilla Press.

Lardiere, D. (2007) *Ultimate Attainment in Second Language Acquisition: A Case Study*. Mahwah, NJ: Lawrence Erlbaum.

Larsen-Freeman, D. (2006) Second language acquisition and the issue of fossilization: There is no end, and there is no state. In Z-H. Han and T. Odlin (eds) *Studies of Fossilization in Second Language Acquisition* (pp. 189–200). Clevedon: Multilingual Matters.

Lefebvre, C. (1998) *Creole Genesis and the Acquisition of Grammar: The Case of Haitian Creole*. Cambridge: Cambridge University Press.

Leung, Y.I. (2001) The initial state of L3A: Full transfer and failed features? In X. Bonch-Bruevich, W. Crawford, J. Hellermann, C. Higgins and H. Nguyen (eds) *The Past, Present, and Future of Second Language Research: Selected Proceedings of the 2000 Second Language Research Forum* (pp. 55–75). Somerville, MA: Cascadilla Press.

Levelt, W. (1989) *Speaking: From Intention to Articulation*. Cambridge, MA: MIT Press.

Levin, B. (1993) *English Verb Classes and Alternations: A Preliminary Investigation.* Chicago, IL: University of Chicago Press.

Levin, B. and Rapoport, T. (1988) Lexical subordination. *Papers from the 24th Regional Meeting of the Chicago Linguistics Society* 275–289.

Levin, B. and Rappaport Hovav, M. (2005). *Argument Realization.* Cambridge: Cambridge University Press.

Levinson, S.C. (1996) Frames of reference and Molyneux's question. In P. Bloom, M.A. Peterson, L. Nadel and M.F. Garrett (eds) *Language and Space* (pp. 109–169). Cambridge, MA: MIT Press.

Levinson, S. (1997) From outer to inner space: Linguistic categories and non-linguistic thinking. In J. Nuyts and E. Pederson (eds) *Language and Linguistic Categorization* (pp. 13–45). Cambridge: Cambridge University Press.

Levinson, S.C. (2003a) *Space in Language and Cognition. Explorations in Cognitive Diversity.* Cambridge: Cambridge University Press.

Levinson, S.C. (2003b) Language and mind: Let's get the issues straight. In D. Gentner and S. Goldin-Meadow (eds) *Language in Mind: Advances in the Study of Language and Cognition* (pp. 25–46).Cambridge, MA: MIT Press.

Levinson, S., Kita, S., Haun, D. and Rasch, B. (2002) Returning the tables: Language affects spatial reasoning. *Cognition* 84, 155–188.

Li, C. and Thompson, S. (1987) Chinese. In B. Comrie (ed.) *The World's Major Languages* (pp. 811–833). Oxford: University Press.

Li, P. and Gleitman, L. (2002) Turning the tables: Language and spatial reasoning. *Cognition* 83 (3), 265–294.

Liu, D. and Gleason, J.I. (2002) Acquisition of the article *the* by nonnative speakers of English: An analysis of four nongeneric uses. *Studies in Second Language Acquisition* 24 (1), 1–26.

Loewenstein, J. and Gentner, D. (2005) Relational language and the development of relational mapping. *Cognitive Psychology* 50, 315–353.

Loftus, E. and Palmer, J. (1974) Reconstruction of automobile: An example of the interaction between language and memory. *Journal of Verbal Learning and Verbal Behavior* 13, 585–589.

Long, M.H. (1996) The role of the linguistic environment in second language acquisition. In W.C. Ritchie and T.K. Bhatia (eds) *Handbook of Second Language Acquisition* (pp. 413–468). New York: Academic Press.

Long, M.H. (2003) Stabilization and fossilization in interlanguage development. In C. Doughty and M.H. Long (eds) *The Handbook of Second Language Acquisition* (pp. 487–536). Oxford: Blackwell.

Loschky, L. and Bley-Vroman, R. (1993) Grammar and task-based methodology. In G. Crookes and S. Gass (eds) *Tasks and Language Learning: Integrating Theory and Practice* (pp. 123–167). Clevedon: Multilingual Matters.

Lucy, J.A. (1992a) *Language Diversity and Thought. A Reformulation of the Linguistic Relativity Hypothesis.* Cambridge: Cambridge University Press.

Lucy, J.A. (1992b) *Grammatical Categories and Cognition. A Case Study of the Linguistic Relativity Hypothesis.* Cambridge: Cambridge University Press.

Lucy, J.A. (1996) The scope of linguistic relativity: An analysis and review of empirical research. In J.J. Gumperz and S.C. Levinson (eds) *Rethinking Linguistic Relativity* (pp. 37–69). Cambridge: Cambridge University Press.

Lucy, J.A. (2000) Introductory comments. In S. Niemeier and R. Dirven (eds) *Evidence for Linguistic Relativity* (pp. x–xxi). Amsterdam: John Benjamins.

Lucy, J. and Gaskins, S. (2001) Grammatical categories and the development of classification preferences: A comparative approach. In M. Bowerman and S. Levinson (eds) *Language Acquisition and Conceptual Development* (pp. 257–283). Cambridge: Cambridge University Press.

Lyons, C. (1999) *Definiteness*. Cambridge: Cambridge University Press.

Lyons, J. (1977) *Semantics* (Vols. I–II). Cambridge: Cambridge University Press.

Mackey, A. and Gass, S. (2005) *Second Language Research: Methodology and Design*. Mahwah, NJ: Lawrence Erlbaum.

Mackey, A., Gass, S. and McDonough, K. (2000) How do learners perceive interaction feedback? *Studies in Second Language Acquisition* 22 (4), 471–498.

Majsak, T. A. and Rakhilina, E. V. (eds) (2007) *Glagoly dvizheniia v vode: Leksicheskaia tipologiia*. Moscow: Indrik.

Maratsos, M. (1976) *The Use of Definite and Indefinite Reference in Young Children: An Experimental Study of Semantic Acquisition*. Cambridge: Cambridge University Press.

Maratsos, M., Katis, D. and Margheri, A. (2000) Can grammar make you feel different? In S. Niemeier and R. Dirven (eds) *Evidence for Linguistic Relativity* (pp. 53–70). Amsterdam: Benjamins.

Marcos, L.R. (1979) Nonverbal behavior and thought processing. *Archives of General Psychiatry* 36, 940–943.

Mayer, M. (1969) *Frog, Where Are You?* New York: Dial Press.

McDonough, L., Choi, S. and Mandler, J.M. (2003) Understanding spatial relations: Flexible infants, lexical adults. *Cognitive Psychology* 46 (3), 229–259.

McNeill, D. (1992) *Hand and Mind*. Chicago: The University of Chicago Press.

McNeill, D. (1997) Growth points cross-linguistically. In J. Nuyts and E. Pederson (eds) *Language and Conceptualization: Language, Culture and Cognition* (Vol. 1, pp. 190–212). Cambridge: Cambridge University Press.

McNeill, D. (2000) Analogic/analytic representations in cross-linguistic differences in thinking for speaking. *Cognitive Linguistics* 11 (1/2), 43–60.

McNeill, D. (2005) *Gesture and Thought*. Chicago: University of Chicago Press.

McNeill, D. and Duncan, S. (2000) Growth points in thinking-for-speaking. In D. McNeill (ed.) *Language and Gesture* (pp. 141–161). Cambridge: Cambridge University Press.

Meara, P. (1996) The dimensions of lexical competence. In G. Brown, K. Malmkjaer, and J. Williams (eds) *Performance and Competence in Second Language Acquisition* (pp. 35–53). Cambridge: Cambridge University Press.

Mel'čuk, I.A. (1985) Lexicography and verbal government: On a dictionary by Ju D. Apreszjan and E. Páll. *Folia Linguistica* 19, 253–266.

Miller, J.L. (1995) On the internal structure of phonetic categories: A progress report. In J. Mehler and S. Franck (eds) *Cognition on Cognition* (pp. 333–346). Cambridge, MA: MIT Press.

Montrul, S. (2001) The acquisition of causative/inchoative verbs in L2 Turkish. *Language Acquisition* 9 (1), 1–58.

Murav'eva, L.S. (2006) *Verbs of Motion in Russian (for English-Speaking Students)*. Moscow: Russkii Iazyk.

Myers-Scotton, C. and Jake, J. (2001) Explaining aspects of codeswitching and their implications. In J. Nichol and T. Langendoen (eds) *Bilingualism* (pp. 84–116). Oxford: Blackwell.

Naigles, L. R., Eisenberg, A. R., Kako, E., Highter, M. and McGraw, N. (1998) Speaking of motion: Verb use in English and Spanish. *Language and Cognition Processes* 13, 521–549.

Nakahama, Y. (2003) Cross-linguistic influence on the development of referential topic management in L2 Japanese oral narratives. Unpublished PhD dissertation, Georgetown University.

Nation, I.S.P. (1990) *Teaching and Learning Vocabulary*. Boston: Heinle & Heinle.

Nation, I.S.P. (2001) *Learning Vocabulary in Another Language*. Cambridge: Cambridge University Press.

Navarro, S. and Nicoladis, E. (2005) Describing motion events in adult L2 Spanish narratives. In D. Eddington (ed.) *Selected Proceedings of the 6th Conference on the Acquisition of Spanish and Portuguese as First and Second Languages* (pp. 102–107). Somerville, MA: Cascadilla Proceedings Project.

Negueruela, E. and Lantolf, J.P. (2006) Concept-based instruction and the acquisition of L2 Spanish. In R. Salaberry and B.A. Lafford (eds) *The Art of Teaching Spanish: Second Language Acquisition from Research to Praxis* (pp. 79–102). Washington, DC: Georgetown University Press.

Negueruela, E., Lantolf, J.P., Jordan, S.R. and Gelabert, J. (2004) The "private function" of gesture in second language speaking activity: A study of motion verbs and gesturing in English and Spanish. *International Journal of Applied Linguistics* 14 (1), 113–147.

Ochs, E. and Schieffelin, B. (1989) Language has a heart. *Text* 9, 7–25.

Odlin, T. (1989) *Language Transfer: Crosslinguistic Influence in Language Learning.* Cambridge: Cambridge University Press.

Odlin, T. (2005) Crosslinguistic influence and conceptual transfer: What are the concepts? *Annual Review of Applied Linguistics* 25, 3–25.

Odlin, T. (2008a) Conceptual transfer and meaning extensions. In P. Robinson and N.C. Ellis (eds) *Handbook of Cognitive Linguistics and Second Language Acquisition* (pp. 306–340). New York/London: Routledge.

Odlin, T. (2008b) Focus constructions and language transfer. In D. Gabryś-Barker (ed.) *Morphosyntactic Issues in Second Language Acquisition Studies* (pp. 3–28). Clevedon: Multilingual Matters.

Ogden, C.K. and Richards, I.A. (1923) *The Meaning of Meaning: A Study of the Influence of Language upon Thought and of the Science of Symbolism.* New York: Harcourt, Brace and World.

Özçalişkan, Ş. (under review). *Doors, Fences, and Thresholds: The Many Ways of Crossing a Boundary in English and Turkish.*

Özçalişkan, Ş. and Slobin, D.I. (1998) Learning how to search for the frog: Expression of manner of motion in English, Spanish, and Turkish. In A. Greenhill, H. Littelfield and C. Tano (eds) *Proceedings of the 23rd Annual Boston University Conference on Language Development* (pp. 541–552). Sommerville, MA: Cascadilla Press.

Özçalişkan, Ş. and Slobin, D.I. (2000) Expression of manner of movement in monolingual and bilingual adult narratives: Turkish vs. English. In A. Göksel and C. Kerslake (eds) *Studies on Turkish and Turkic Languages* (pp. 253–262). Wiesbaden, Germany: Harrasowitz Verlag.

Özyürek, A. (2002) Speech–gesture relationship across languages and in second language learners: Implications for spatial thinking for speaking. In B. Skarabela, S. Fish and A.H.-J. Do (eds) *Proceedings of the 26th Annual Boston University Conference on Language Development* (Vol. 2, pp. 500–509). Somerville, MA: Cascadilla Press.

Özyürek, A. and Kita, S. (1999) Expressing manner and path in English and Turkish: Differences in speech, gesture, and conceptualization. In M. Hahn and S.C. Stoness (eds) *Proceedings of the 21st Cognitive Science Meeting* (pp. 507–512). Hillsdale, NJ: Lawrence Erlbaum Associates.

Özyürek, A., Kita, S., Allen, S., Furman, R. and Brown, A. (2005) How does linguistic framing influence co-speech gestures? Insights from crosslinguistic differences and similarities. *Gesture* 5 (1/2), 216–241.

Pahomov, G. (1977) Bull, boar, and orbit/trajectory: On presenting the verbs of motion. *Russian Language Journal* 31, 1–5.

Paribakht, T.S. (2005) The influence of first language lexicalization on second language lexical inferencing: A study of Farsi-speaking learners of English as a foreign language. *Language Learning* 55 (4), 701–748.

Pavlenko, A. and Driagina, V. (2007) Russian emotion vocabulary in American learners' narratives. *The Modern Language Journal* 91, 213–234.

Pavlenko, A. and Jarvis, S. (2001) Conceptual transfer: New perspectives on the study of cross-linguistic influence. *Cognition in Language Use. Selected Papers from the 7th International Pragmatics Conference* (pp. 288–301). Antwerp: IPRA.

Pavlenko, A. and Jarvis, S. (2002) Bidirectional transfer. *Applied Linguistics* 23 (2), 190–214.

Papafragou, A., Massey C. and Gleitman, L. (2002) Shake, rattle, 'n' roll: The representation of motion in language and cognition. *Cognition* 84, 189–219.

Pedersen, B. (2000) Lexical ambiguity in machine translation: Expressing regularities in the polysemy of Danish motion verbs. *CST (Center for Sprogteknologi) Working Papers* 2, 1–182.

Pederson, E., Danziger, E., Wilkins, D., Levinson, S.C., Kita, S. and Senft, G. (1998) Semantic typology and spatial conceptualisation. *Language* 74 (3), 557–589.

Perdue, C. (1993) *Adult Language Acquisition: Cross-Linguistic Perspectives*. Cambridge: Cambridge University Press.

Peyraube, A. (2006). Motion events in Chinese: A diachronic study of directional complements. In M. Hickmann and S. Robert (eds) *Space in Languages: Linguistic Systems and Cognitive Categories* (121–138). Amsterdam: John Benjamins.

Pica, P., Lemer, C., Izard, V. and Dehaene, S. (2004) Exact and approximate arithmetic in an Amazonian indigene group. *Science* 306, 499–503.

Pinker, S. (1989) *Learnability and Cognition: The Acquisition of Argument Structure*. Cambridge, MA: MIT Press.

Pinker, S. (1994) *The Language Instinct: How the Mind Creates Language*. New York: Morrow.

Pinker, S. (2007) *The Stuff of Thought: Language as a Window into Human Nature*. Penguin: New York.

Pullum, G. (1991) *The Great Eskimo Vocabulary Hoax, and Other Irreverent Essays on the Study of Language*. Chicago: University of Chicago Press.

Read, J. (1993) The development of a new measure of L2 vocabulary knowledge. *Language Testing* 10, 355–371.

Read, J. (2000) *Assessing Vocabulary*. Cambridge: Cambridge University Press.

Regier, T., Kay, P. and Cook, R. (2005) Focal colors are universal after all. *Proceedings of the National Academy of Sciences* 102 (23), 8386–8391.

Rifkin, B. (1996) *Grammar in Context*. New York: McGraw-Hill.

Robertson, D. (2000) Variability in the use of the English article system by Chinese learners of English. *Second Language Research* 16 (2), 135–172.

Roberson, D., Davidoff, J., Davies, I.R. and Shapiro, L.R. (2005) Color categories: Evidence for the cultural relativity hypothesis. *Cognitive Psychology* 50 (4), 378–411.

Robinson, P. and Ellis, N.C. (eds) (2008) *Handbook of Cognitive Linguistics and Second Language Acquisition*. New York/London: Routledge.

Rosch, E. and Mervis, C.B. (1975) Family resemblances: Studies in the internal structure of categories. *Cognitive Psychology* 7, 573–605.

Samuda, V. and Bygate, M. (2008) *Tasks in Second Language Learning*. Houndmills: Palgrave Macmillian.

Saussure, F.de (1983 [1916]) *Course in General Linguistics* (translated and annotated by R. Harris). London: Duckworth.

Schacter, D.L. and Badgaiyan, R.D. (2001) Neuroimaging of priming: New perspectives on implicit and explicit memory. *Current Directions in Psychological Science* 10, 1–4.

Schulman, B.W. (2004) A crosslinguistic investigation of the speech–gesture relationship in motion event descriptions. Unpublished PhD dissertation, Department of Psychology, The University of Chicago.

Schumann, J. (1978) *The Pidginization Process: A Model for Second Language Acquisition*. Rowley, MA: Newbury House.

Schwartz, B.D., Dekydtspotter, L. and Sprouse, R.A. (2003) Pouring the fire with gasoline: Questioning conclusions on L2 argument structure. In J.M. Liceras, H. Zobl and H. Goodluck (eds) *Proceedings of the 6th Generative Approaches to Second Language Acquisition Conference (GASLA 2002)* (pp. 248–259). Somerville, MA: Cascadilla.

Schwartz, B.D. and R.A. Sprouse (1994) Word order and nominative Case in nonnative language acquisition: A longitudinal study of (L1 Turkish) German interlanguage. In T. Hoekstra and B. D. Schwartz (eds) *Language Acquisition Studies in Generative Grammar* (pp. 317–368). Amsterdam: John Benjamins.

Schwartz, B.D. and Sprouse, R.A. (1996) L2 cognitive states and the full transfer/full access model. *Second Language Research* 12, 40–72.

Selinker, L. (1992) *Rediscovering Interlanguage*. London: Longman.

Selinker, L. (2006) Afterword: Fossilization or 'Does Your Mind Mind'? In Z-H. Han and T. Odlin (eds) *Studies of Fossilization in Second Language Acquisition* (pp. 201–210). Clevedon: Multilingual Matters.

Selinker, L. and Lakshmanan, U. (1992) Language transfer and fossilization: The multiple effects principle. In M.S. Gass and L. Selinker (eds) *Language Transfer in Language Learning* (pp. 190–216). Philadelphia: John Benjamins.

Sera, M.D., Gathje, J. and del Castillo Pintado, J. (1999) Language and ontological knowledge: The contrast between objects and events made by Spanish and English speakers. *Journal of Memory and Language* 41 (3), 303–326.

Skvortsova, G. (2004) *Verbs of Motion – Without Mistakes*. Moscow: Russkii Iazyk.

Slobin, D. (1973) Cognitive prerequisites for the development of grammar. In C. Ferguson and D. Slobin (eds) *Studies of Child Language Development* (pp. 175–208). New York: Holt, Rinehart and Winston.

Slobin, D.I. (1987) Thinking for speaking. In J. Aske, N. Beery, L. Michaelis and H. Filip (eds) *Proceedings of the 13th Annual Meeting of the Berkley Linguistic Society* (pp. 435–444). Berkeley, CA: Berkeley Linguistic Society.

Slobin, D.I. (1991) Learning to think for speaking: Native language, cognition, and rhetorical style. *Pragmatics* 1, 7–26.

Slobin, D.I. (1993a) Is spatial language a special case? *Behavioral and Brain Sciences* 16, 249–251.

Slobin, D. (1993b) Adult language acquisition: A view from child language study. In C. Perdue (ed.) *Adult Language Acquisition: Cross-linguistic Perspectives. Volume II: The Results* (pp. 239–252). Cambridge: Cambridge University Press.

Slobin, D.I. (1996a) From "thought and language" to "thinking for speaking". In J. Gumperz and S. Levinson (eds) *Rethinking Linguistic Relativity. Studies in the Social and Cultural Foundations of Language* (Vol. 17, pp. 70–96). Cambridge: Cambridge University Press.

Slobin, D.I. (1996b) Two ways to travel: Verbs of motion in English and Spanish. In M. Shibatani and S.A. Thompson (eds) *Grammatical Constructions: Their Form and Meaning* (pp. 195–220). Oxford: Clarendon Press.

Slobin, D.I. (1997) Mind, code, and text. In J. Bybee, J. Haiman and S.A. Thompson (eds) *Essays on Language Function and Language Type: Dedicated to T. Givón* (pp. 437–467). Amsterdam/Philadelphia: John Benjamins.

Slobin, D.I. (1998) A typological perspective on learning to talk about space. In H. Ragnarsdóttir and S. Strömqvist (eds) *Learning to Talk about Time and Space. Proceedings of the 3rd NELAS Conference* (pp. 1–30). Reykjavík and Göteborg: University Colleague of Education and Department of Linguistics, University of Göteborg.

Slobin, D.I. (2000) Verbalized events: A dynamic approach to linguistic relativity and determinism. In S. Neimeier and R. Dirven (eds) *Evidence for Linguistic Relativity* (pp. 107–138). Amsterdam/Philadelphia: John Benjamins.

Slobin, D.I. (2003) Language and thought online: Cognitive consequences of linguistic relativity. In D. Gentner and S. Goldin-Meadow (eds) *Language in Mind: Advances in the Study of Language and Thought* (pp. 157–192). Cambridge, MA: MIT Press.

Slobin, D.I. (2004) The many ways to search for a frog: Linguistic typology and the expression of motion events. In S. Strömqvist and L. Verhoeven (eds) *Relating Events in Narrative. Typological and Contextual Perspectives* (pp. 219–257). Mahwah, NJ: Lawrence Erlbaum Associates.

Slobin, D.I. (2006) What makes manner of motion salient? Explorations in linguistic typology, discourse, and cognition. In M. Hickmann and S. Robert (eds) *Space in Languages: Linguistic Systems and Cognitive Categories* (pp. 59–81). Amsterdam/ Philadelphia, PA: John Benjamins.

Slobin, D.I. (2007) Language and thought online: Cognitive consequences of linguistic relativity. In V. Evans, B.K. Bergen and J. Zinken (eds) *The Cognitive Linguistics Reader* (pp. 902–928). London: Equinox Publishing Ltd.

Slobin, D.I. and Hoiting, N. (1994) Reference to movement in spoken and signed languages: Typological considerations. *Proceedings of the 20th Annual Meeting of the Berkeley Linguistics Society* (pp. 487–503). Berkeley, CA: Berkeley Linguistics Society.

Smoczynska, M. (1985) The acquisition of Polish. *The Crosslinguistic Study of Language Acquisition: The Data* (Vol. 1, pp. 595–686). Hillsdale, NJ: Lawrence Erlbaum.

Snyder, W. (1995) Language acquisition and language variation: The role of morphology. Doctoral dissertation, MIT.

Sperber, D. and Wilson D. (1995 [1986]) *Relevance: Communication and Cognition* (2nd edn). Oxford: Blackwell.

Sprouse, R.A. (2006) Full transfer and relexification: Second language acquisition and creole genesis. In C. Lefebvre, L. White and C. Jourdan (eds) *L2 Acquisition and Creole Genesis: Dialogues* (pp. 169–181). Amsterdam: John Benjamins.

Stam, G. (1998) Changes in patterns of thinking about motion with L2 acquisition. In S. Santi, I. Guaïtella, C. Cavé and G. Konopczynski (eds) *Oralité et gestualité: Communication Multimodale, Interaction* (pp. 615–619). Paris: L'Harmattan.

Stam, G. (2001) Gesture and second language acquisition. Paper presented at TESOL Convention, St. Louis, Missouri, March.

Stam, G. (2006a) Changes in patterns of thinking with second language acquisition. Unpublished PhD dissertation, Committee on Cognition and Communication, Department of Psychology, The University of Chicago.

Stam, G. (2006b) Thinking for speaking about motion: L1 and L2 speech and gesture. *IRAL* 44 (2), 145–171.

Stam, G. (2007) Second language acquisition from a McNeillian perspective. In E. Levy, S. Duncan and J. Cassell (eds) *Gesture and the Dynamic Dimension of Language: Essays in Honor of David McNeill* (pp. 117–124). Amsterdam: John Benjamins.

Stam, G. (2008) What gestures reveal about second language acquisition. In S. McCafferty and G. Stam (eds) *Gesture: Second Language Acquisition and Classroom Research* (pp. 231–255). New York: Routledge.

Stam, G. and McCafferty, S.G. (2008) Gesture studies and second language acquisition: A review. In S. McCafferty and G. Stam (eds) *Gesture: Second Language Acquisition and Classroom Research* (pp. 3–24). New York: Routledge.

Stilman, L. (1951) *Russian Verbs of Motion: Going, Carrying, Leading.* New York: King's Crown Press.

Stringer, D. (2002) The syntax of paths and boundaries. In M. Andronis, C. Ball, H. Elston and S. Neuvel (eds) *CLS 37: The Panels. Papers from the 37th Meeting of the Chicago Linguistics Society, Vol. 2*, 139–154.

Stringer, D. (2005) Paths in first language acquisition: Motion through space in English, French and Japanese. Doctoral dissertation, University of Durham.

Stringer, D. (2007) Motion events in L2 acquisition: A lexicalist account. In H. Caunt-Nulton, S. Kulatilake and I.H. Woo (eds) *BUCLD 31: Proceedings of the 31st annual Boston University Conference on Language Development, Vol. II* (pp. 585–596). Somerville, MA: Cascadilla.

Talmy, L. (1985). Lexicalization patterns: Semantic structure in lexical forms. In T. Shopen (ed.) *Language Typology and Syntactic Description: Grammatical Categories and the Lexicon* (Vol. 3, pp. 36–149). Cambridge: Cambridge University Press.

Talmy, L. (1991) Path to realization: A typology of event conflation. In *Proceedings of the 17th Annual Meeting of the Berkeley Linguistics Society* (pp. 480–519). Berkeley, CA: Berkeley Linguistics Society.

Talmy, L. (2000a) *Toward a Cognitive Semantics: Concept Structuring Systems* (Vol. 1). Cambridge, MA: MIT Press.

Talmy, L. (2000b) *Toward a Cognitive Semantics: Typology and Process in Concept Structuring* (Vol. 2). Cambridge, MA: MIT Press.

Talmy, L. (2006) The representation of spatial structure in spoken and signed language. In M. Hickmann and S. Robert (eds) *Space in Languages: Linguistic Systems and Cognitive Categories* (pp. 207–238). Amsterdam/Philadelphia: John Benjamins.

Talmy, L. (2008) Aspects of attention in language. In P. Robinson and N.C. Ellis (eds) *Handbook of Cognitive Linguistics and Second Language Acquisition* (pp. 27–38). New York/London: Routledge.

Tarone, E. (1982) Systematicity and attention in interlanguage. *Language Learning* 32 (1), 69–84.

Tarone, E. and Liu, G. (1996) Situational context, variation, and second language acquisition theory. In G. Cook and B. Seidlehofer (eds) *Principle and Practice in Applied Linguistics* (pp. 107–124). Oxford: Oxford University Press.

Thomas, M. (1989) The acquisition of English articles by first- and second-language learners. *Applied Psycholinguistics* 10, 335–355.

Titelbaum, O.A. (1990) Prefixed Russian verbs of transposition. *Russian Linguistics* 14, 20–23.

Tomasello, M. (1998) Cognitive linguistics. In W. Bechtel and G. Graham (eds) *A Companion to Cognitive Science*. Oxford: Blackwell.

Trenkic, D. (2002) Establishing the definiteness status of referents in dialogue (in languages with and without articles). *University of Cambridge Working Papers in English and Applied Linguistics* 7, 107–131.

Trenkic, D. (2007) Variability in L2 article production: Beyond the representational deficit vs. processing constraints debate. *Second Language Research* 23, 289–327.

Trenkic, D. (2008) The representation of English articles in second language grammars: Determiners or adjectives? *Bilingualism: Language and Cognition* 11, 1–18.

Tsekos Phillips, L. (2007) Motion events in Spanish as a foreign language. Unpublished Master's thesis, University of Pittsburgh.

Tulving, E. and Schacter, D.L. (1990) Priming and human memory systems. *Science* 247, 301–306.

Tyler, A. (2008) Cognitive linguistics and second language instruction. In P. Robinson and N. Ellis (eds) *Handbook of Cognitive Linguistics and Second Language Acquisition* (pp. 456–488). New York: Routledge.

VanPatten, B. (1996) *Input Processing and Grammar Instruction: Theory and Research*. Norwood, NJ: Ablex.

VanPatten, B., Williams, J. and Rott, S. (2004) Form-meaning connections in second language acquisition: An introduction. In B. VanPatten, J. Williams, S. Rott and

M. Overstreet (eds) *Form-Meaning Connections in Second Language Acquisition* (pp. 1–26). Mahwah, NJ: Lawrence Erlbaum.

Vinogradov, V.V. (ed.) (1960) *Grammar of the Russian Language*. Moscow: Izdatel'stvo Akademii Nauk SSSR.

von Humboldt, W. (1836/1999) In M. Losonsky (ed.) *On Language: On the Diversity of Human Language Construction and Its Influence on the Mental Development of the Human Species* (P. Heath, trans.). Cambridge: Cambridge University Press.

von Humboldt, W. (1836) *Über die Verschiedenheit des menschlichen sprachbaues und ihren Einfluss auf die geistige Entwickelung des Menschengeschlechts. [On the Diversity of Human Language Construction and Its Influence on Human Development]*. Bonn: Dümmler.

von Stutterheim, C. (2003) Linguistic structure and information organization: The case of very advanced learners. *EUROSLA Yearbook* 3, 183–206.

von Stutterheim, C. and Klein, W. (1987) A concept-oriented approach to second language studies. In C. Pfaff (ed.) *First and Second Language Acquisition Process* (pp. 191–205). Cambridge, MA: Newbury House.

Ward, D. (1965) *The Russian Language Today. System and Anomaly*. London: Hutchinson University Library.

Wei, L. (2000) Unequal election of morphemes in adult second language acquisition order in second language acquisition. *ITL Review of Applied Linguistics* 139–140, 77–100.

White, L. (2003) On the nature of interlanguage representation: Universal grammar in the second language. In C. Doughty and M. Long (eds) *Handbook of Second Language Acquisition* (pp. 19–42). Blackwell.

Whitley, M. (2002) *Spanish/English Contrasts*. Washington, DC: Georgetown University Press.

Whorf, B.L. (1956) Language, thought and reality. In J.B. Carroll (ed.) *Selected Writings of Benjamin Lee Whorf*. Cambridge, MA: MIT Press.

Wierzbicka, A. (1985) *Lexicography and Conceptual Analysis*. Ann Arbor, MI: Karoma.

Yoshioka, K. (2008) Linguistic and gestural introduction of Ground reference in L1 and L2 narrative. In S. McCafferty and G. Stam (eds) *Gesture: Second Language Acquisition and Classroom Research* (pp. 211–230). New York: Routledge.

Yoshioka, K. and Kellerman, E. (2006) Gestural introduction of ground reference in L2 narrative discourse. *IRAL* 44 (2), 173–195.

Young, R. (1996) Form–function relations in articles in English interlanguage. In R. Bayley and D.R. Preston (eds) *Second Language Acquisition and Linguistic Variation* (pp. 135–175). Amsterdam: John Benjamins.

Yu, L. (1996) The role of L1 in the acquisition of motion verbs in English by Chinese and Japanese learners. *Canadian Modern Language Review* 53, 191–218.

Zalizniak, A. (2005) Crossing spaces in the Russian linguistic world view. In I. Levontina and A. Shmelev (eds) *The Key Ideas in the Russian Linguistic World View* (pp. 96–110). Moscow: Iazyki Slavianskoi Kul'tury.

Zlatev, J. and Yangklang, P. (2004) A third way to travel: The place of Thai in motion-event typology. In S. Strömqvist and L. Verhoeven (eds) *Relating Events in Narrative. Typological and Contextual Perspectives* (pp. 159–190). Mahwah, NJ: Lawrence Erlbaum.

Zobl, H. (1982) A direction for contrastive analysis: The comparative study of developmental sequences. *TESOL Quarterly* 16 (2), 169–183.

Index